A Practitioner's Guide to ... s

GW01454189

First published in 2003

A Practitioner's Guide to Legacies

by

Martyn Frost FCIB, TEP
Head of Fiduciary Standards, Barclays Bank Trust Company Limited

Paul Saunders FCIB, TEP
Senior Fiduciary Standards Manager, Barclays Bank Trust Company Limited

Arabella Saker
Solicitor, Allen & Overy

Geoffrey Shindler MA, LLM (Cantab), TEP
Partner, Halliwell Landau

Tim Stone TEP
Head of Legal Services, Royal National Institute of the Blind
Founding Chairman, Institute of Legacy Management

Richard Wilson LLB, LLM
of the Middle Temple, Barrister

™

LexisNexis™ UK

Members of the LexisNexis Group worldwide

United Kingdom	LexisNexis UK, a Division of Reed Elsevier (UK) Ltd, Halsbury House, 35 Chancery Lane, LONDON, WC2A 1EL, and 4 Hill Street, EDINBURGH EH2 3JZ
Argentina	LexisNexis Argentina, BUENOS AIRES
Australia	LexisNexis Butterworths, CHATSWOOD, New South Wales
Austria	LexisNexis Verlag ARD Orac GmbH & Co KG, VIENNA
Canada	LexisNexis Butterworths, MARKHAM, Ontario
Chile	LexisNexis Chile Ltda, SANTIAGO DE CHILE
Czech Republic	Nakladatelství Orac sro, PRAGUE
France	Editions du Juris-Classeur SA, PARIS
Germany	LexisNexis Deutschland GmbH, FRANKFURT and MUNSTER
Hong Kong	LexisNexis Butterworths, HONG KONG
Hungary	HVG-Orac, BUDAPEST
India	LexisNexis Butterworths, NEW DELHI
Ireland	Butterworths (Ireland) Ltd, DUBLIN
Italy	Giuffrè Editore, MILAN
Malaysia	Malayan Law Journal Sdn Bhd, KUALA LUMPUR
New Zealand	LexisNexis Butterworths, WELLINGTON
Poland	Wydawnictwo Prawnicze LexisNexis, WARSAW
Singapore	LexisNexis Butterworths, SINGAPORE
South Africa	LexisNexis Butterworths, Durban
Switzerland	Stämpfli Verlag AG, BERNE
USA	LexisNexis, DAYTON, Ohio

© Reed Elsevier (UK) Ltd 2003

A CIP Catalogue record for this book is available from the British Library.

First published 2003

ISBN 0 7545 1454 4

Typeset by Kerrypress Ltd, Luton, Beds

Printed and bound in Great Britain by The Cromwell Press Limited, Trowbridge, Wiltshire

Visit LexisNexis UK at www.lexisnexis.co.uk

Preface

This book has been an unusual exercise for the authors. Most books concerning wills or legacies have been written with the professionals involved in this area of law in mind. In other words, authors have usually been writing about wills and probate for their peers or for their students. However this book was conceived with the 'customer' in mind, to try to help those who are routinely involved in receiving legacies understand what the process is.

The legatee is the person we have in mind in administering estates. The distribution to them is the end product of the labour of administration. Much of the administration process must seem arcane (even archaic) to the non-professional, although in reality there is much that is sound and sensible about the process. However, where beneficiaries, such as charities, routinely receive substantial legacies that are vital to their future work, they are becoming much more interested in the detail of the process that may determine how much they get and when.

This then is our attempt at setting out a beneficiaries' guide to the process. All of the authors have been involved for many years in many different aspects of the administration of estates, although only one has also been involved as a charity legacy officer. We hope that the approach that the authors have taken will prove useful to beneficiaries and the authors will welcome readers' views on how far we have managed to meet their needs. In particular readers' views on areas that might need more detail, or even areas that we have omitted and could usefully address in future editions, will be very helpful.

Martyn Frost
Barclays Bank Trust Company Limited, Northwich

Contents

Table of Cases

C

D

E

F

G

H

L

M

T

Table of Statutes

References in the right-hand column are to paragraph numbers. Paragraph references printed in **bold** type indicate where the legislation is set out in part or in full.

Table of Statutory Instruments

References in the right-hand column are to paragraph numbers.

Chapter 1

Introduction

1.1   The importance of legacies to charities in the UK is set out in CHAPTER 9. The main aim of this work is to offer practical guidance on those legacies. Therefore, in considering legacies it is necessary to look quite widely at the factors affecting them (construction of wills, taxation etc). It is also understood that sometimes those who manage the legacy interests of charities may not be wholly familiar with the overall subject of wills. This introduction therefore tries to provide a context for legacies by outlining the important features of wills, and their administration, which provide those legacies.

This book is concerned with the law of wills and probate in England and Wales. It does not deal with the law outside that jurisdiction. The law is stated as at 31 December 2002.

What is a will?

1.2   A will is a written statement of how an individual ('testator' if male and 'testatrix' (plural 'testatrices') if female) wishes his or her wealth to be disposed of after death. A written will is capable of being revoked by the testator at any time before his death, whether or not it is replaced by another will, unless he has entered into a valid contract not to do so. The terms of the will do not take effect until his death. This latter point is vital in the understanding of the position of potential beneficiaries: the named beneficiaries have no rights under the will before the testator's death, except in two important cases. It is possible for the beneficiaries to have some right to what is bequeathed in the will before the testator's death where:

(a)   the testator had – under a valid contract – undertaken to leave the beneficiary the bequest; or

(b)   the testator had promised the beneficiary the benefit under the will and the beneficiary had, relying on that promise, acted to his detriment or performed substantive services for the testator (this is known as proprietary estoppel, a complex area on which, in practice, professional advice will be required: see *Gillett v Holt [2000] WTLR 195*).

The terms of a will may be amended in detail by a codicil, which must, like the will itself, be executed in conformance with the Wills Act 1837.

A will is, in itself, a fairly simple concept but, because it involves the transfer of wealth from the testator to his legatees (also known as beneficiaries), it has over the years become a matter of great interest for various parties:

- the testator;
- the government;
- the executor of the will;
- the beneficiaries;
- the surviving members of the family;
- the dependants of the testator;
- the creditors of the testator.

The collision of these varied interests inevitably means that a substantial body of case law has accumulated in an attempt to resolve clashes of interest. We can develop a further understanding of why this is so by looking at some of the reasons behind these various parties being interested in the estate.

The testator

1.3   Being the owner of wealth there is a natural interest on the part of the testator in establishing formally who should receive the various parts of his estate. These wishes are usually driven by the testator's unique understanding of whom he may consider deserving, or worthy, of his bounty. Unfortunately, having owned the wealth during his lifetime, the testator often has an understandable natural reluctance to relinquish control of it. All too often the testator tries to control that wealth from beyond the grave through the conditions he imposes within the terms of the will.

It is also fair to say that the testator's view of which of his relatives are deserving of what amount of benefit does not always accord with those beneficiaries' own views. Further, it is far from unknown for testators to drop hints about what might be in their wills and this often leads to false expectations on the part of the beneficiaries. Even worse can be the position where the testator tries to obtain services from, or the attention of, his relatives by promises of what will be in his will.

The government

1.4   The interest of the government of the day in the general question of how property devolves on death has always been substantial, although its reasons for this interest have altered over the centuries. Almost until the early part of the 20th century, political power derived to a significant extent from wealth and for much of this time a large amount of wealth derived from land. In feudal times, the ultimate ownership of the land by the Crown meant that there was always a royal interest in how land was devolved, as that would affect local and regional political power.

Although this has now changed, there is still much government interest in succession on death for the following reasons.

- The social policy of the government on the support of dependants (abandonment without support would place a greater burden on the state through the benefit system).

- The effect on taxation policies for the raising of government revenue and/or the redistribution of wealth.

- The desirability of understood and settled methods of succession which prevent dispute and lessen the risk of fraud.

- Other social policy interests, such as the age of majority; opposition to permanent alienation of property; limits on accumulation of income; single-sex relationships etc.

The executor

1.5   There will be a closer look at the role of the executor later (see 1.23–1.26 below), but as the person charged by the will with carrying out the wishes of the testator, the executor has obligations to most of the interested parties and needs to be aware of the exact nature of his rights and duties. His position is, therefore, one where his interests may collide with any of the other interested parties and his task would be impossible in the absence of a clear framework of law within which to operate.

The beneficiaries

1.6   Those who will receive the wealth of the testator quite naturally want their inheritance as soon as possible and also want the maximum value that they can receive. It is not always possible to meet these wishes as well as the beneficiaries might like, because of the executors' duties towards the testator (conditions in the will that may limit the beneficiaries' interests), creditors (debts), the government (taxes), the other beneficiaries (competing interests) and dependants or other family members (claims against the estate).

The surviving family members

1.7   The surviving family members may well have expectations, reasonable or otherwise, of inheritance from the testator. Failure by the testator to do what the family members feel is expected of him is a frequent source of dispute and general ill-feeling within the family (and the executor may well be caught in the middle of the contending parties).

The law does recognise, to a degree, that some classes of relatives have a right to look to the estate for support if they are left unsupported by the testator (Inheritance (Provision for Family and Dependants) Act 1975). A claim made in this way against the estate obviously has implications for all who would otherwise take the estate (and also causes delay in distributing the estate which such a claim causes).

The dependants of the testator

1.8   As in the position of family members, referred to in 1.7 above, there may be non-family members who were dependent upon the testator, who also have a right to look to the testator's estate for support. These interests from outside the family may often be extra-marital partners and issue whose claims are disputed and indeed resented by family members.

The creditors of the testator

1.9   Gifts in wills cannot defeat the interests of legitimate creditors of the testator. The rights of creditors will have priority over those of the beneficiaries, so much so that, if the sums due to the creditors exhaust the estate, then the beneficiaries will receive nothing.

This fairly simple outline illustrates that in some ways the devolution of an estate is a bundle of contending interests and the difficulty, or ease, of the administration of the estate will depend upon the extent to which the competing interests come into conflict.

What makes a valid will?

1.10   Leaving to one side privileged wills or foreign wills, the validity of a will is governed by section 9 Wills Act 1837 (as substituted – in relation to wills taking effect after 1982 – by the Administration of Justice Act 1982, ss 17 and 73(6)):

'No will shall be valid unless –

(a)   it is in writing, and signed by the testator, or by some other person in his presence and by his direction; and

(b)   it appears that the testator intended by his signature to give effect to the will; and

(c)   the signature is made or acknowledged by the testator in the presence of two or more witnesses present at the same time; and

(d)   each witness either –

(i)   attests and signs the will; or

(ii)   acknowledges his signature,

in the presence of the testator (but not necessarily in the presence of any other witness),

but no form of attestation shall be necessary.'

It is beyond the scope of this book to deal in detail with the considerable body of law that surrounds these provisions, but some important general points can be made about the validity of wills.

Formalities

1.11 There is no requirement that the will be dated, although it is helpful if it is.

The testator's signature on a will can be by way of mark, or it can be made by another person (at the direction of the testator and in his presence). However made, the requirement of a signature is mandatory.

Where the testator uses a mark, or where the will is signed by another person, the method of signing (execution) should be recited in that part at the end of the will containing the signature and witnesses signatures (properly called the 'testimonium and attestation'). A will is signed by a mark usually where the testator is illiterate or where physical incapacity prevents a full signature.

Signature by another, on behalf of the testator, will usually be where physical incapacity prevents even a mark. This method is often used for signing on behalf of a blind person (although of course the blind person could, if he wishes, sign the will himself). In the case of a blind testator, the will will be read over to him if it is in conventional typed form.

It should be stressed that the requirement that a will is 'in writing' means just that (Interpretation Act 1978, Sch 1 defines writing as including various forms, all of which must be visible). Electronic methods of storing images of documents, tape recorded wills, video taped wills, computer files, death bed letters, unattested scribblings and all the other elements found in plays or novels remain just what they are – fiction. A written document is still the basic requirement of a valid English will. Wills do not have to be written in the English language and they do not have to be in the testator's own writing, but they do have to be written. There is no requirement that they are written on paper, but conventionally they usually are, as it is the easiest medium for recording writing. Testators have had a tendency to try to find alternatives to paper (*Re Barnes Goods (1926) 43 TLR 71* (an eggshell); *Re Slavinsky's Estate (1989) 53 SASR 221* (a wall)), but this is to be discouraged for obvious practical reasons.

These formal requirements for a valid will are strictly adhered to by the court. Whilst the court will go as far as it reasonably can to find that a will is valid (e.g. see the recent *Re Cynthia Chapman deceased (1998/99) ITELR 169*), there is no question of a court overlooking the absence of any of these requirements, or finding a will valid when one of these elements fails (some overseas jurisdictions, e.g. several of the Australian states, allow for substantial compliance by giving their courts the discretion to admit a will to probate where the court is satisfied that it correctly reflects the wishes of the testator even though some element of formality may be absent). The strictness of the statutory requirements in England clearly places a degree of responsibility on any professional involved in will preparation.

There is a duty of care on the professional regarding the correct execution of a will, where he has prepared it or where he is instructed regarding its execution. Should the professional fail to ensure correct execution of the will, there may be a claim against him by disappointed beneficiaries under the failed will (see *Ross v Caunters [1980] Ch 297*; *Esterhuizen v Allied Dunbar [1998] FLR 668*; *Gray v Richards Butler [2002] WTLR 143*) (or under a will that he has failed to prepare (*White v Jones [1995] 2 AC 207*)). Therefore, where it is discovered that a bequest has failed because of the invalid execution of the will (or a failure to prepare the will before the deceased's death), the disappointed beneficiary should always at minimum ask sufficient questions to determine the circumstances and identify if there are grounds to take legal advice about redress for loss of benefit under the will which did not come into effect.

The requirements of the Wills Act 1837 control the validity of all testamentary documents and any informal documents that attempt to dispose of or control the testator's personal estate after death are invalid unless they conform to the terms of the Act. This point is of importance for the informal letters that are frequently left by testators for the guidance of executors. While such guidance may be of assistance, the testator cannot reserve the right to dispose of his wealth informally by such a letter unless it is also executed in accordance with the Act, or it exists at the date of the will and its terms are expressly incorporated by reference, thereby becoming part of the will and admitted to probate.

However, there is an exception, which in practice is rarely encountered, which permits informal wills (i.e. those that need not meet any of the formal requirements of the Wills Act 1837) to be made by members of the armed forces being in actual military service and by seamen being at sea (Wills Act 1837, s 11; and generally Wills (Soldiers and Sailors) Act 1918).

Witnessing

1.12   The passage from section 9 Wills Act 1837 quoted at 1.10 above, refers to the necessity of two witnesses witnessing (alternatively called attesting) a testator's signature. For understandable reasons, the Act requires that a will should not be witnessed by a beneficiary under it, nor by the spouse of a beneficiary (Wills Act 1837, s 15; although the marriage of a beneficiary to a witness after the execution of the will does not affect the gift: *Thorpe v Bestwick (1881) 6 QBD 311*). If a beneficiary, or the beneficiary's spouse, is one of the two witnesses to the will, the will is regarded as validly executed (if the execution was correct in all other regards), but the gift to that particular beneficiary will fail.

The witnessing of a will is not invalid simply because one of the witnesses is not competent to be called as witness in a probate action (i.e. because they are either not mentally competent or conceivably so far under age so not to be capable of giving evidence: s 14, Wills Act 1837), but for obvious reason such witnesses are best avoided. A blind person cannot witness a will (*In the Estate of Gibson [1949] P 434*).

Revocation

1.13   The process of revocation of a will is also subject to statutory control, with the specific requirements being set out, mainly, in section 20 Wills Act 1837. Revocation, like the execution of a will, requires the testator to have the intention to do the act and the mental capacity to understand the act and its consequences (see 1.20 below on capacity). Intention to revoke can cause problems when the testator's intention was conditional upon his revocation reviving a previous will or, if there is no previous will, the intestacy rules meeting his intention. In these circumstances, where the intention to revoke is not unqualified, and if the expectation of the testator is not met, the testator would not have sufficient intention to revoke the original will. This is known as the doctrine of dependent relative revocation. This doctrine can also apply where the testator revokes a will with the intention of executing a new one, but fails to do so. Here the position is more complicated, as it is necessary to determine if the testator intended to revoke the original, whatever happens, or if the revocation would not happen if the later will was not executed. Where it is thought that revocation may be conditional and affected by the doctrine of dependent relative revocation, professional legal advice should be taken.

Revocation of a will or codicil may be effected under the following circumstances.

- Marriage of the testator will revoke the last will, unless the will was expressly made in expectation of marriage to a particular person and it was intended that the marriage should not revoke the will (Wills Act 1837, s 18). Divorce does not have the same effect (see later at 8.5);

- A later will that specifically revokes the earlier will (Wills Act 1837, s 20). Revocation of part of an earlier will may be effected by a later codicil. It is more than merely good practice that wills conventionally commence by revoking all previous dispositions, for without this the earlier will is *not* revoked by the later will and the two documents would be read together, with the dispositions in the later document prevailing over the former where the two documents are inconsistent. It is most unusual for this situation to arise through the deliberate intention of the testator; it is more usually through mistake in the second will;

- '. . . by the burning, tearing, or otherwise destroying [the will] by the testator, or by some other person in his presence and by his instruction' (Wills Act 1837, s 20). When taken together, these words require something more than symbolic destruction (e.g. writing 'cancelled' across the face of the will). They require an act of actual destruction (literally tearing or cutting up or burning, but also cutting off or obliterating the signature).

The Act also requires that if this is not done by the testator, but is done by a third party, then it must be done at the direction of the testator and also in his presence.

Unattested alterations

1.14 Where wills are not held in professional safe custody, but are retained by the testator, they are sometimes found with post-execution alterations which have been made by the testator without professional advice or supervision. These alterations may be:

- bequests written in between the lines (interlineations);

- amended figures or words of some legacies;

- crossings out;

- cuttings out;

- obliterations.

Unless evidence can be produced to show that any of these alterations were made before execution, or that the will has been re-executed in accordance with the Wills Act 1837 after the alteration, the alterations will not generally take effect and the will will be read in its original terms without the alterations. In practice, however, where the amendment has had the effect of making the original impossible to read (e.g. obliteration or cutting out) the original words cannot take effect (thus, despite the terms of the Wills Act 1837, making such unattested alterations effective in practice). The court, or Probate Registry, will make every attempt to read obliterated words short of using artificial means such as X-rays.

Loss

1.15 It is an unfortunate fact of life that wills are occasionally lost. The loss or destruction of a will does not necessarily mean that the terms of the will have ceased to be valid and enforceable. Where, after death, the will cannot be found but it was last traced to the possession of the testator there is a rebuttable presumption that he destroyed it with the intention to revoke it (*Eckersley v Platt (1866) LR 1 P & D 281*).

Where this presumption is rebutted by the evidence, or where the loss occurred when the will was in the safekeeping of someone else, evidence of the will and its contents may be provided from various sources. Most commonly this evidence is provided by copy wills held by the person who prepared the will. But even without a copy of the will it may be possible to establish most or all of the terms to the satisfaction of the court – most famously, when the former Chancellor, Lord St Leonards (who had written of the need for all men to make wills in spite of being able to list many judges and lawyers who had not) died in

1875, his will was lost, but the court accepted his daughter's recital of its terms. It was said he used to like her to read its terms over to him during his last illness.

Preparation of wills

1.16   There is no requirement that a will must be professionally prepared. A testator may, if he has the skills, write out his own will (known as a 'holograph will' if it is in his own handwriting). He may, as an alternative, purchase a pre-printed will form that contains certain information to assist him in the requirements (but rarely with the terms) of the will. Experience of self-made wills is such that they should be discouraged emphatically; the scope for error, giving rise to invalidity or dispute, is far too great. Errors commonly found are:

- inaccurate descriptions, or descriptions which are so unique to the testator's understanding that others cannot be sure of their meaning;

- failure to deal with all of the estate, or attempting to deal with assets which were not part of the free estate;

- inconsistent bequests;

- meaningless drafting, often as a result of copying parts of professionally drafted wills without understanding their meaning or effect;

- failure to understand the need for alternative provisions in the event of failure of a gift; and

- invalidity of the will through incorrect execution.

In practice such wills tend to give the executor a great deal of trouble, which in turn frequently leads to legal bills way in excess of the marginal amount of fees saved through not having the will professionally prepared in the first place. As such costs are payable out of the estate they have the effect of reducing the value of the beneficiaries' inheritances.

Wills are more usefully obtained from:

- solicitors;

- trust companies; or

- professional will-writing companies.

Solicitors

1.17   Undoubtedly where the proposed terms of the will are complex, or the personal circumstances of the testator are complex, the will should be prepared by a solicitor experienced in such work.

Trust companies

1.18 Most commercial trust companies have the facilities to prepare wills either themselves or through supply arrangements with solicitors. Their market is principally those customers who may want to use the trust company's services as executor or trustee, but this is by no means exclusively so. The major trust companies in England and Wales are all part of larger financial institutions and, in some cases, those institutions also use their trust company to supply wills to their customers (sometimes without charge) when the customers purchase another product such as a life policy or bank account.

Will-writing companies

1.19 The third possibility is a professional will-writing company, which will often be independent. They vary in size and experience.

Who may make a will?

1.20 Anyone over 18 can make a will (or under that age if within the class entitled to make a privileged will; see 1.11 above) provided they have animus testandi. Animus testandi can be summarised as having the intention to make a will at the same time as having the mental capacity to do so and being able to exercise both free from coercion and the undue influence of others.

The requisite mental capacity has previously been defined in *Banks v Goodfellow (1870) LR 5 QB 549:*

> 'as to the testator's capacity, he must, in the language of the law, have a sound disposing mind and memory. In other words, he ought to be capable of making his will with an understanding of the nature of the business in which he is engaged, a recollection of the property he means to dispose of, of the persons who are the objects of his bounty, and the manner in which it is to be distributed between them. It is not necessary that he should view his will with the eye of a lawyer, and comprehend its provisions in their legal form. It is sufficient that he has such a mind and memory as will enable him to understand the elements of which it is composed, and the disposition of his property in its simple forms.'

Published guidance for doctors and lawyers (*Assessment of Mental Capacity; Guidance for Doctors and Lawyers* (1995) jointly published by the Law Society and the British Medical Association) summarises the position as follows.

When making a will a testator should understand:

(a)   *The nature of the act*; that is that:

    (i)   he will die;

    (ii)   the will will operate from death, but not before;

(iii) the will can be changed or revoked by him at any time before he dies.

(b) *The effect of making a will*; that is:

    (i) who the executor is and why the executor has been appointed;

    (ii) who gets what benefit under the will;

    (iii) the nature of the gifts made in the will, i.e. if they are conditional or limited;

    (iv) that if he spends or gives away his assets during his lifetime that the beneficiaries may receive nothing;

    (v) that the beneficiary might die before he does;

    (vi) whether or not he has already made a will and, if he has, how the proposed terms of the new will differ.

(c) *The extent of the property that he owns*; the use of the word 'extent' is deliberate. It is not synonymous with 'value'. Whilst the approximately value is relevant, it is the amount of assets, their number and type that is important. A testator should comprehend:

    (i) the extent of the property owned solely by him;

    (ii) that jointly owned assets may pass to the other joint owner irrespective of the provisions of the will:

    (iii) that some benefits on death might be unaffected by the will (pension interests or life policies payable to others;

    (iv) that the extent of his property could change during his lifetime.

(d) *The claims of others*; a testator should understand the claims that he ought to give effect to and his reason for preferring some to others e.g. that some possible beneficiaries:

    (i) may already have received adequate provision from the testator;

    (ii) may be financially better-off than others;

    (iii) may have been more attentive and caring of the testator than others;

    (iv) may be in greater need of assistance because of age, gender, or physical or mental problems.

It is almost needless to add that this area has proved to be particularly prone to litigation. There are several reasons for this:

- The claim that someone lacks capacity is often the first reaction of those disappointed by their benefit, or lack of it, under a will. The law does not presume that eccentricity is the same as incapacity and thus terms which are capricious may be upheld by a court, whilst the disappointed beneficiary can only rationalise his disappointment by insisting that his relative must have lacked capacity.

- Longevity is a feature of modern society, but one of the disadvantages of old age is a greater likelihood of mental impairment through age and disease. This tends to make the elderly more vulnerable to the unscrupulous or the outright criminal.

- Another feature of society is the dependence upon nursing homes and carers for the maintenance of the elderly. Whilst it must be stressed that by far the greater majority of staff in such roles act solely with the benefit of their patients in mind, the dependence of the elderly upon them can place the carer in a position that can be abused.

- The dividing line between having the mental capacity to make a will and not having that capacity is not a division that can be clearly drawn or described. A feature of mental incapacity claims against wills is the conflicting nature of the evidence with witnesses, even medically qualified witnesses, often holding opposite, but nonetheless genuine, opinions about capacity.

- It is also true that today's society is wealthier and that the elderly have shared in this growth in wealth, hence making their estates more likely to attract disputes.

Even where a testator has the necessary mental capacity to make a will, he must also act free from coercion by others. He must not be compelled or induced to sign by threats, force, fear or even blackmail. He must also act free from the undue influence of others. Undue influence must be distinguished from mere persuasion; *Hall v Hall (1868) LR 1 P & D 481*:

> 'Persuasion appeals to the affections or ties of kindred, to a sentiment of gratitude for past services, or pity for future destination or the like – these are all legitimate and may fairly be pressed on the testator. On the other hand, pressure on whatever character . . . if so exerted as to overpower the volition without convincing the judgement . . . will constitute undue influence, though no force is either used or threatened. In a word a testator may be led but not driven.'

If someone lacks the mental capacity to make a will, but it is thought to be in his interests that he should have a will, the court may make provision for one to be drawn up and executed on his behalf (Mental Health Act 1983, s 96). Those who may apply for such a will are specified in rule 18 of the Court of Protection Rules 2001 and are:

(a)   any receiver for the patient;

(b)   anyone who has a pending application to be a receiver for the patient;

(c)   anyone entitled to inherit under any known will or intestacy of the patient;

(d)   anyone that the patient might be expected to make provision for;

(e)   an attorney for the patient acting under a registered enduring power of attorney;

(f)   anyone else that the court may authorise.

When executing his will, the testator must also know of the contents of the will and approve of them. Lack of knowledge and approval strikes at the testamentary intention of the testator and, if proved, will lead to the will being invalid (*Wintle v Nye [1959] 1 All ER 552*).

What may be disposed of by will?

1.21   Generally any assets owned by the testator may be disposed of by his will, but there are important exceptions.

- Property which is owned jointly with another as beneficial joint tenants will pass by survivorship outside of the terms of the will in favour of the surviving joint owner. Contrast this with property that is owned as tenants in common, where the testator's share is an asset of his estate. It is therefore always essential to identify exactly the way in which any joint property is owned.

- Most pension fund interests are, by the terms of the pension trust deed, not payable to the member's executors. Although the fund may continue to pay benefits to a surviving spouse or dependant, generally these are controlled by the trust deed and not the will of the deceased pension fund member.

- Annuities which are not capital protected cease on the death of the annuitant, generally speaking.

- Property held by the deceased as a trustee for others remains subject to that trust and not the terms of the trustee's will.

- Life policies written in trust for others are written under a trust and their devolution is not governed by the will but by the terms of the trust deed (as would also be the case for any other assets in the name of the testator, but not owned by him and subject to separate trusts).

- A donatio mortis causa is a deathbed gift made in the face of death, which is also dependent upon death occurring. To this extent it is somewhere between a life-time gift and gift by will, but it is nonetheless a gift and the subject of the gift will not pass under the will.

- Foreign assets owned by the testator may, or may not, devolve according to the terms of an English will. These assets will be governed by the law of the country in which they are situate and the extent to which the assets will pass under an English will will depend upon the law of that country. This point is particularly relevant for foreign real property and for property which may be subject to foreign forced heirship rules.

Foreign aspects

1.22   Under English law (Wills Act 1963, s.1):

'A will shall be treated as properly executed if its execution conformed to the internal law in force in the territory where it was executed, or in the territory where, at the time of its execution or of the testator's death, he was domiciled or had his habitual residence, or in a state of which, at either of those times, he was a national.'

A will which does not conform to section 9 Wills Act 1837 may be saved from failure if the circumstances of its execution are examined to see if this provision might save it.

Where a will deals with foreign property it involves a collision between the requirements of English law and the law of the country in which the property is situate. This gives rise to the possibility of the validity of the will and its terms being subject to two tests of validity; one from each country's law. A will may be valid under English law because it conforms to the requirements of the Wills Act 1837 – this is described as 'formal validity'. However, where the will bequeaths foreign property, it is both the ability to bequeath that property and the terms of the bequest that are subject to the requirement of validity under the foreign law – 'essential validity'. Thus it is possible that while the will itself maybe valid, one or more of the bequests in it may not be.

What is an executor?

1.23   Nearly all wills will contain the appointment of an executor. It is not essential that they do so, but it is unusual where they do not. Where a will does not appoint an executor, or the executor named is dead or is unwilling or unable to act, an administrator will carry out similar functions to the executor. The order of preference for who may act as an administrator is set out in the Non-Contentious Probate Rules 1987 (SI 1987/2024).

An executor's powers to deal with the will date from the death of the testator. This is from when his will has legal effect (an administrator's authority dates from his Letters of Administration). However, although the will bestows the authority on the executor, the executor has no proof of the title that he can use to obtain control of assets etc, because anyone asked to accept his authority cannot be sure that the will is valid, even if the original was produced to them. Proof of the title is obtained by applying to the court (through the Probate Registry) for recognition of the validity of the will. Proof is given to an executor in the form of a Grant of Probate or, where an administrator is involved, a Grant of Letters of Administration. Collectively these documents are known as grants of representation and they are described further at 1.26 below.

A personal representative is often described as 'standing in the shoes of the testator'. This is apt in the sense that he has all of the rights and obligations that the testator had while he was alive.

- He is the legal owner of the assets of the testator's estate which he is bound to collect, control and manage in the best interests of those entitled to the estate. He is given extensive statutory powers in order to accomplish this.

- He has the responsibility for the debts of the deceased, including the funeral expenses. He also has the duty to dispose of the body (*Williams v Williams (1882) 20 Ch D 659*), although in the absence of dispute he would usually leave arrangements to the family. The funeral wishes of the testator expressed in his will are not binding on the executor although they will normally be observed wherever possible.

- He is bound to account to the Revenue for all taxes due, including those arising because of the testator's death.

- He is bound to carry out the terms of the testator's will in so far as those terms are lawful and to account to the beneficiaries for the distributable estate.

- Whilst the personal representative has the right to reimbursement of expenses incurred, he does incur these personally as the estate does not constitute a separate legal entity capable of entering into contracts or incurring obligations itself.

- His liability for any failure to meet his duties is personal and this may be enforced against him at the suit of the beneficiaries affected by his actions or inactions.

Who acts as an executor?

1.24   A testator may appoint whoever he wishes to be his executor. He should select someone reliable and of sound judgement. There is no requirement that the executor be free from conflicts of interest in carrying out his duties, but the writer's view is that avoiding conflicts of interest is much to be preferred. There is no legal requirement that the executor be a member of the family or a beneficiary under the will.

There is no rule to prevent a minor or person of unsound mind being appointed as executor, but such persons cannot apply for a grant until of age or free from their disability. Depending upon circumstances, others may apply for grants during the period when minors or persons of unsound mind are under disability.

The executor need not be an individual: a corporation, usually a trust corporation, can act. An unincorporated body such as a partnership may not apply, although the individual partners may apply in their own names.

Executors' fees

1.25   Prior to the Trustee Act 2000 there was no statutory authority for an executor (or trustee) to charge for his services. The position was that an executor was regarded as being in a position of trust and good faith that did not require remuneration, only the reimbursement of expenses reasonably incurred in carrying out his office. Therefore the only remuneration allowed was that expressly authorised under the terms of the will itself. This led to the development of charging clauses authorising professional individuals to charge their appropriate professional fees and also to clauses authorising trust corporations to charge their published fee scales for acting as executor. Where there is a charging clause, it should be read carefully as some modern charging clauses extend the right to remuneration beyond the traditional solicitor/accountant authority. Prior to the Trustee Act 2000, fees authorised under a will were deemed to be legacies under the will, but since the passing of the Act, this is no longer the case and all remuneration – whether expressly authorised or charged under the Act (see below) – is treated as an expense of the estate. By preventing the fee authority from being treated as a legacy, this reform removes the threat of the fees (a legacy) abating with the other gifts if there is insufficient in the estate to pay all the gifts in full.

Since the Trustee Act 2000, there has been a statutory basis to charging which is an alternative to a remuneration expressly authorised in the will. The provisions of Part V of the Act authorise trust corporations to charge reasonable remuneration for their services. They also permit a professional trustee to charge similarly, with the consent in writing of any other trustees. A trustee acts in a professional capacity if he acts in the course of a profession or business which consists of or includes administering estates or trusts or some aspect of them. The Act does not provide any statutory authority for non-professional trustees to charge fees for their work.

Grant of representation

1.26   As referred to at 1.23 (above), a grant of representation is essential proof of the validity of the will and hence the personal representative's title to the assets and his standing to act in the estate. The document is comprised of a front sheet which recites the name, etc of the testator and shows the name of the executor(s) who obtained probate. The original and any copies issued by the Probate Registry will be embossed with the probate court seal (without which the document has no validity). The original will is retained by the Probate Registry and the original grant will have a photocopy of the grant bound to it.

The procedures for obtaining a grant without litigation are contained in the Non-Contentious Probate Rules 1987 (SI 1987/2024). A grant of representation to a will may be obtained after seven days have elapsed from death. Where there is no will the time period before a grant may be issued is 14 days. In theory, these time periods are to allow for adequate searches to be made for other wills. There is no corresponding upper limit to the period within which a grant must be obtained.

It is worth noting that the grant of representation is vital to the administration of the estate and that without it a personal representative cannot take control of the assets and progress the administration. Therefore in modern probate practice stress is placed on commencing the enquiries necessary to make the probate application and making the application itself as quickly as possible after the testator's death.

In order to obtain a grant (at the time of writing, there was a consultation document recently issued by the Lord Chancellor's Department on the reform of this process) the personal representative is required to prepare an account for the Inland Revenue, showing all of the assets and liabilities and their values, in order that any inheritance tax due may be paid before the grant is issued. A grant will not be issued without proof that the inheritance tax due has been paid. This can pose difficulties for the executor for although this tax must be paid prior to the issue of the grant, the executor cannot collect the assets until he has the grant. Therefore in practice the executor either:

(a)   negotiates a loan; or

(b)   agrees with the banks or building societies where the testator maintained accounts that funds may be released by way of cheques drawn on the accounts payable to the Revenue. In order to obtain funds to meet tax in this way the banks or building societies will require that they are indemnified against loss by the executor personally. With effect from 31 March 2003, the British Bankers' Association and the Building Societies Association have agreed a process with the Inland Revenue for payments on account of inheritance tax to be made by transfer from an account direct to the Revenue where the personal representative requests it and gives the appropriate undertakings.

Although it may not be possible to ascertain exactly all of the information that the Revenue require at this time, the personal representative must make the fullest enquiries that are reasonably practical in the circumstances. Failure to act to this standard may make the personal representative liable to penalties assessed by the Revenue (see *IRC v Robertson [2002] WTLR 907* on the standard required). Penalties incurred in this way may well, depending upon the circumstances, be a personal liability of the personal representative that is not reimbursed from the estate.

In addition to paying inheritance tax that is due, the personal representative is also required to submit an oath setting out:

●   the date and place of death;

●   the age of the deceased; and

●   the domicile of the deceased.

The oath must be accompanied by the original will and the originals of any codicils to it.

An exception to the above process for the Inland Revenue Account, is the 'excepted estates' procedure. For smaller estates Inland Revenue Accounts are not required. The regulations governing this process are updated fairly frequently and reference should be made to them when required. At the time of writing the upper limit of value for the excepted estate procedure is £220,000. Where this procedure can be used the process for obtaining a grant of representation is simplified and thus should involve less professional fees.

Personal applications for a grant may be made by individuals, with or without professional assistance. As the law stands at present a trust corporation may not make its own applications, but must use a solicitor to make the application for them. At the time of writing, there is a consultation process under way which may reform this aspect of the law and give wider access to probate applications. Where any executor or administrator uses a solicitor to prepare the probate papers and make the probate application the professional costs incurred are an expense properly repayable to the executor out of the estate.

The above brief summary is based on a standard non-contentious application for a common form grant. In addition there is a more complex procedure for obtaining grants in contentious proceedings. There are also a number of special grants which may give limited powers only (both limited in time and scope). A special grant will show on its front sheet the type of grant that it is and make reference to its limited terms.

Chapter 2

Types of legacies

Introduction

2.1   This section contains a description of the types of gift made by will and their main features. For further practical guidance on how they are to be construed or how, for example, they may fail, reference should be made to the subsequent sections of the book.

Specific legacies

2.2   For a legacy to be a specific legacy it must be a bequest of an identifiable thing that is owned by the testator and which can be distinguished from the remainder of his estate. Generally speaking such legacies will be described in a will as 'my' or 'belonging to me'. The will must also show an intention that the item is to pass in specie and not have a direction that it is to be sold and the proceeds paid to the legatee instead (*Bothamley v Sherson (1875) LR 20 Eq 304*), for such a direction would make the legacy demonstrative.

It is important that the testator identifies the item as belonging to him. A bequest of a specified amount of stock, for example, which is not characterised as being the testator's, has been held not to be a specific legacy, but a general legacy, notwithstanding that the testator owned that precise amount of stock. Good drafting should always attempt precise definition, including present ownership, in order not only to accurately identify the subject matter, but also to prevent doubt as to whether or not the legacy is intended to be specific.

Income

2.3   Unless the will provides otherwise, a specific legacy or devise carries the income arising from the date of death of the testator.

The above applies to any specific gift, even if it is a contingent or future gift, unless the testator specifically disposes of the intermediate income (Law of Property Act 1925, s 175).

The Apportionment Act 1870 directs that payments in the nature of income are to be treated as accruing from day to day. Irrespective of the date of payment, the statutory apportionment of any dividend or rent is made by reference to the period during which it is stated to accrue: e.g. a dividend may be 'for the year ended 31 March 2002', so that if the testator had died on, say, 30 June 2001, roughly three-quarters of the dividend would be due to the specific legatee.

Most modern wills contain an express direction that no apportionment shall be made. By such a will, any income receipt (or expenditure incurred) after the date of the testator's death will attach to the legacy. Care must be taken, however, as the form of wording of such clauses may vary. Some direct the benefit of the income stream (or liabilities) by reference to the due date of payment, others to the date of receipt. Whilst the former is clear, the latter may be uncertain – is a dividend 'received' when the dividend cheque appears on the proverbial door-mat; when the executor pays it into the estate bank account; or when the cheque is eventually debited to the drawer's account?

One might look to the rules for the making of a gift, where the relevant date is the date that the cheque is debited to the donor's account, on the basis that payment could be stopped at any point up until then. A cheque is not an assignment of any money standing to the credit of the drawer's account (*Hopkinson v Forster (1874) LR 19 Eq 74*), so that no 'debt' arises until the cheque is presented for payment at the drawer's bankers (*Schroeder v Central Bank of London (1876) 24 WR 710*). However, the payment of a dividend is a contractual matter, once the dividend has been declared, and so would the paying company have any right to stop the cheque? Reliance upon the date that dividends etc are 'received' may therefore give rise to debate. It is unfortunate that what would normally be a 'simplifying' clause should introduce uncertainty.

Taxation issues

Inheritance tax

2.4   Section 211 Inheritance Tax Act 1984 (IHTA 1984) provides that inheritance tax on UK assets is a testamentary expense and, in the absence of a contrary intention in the will, residue will bear the tax on prior legacies and devises to the extent that such specific gifts are UK assets. There is no need for the will to provide that any such gift is 'free of tax'. The fact that a will states that some gifts are 'free of tax' but is silent on others, does not cause those other gifts to be subject to tax – clear words imposing a charge to tax must be used if the residuary estate is to be relieved of the liability.

The words 'free of tax' will only relieve the gift of UK inheritance tax, and not of any similar tax payable in respect of the asset in a foreign country. More particular words are necessary in such instance, specifically directing that the gift is free of all taxes and duties whatsoever (there are many forms of words that may be used and each situation will need to be considered on its own merits).

If a foreign asset is specifically gifted, the beneficiary will be liable both for the foreign taxes relating to that asset, and for the proportionate part of the UK inheritance tax.

Capital gains tax

2.5   No capital gains tax is payable by the specific legatee upon receipt of the specified asset(s).

When the subject matter of the legacy is appropriated to him, the beneficiary is deemed to have received it as 'legatee' under section 62(4) Taxation of Chargeable Gains Act 1992 (TCGA 1992) at the date of death value. Where the value of the asset has been determined for inheritance tax, this is the value used for capital gains tax (TCGA 1992, s 274). If no inheritance tax is payable in respect of the gift, the usual valuation rules apply to determine 'market value' as at the date of death (TCGA 1992, s 273).

If the legal personal representative (LPR) should sell the subject matter of the legacy (or a part of it) before any appropriation is made to the beneficiary, the disposal is that of the LPR, not the beneficiary. Accordingly, any gain will be assessable upon the LPR (subject to being offset by any capital gains tax allowance or loss otherwise available to the LPR), and any actual loss will accrue to the estate.

If a loss arises on a sale by the LPR before appropriation, the LPR may claim relief against inheritance tax under section 179 IHTA 1984 (sale of investments within 12 months of death) or section 191 IHTA 1984 (sale of land within three years of death). In certain circumstances the latter may be extended to four years (IHTA 1984, s 197A). Each relief applies to the net loss on sales of relevant assets within the specified period, not losses on individual sales.

Any relief granted will benefit the estate generally and result in the loss on sale effectively being limited to the amount of the sale expenses. Such loss is the LPR's loss and is not available for the specific legatee to set against his personal gains for capital gains tax purposes.

Income tax

2.6   Upon the asset being appropriated to the beneficiary, the appropriation will 'relate back' to the date of death so that the income due to the beneficiary (see 2.3 above) will be treated for taxation purposes as if it was his income and not income of the estate (i.e. the beneficiary will be taxed on that income on the 'income arising' basis). If the asset has been sold by the LPR, the 'relation back' will be triggered by the payment of the proceeds (or part of them) to, or on behalf of, the beneficiary.

Until the specifically bequeathed asset (s), or the proceeds of sale, is appropriated to the beneficiary entitled, income received on it is the executor's income and subject to tax in the executor's hands, even if received 'gross'. This is so even if it is payable to the specific legatee in due course. Income payable on such assets post-appropriation is received by the executor as 'bare trustee' and is taxable in the hands of the beneficiary (NB: if the beneficiary's place of abode is outside of the UK, however, the executor may be required to deduct tax and account to the beneficiary for the net income only).

Stamp duty

2.7   The transfer or conveyance by which title to the asset is vested in the name of the beneficiary, or his nominee, will be exempt from stamp duty if it is endorsed with the relevant certificate referring to category B of the Schedule to the Stamp Duty (Exempt Instruments) Regulations 1987 (SI 1987/516).

If the transfer or conveyance does not carry the appropriate certificate, it should be submitted to the Stamp Office for adjudication and will be subject to stamp duty at the fixed rate of £5.

Specific devise

2.8   A specific legacy of realty is more properly known as a specific devise and the legatee as a devisee.

Generally speaking, 'realty' (or real property) is freehold land with all other property (including other interests in land) being described as 'personalty'. The difference between the two is historical and the way in which the two categories of property are treated has tended to become more similar, although technically there still remain some significant distinctions.

General legacies

Gifts of things

2.9   Gifts by will of items that are not owned by the testator but are capable of being acquired by the personal representative are general legacies. Thus a bequest of '1,000 £1 shares of Barclays plc' would require the personal representative to purchase sufficient stock to satisfy the legacy. These are comparatively rare in modern wills unless they arise through drafting error (see 5.10 for rectification).

Income

2.10   Interest on general legacies normally runs from the first anniversary of the testator's death. It is payable on the amount of the legacy which remains outstanding at that date. A direction that the legacy is to be paid 'as soon as possible', or 'within four years' of the testator's demise does not alter the date upon which interest will start running (see *Theobald on Wills*, (15th edition, Sweet & Maxwell) p 270, note 67).

The interest will accrue on a daily basis, on the amount of the legacy that remains outstanding. When any distribution is made in part satisfaction of the legacy, it is first applied to discharge the interest accrued to that date, and any surplus used to reduce the outstanding balance of the legacy (*Re Morley's Estate, Hollenden v Morley [1937] 3 All ER 204*).

Unless the will specifies a particular rate, interest is payable at 6% simple (Rules of the Supreme Court (Amendment No 2) Order 1983, SI 1983/1181), even if the residuary estate has been producing income at a higher rate (*Re Campbell, Campbell v Campbell [1893] 3 Ch 468*).

There are a number of exceptions to the rule that interest only runs from the first anniversary of death. The principal ones are as follows (legacies to executors are also an exception to the general rule, and are considered separately, see 2.38–2.43):

(a) *Spouses*: if the legacy is directed to be paid 'immediately' it will carry interest from the date of death, otherwise the general rule applies.

(b) *Persons in respect of whom the testator stands in loco parentis (this includes a minor child of the testator)*: provided that the gift is directly to the minor (and not to trustees on his behalf), and is payable upon him attaining full age, or marrying under that age. Interest runs from the date of death.

(c) *Legacies for the maintenance of minors*: where the income of a legacy is given to a minor for his maintenance (*Re Richards (1869) LR 8 Eq 119*) or education (*Re Selby-Walker, Public Trustee v Selby-Walker [1949] 2 All ER 178*), it carries interest from the date of death. The right to income is not affected by the existence, or otherwise, of any relationship between the deceased and the minor. There is no simple definition of a legacy for the maintenance of a minor and, on its own, a power to advance to the minor does not bring the legacy within this exception.

(d) *Legacies in satisfaction of a debt*: if the debt is due from the deceased, interest runs from the date of death (*Clark v Sewell (1744) 3 Atk 96*). However, if the debt is owed by the legatee to a third party, interest runs only from the first anniversary of the testator's death.

(e) *Vested legacies payable at a future date*: interest is given to the legatee to compensate for the delay in payment so that, until the legacy becomes payable, no interest is due (*Re Scadding (1902) 4 OLR 632*). If the intermediate income is not specifically disposed of, it will form part of the residuary estate. This applies whether payment of the legacy is on a fixed date in the future, or is dependent upon some other, uncertain event. If the legacy is payable upon the termination of a life interest, the legatee will usually be entitled to interest from the date of termination of that prior interest.

If the legacy is 'severed' from the estate, this may displace the above, so that interest will run from the first anniversary of death (*Morpeth v Williamson [1926] NZLR 39*). The severance should usually be for some reason connected with the legatee, or because the legacy is given to trustees upon trust for the legatee. If the severance is for administrative purposes only, interest will run only from the due date of payment (*Festing v Allen (1844) 5 Hare 573*).

Where such a legacy is directed to be paid 'with interest', the right to interest commences at the end of the executor's year, although the legatee is not entitled to receive it until the happening of the specified event (*Knight v Knight (1826) 2 Sim & St 490*).

(f)   *Contingent legacies*: will not generally carry income until the happening of the specified event. However, if the legacy is directed to be set aside, other than merely for administrative purposes, it will carry the intermediate income. (A legacy is not 'set aside' unless it is preceded by a vested limited interest or is vested in trustees (*Re Eyre, Johnson v Williams [1917] 1 Ch 351*)).

(g)   *Defeasible legacies*: where a legacy is vested, but is liable to be divested, until the happening of the event which defeats the legacy the legatee is entitled to interest (*Re Buckley's Trusts (1883) 22 Ch D 583*).

In the absence of an acknowledgement by the LPR of the beneficiary's right to interest, the legatee may only be entitled to claim payment of six years' arrears of interest (Limitation Act 1980, although, where this does not apply, in cases of delay the courts are likely to allow no more than six years' arrears to be recovered (*Thomson v Eastwood (1877) 2 App Cas 215*)).

Taxation issues

Inheritance tax

2.11   Section 211 IHTA 1984 provides that inheritance tax on UK assets is a testamentary expense. In the absence of a contrary intention in the will, the residue will bear the tax on prior legacies and devises to the extent that they are comprised of UK assets. There is no need for the will to provide that any such gift is 'free of tax'. The fact that a will might state that some gifts are 'free of tax' but is silent on others, does not cause those other gifts to be subject to tax – clear words imposing a charge to tax must be used if the residuary estate is to be relieved of the liability.

The words 'free of tax' will only relieve the gift of UK inheritance tax, but not of any similar tax payable in a foreign country in respect of any part of the fund from which the legacy is to be satisfied. More particular words are necessary in such instance, specifically directing that the gift is free of all taxes and duties whatsoever (there are many forms of words that may be used and each situation will need to be considered on its own merits).

Capital gains tax

2.12   The satisfaction of a general legacy in cash does not give rise to any capital gains tax issues.

If the legatee receives assets, these will normally be appropriated to him at the value as at the date of appropriation (*Re Charteris, Charteris v Biddulph [1917] 2 Ch 379*). Provided that the value appropriated does not exceed the value of the legacy, the beneficiary will be deemed to acquire the assets at the date of death value, as 'legatee' under section 62(4) TCGA 1992. This will include a gift of 'things' which is satisfied out of assets belonging to the testator at the date of his death.

If the legacy is a 'gift of things' and is satisfied by way of purchase by the LPR, the beneficiary will acquire those 'things' at the LPR's purchase price.

Income tax

2.13   Interest is payable to the legatee without the deduction of tax (Income and Corporation Taxes Act 1988 (ICTA 1988), ss 348, 349), even though it may be payable out of taxed income.

There is an exception, though, where the interest is due to a person 'whose place of abode is outside of the United Kingdom' (ICTA 1988, s 349(2)). In such instances, interest is paid after deduction of tax at the 'rate applicable to savings' (20% in the tax year 2003–04). The LPR must account to the Inland Revenue for the tax deducted (ICTA 1988, s 350) and provide the legatee with a tax deduction certificate.

In the hands of the legatee, the interest is treated as income of the year of receipt, irrespective of the period during which it might have accrued.

Any interest paid on legacies is not allowable as a deduction against the income of the LPR for taxation purposes. However, it is deductible when computing the residuary estate income in the hands of those beneficiaries entitled (ICTA 1988, s 697(1)).

Stamp duty

2.14   The transfer or conveyance by which title to any asset appropriated in satisfaction of a general legacy is vested in the name of the beneficiary, or his nominee, will be exempt from stamp duty if it is endorsed with the relevant certificate referring to category D of the Schedule to the Stamp Duty (Exempt Instruments) Regulations 1987 (SI 1987/516).

If the transfer or conveyance does not carry the appropriate certificate, it should be submitted to the Stamp Office for adjudication and will be subject to stamp duty at the fixed rate of £5.

Demonstrative legacies

2.15   This is a gift of a general nature which is directed to be paid out of a designated fund or property: typically, a legacy described as '£5,000 to A to be paid from my current account with ABC Bank plc'.

This type of legacy is distinct from the specific legacy ('the balance of my current account with ABC Bank plc') as the specific legacy is a legacy only of the thing given (and if that does not exist the gift fails). The demonstrative legacy on the other hand is essentially one of a general gift, an amount which can be paid from the general estate if the designated fund for payment does not exist (*Re Webster, Goss v Webster [1937] 1 All ER 602* where a legacy of £3,000 was payable out of a designated fund; Wright MR observed: 'These words ought, I think, to be construed as meaning "to be paid to him primarily out of the share . . ." ').

If the fund exists, but it is insufficient to pay the legacy, that part of the amount which can be paid from the designated fund is paid, and is a demonstrative legacy, but the balance which can be paid from the estate generally is a general legacy (the distinction between the two parts is important for the purposes of abatement – see 8.16). The testator is, however, at liberty, should he wish, to expressly direct that a demonstrative legacy will only be paid out of the designated fund and from nowhere else.

Demonstrative legacies are not commonly found in modern wills. The general aversion to them is that there is little practical point in them. Modern drafting tends much more to favour the specific and general gifts as being more easily understood and identified. They also have more certainty as to how they may be affected by changes in the testator's estate before death.

Income

2.16   Where the fund out of which the legacy is to be paid still exists, the legacy carries a right to a proportionate share of the income of the fund, equal to the proportion that the legacy bears to the entire fund. In such case, income runs from the date of death.

Where the legacy exceeds the fund out of which it is to be paid (or the fund is not available to satisfy the legacy), the excess is treated as a general legacy (see 2.10 above) and carries the right to income accordingly.

Taxation issues

Inheritance tax

2.17   Section 211 IHTA 1984 provides that inheritance tax on UK assets is a testamentary expense. In the absence of a contrary intention in the will, the residue will bear the tax on a demonstrative legacy to the extent that it is payable out of UK assets. There is no need for the will to provide that any such gift is 'free of tax'. The fact that a will directs that some gifts are 'free of tax' but is silent on others, does not cause those other gifts to be subject to tax – clear words imposing a charge to tax must be used if the residuary estate is to be relieved of the liability.

The words 'free of tax' will only relieve the gift of UK inheritance tax, and not of any similar tax payable in a foreign country in respect of the fund out of which the gift is to be satisfied. More particular words are necessary in such instance, specifically directing that the gift is free of all taxes and duties whatsoever (there are many forms of words that may be used and each situation will need to be considered on its own merits).

If the gift is payable out of a fund comprised of foreign assets, in the absence of specific directions the beneficiary will be liable both for the foreign taxes relating to that fund, and for the proportionate part of the UK inheritance tax.

Capital gains tax

2.18   If assets are appropriated to the beneficiary in satisfaction of their legacy, the rules as they relate to the appropriation of assets in satisfaction of a general legacy (see 2.12 above) apply. Whilst any assets will be re-valued for appropriation as at the date of the appropriation (*Re Charteris, Charteris v Biddulph [1917] 2 Ch 379*), the legatee will be deemed to have acquired them as legatee at the date of value (TCGA 1992, s 62(4)).

Income tax

2.19   The income tax rules follow the nature of the beneficiary's right to income.

Where the beneficiary's right is to a proportionate part of the income of the fund out of which the legacy is payable, such income is taxed in his hands on the 'income arising' basis (this will include where the amount of the legacy exceeds the fund out of which it is payable, in which case the beneficiary will be entitled to the whole of the income of the fund). When the legacy, or that part of the legacy that can be paid out of the designated fund, is satisfied, this triggers the application of 'relation back'. Accordingly, the income is deemed to have been the income of the beneficiary from the date of death.

As identified above, where the fund is insufficient to satisfy the whole of the legacy, the excess is treated as a general legacy. Interest payable upon that part of the legacy is subject to the same rules as for a general legacy, and the income tax position is as set out at 2.13 above.

Stamp duty

2.20   The transfer or conveyance by which title to any asset appropriated in satisfaction of a demonstrative legacy is vested in the name of the beneficiary, or his nominee, will be exempt from stamp duty if it is endorsed with the relevant certificate referring to category D of the Schedule to the Stamp Duty (Exempt Instruments) Regulations 1987 (SI 1987/516).

If the transfer or conveyance does not carry the appropriate certificate, it should be submitted to the Stamp Office for adjudication and will be subject to stamp duty at the fixed rate of £5.

Annuities

2.21   These are gifts of fixed periodic income payments to beneficiaries for life or a shorter period as will be specified in the will. Once common in wills, annuities are far less common today. The post-war effects of inflation have made annuities by will fairly unattractive propositions. Annuities that are secured on land are known as rentcharges (the Administration of Estates Act 1925, s 55(1)(ix) defines a pecuniary legacy as including an annuity).

Annuities can pose a practical problem in the administration and distribution of the estate. Unless the will is drawn in such a way as to limit the estate liability, for example by specifying the value of fund to finance the annuity or by directing that a fund is charged with the annuity to the exoneration of the rest of the estate, all of the estate which is comprised of gifts which would abate before the annuity is charged with the annuity and the annuitant has a right of recourse to capital should the income alone be insufficient. The decisions as to the retention and distribution of residue, where the fund on which the annuity is charged is not limited, require very careful consideration and, where necessary, the agreement of the court (*Re Hill, Westminster Bank Ltd v Wilson [1944] Ch 270*). The executor would have a personal risk should the residue of the estate be distributed and the funds retained prove insufficient to meet the annuity (*May v Bennett (1826) 1 Russ 370*).

An annuitant is the person (legatee) entitled to receive the annuity and in general he is only entitled to receive those income payments specified and not a capital sum in lieu of them. He may, however, have the option to receive a capital payment in lieu in five circumstances.

1.   *Where the will expressly gives him this option*

This will usually be expressed with a specified time in which the option must be exercised. Where this occurs, the will will usually contain a definition of how the capital sum is to be calculated.

2.   *Where the will gives a direction to the executor that an annuity is to be purchased out of the estate (annuities are commercially available from many life companies)*

Where the will directs that a specific sum be set aside from the estate for the purchase of an annuity the annuitant has the option of taking either the annuity or the sum specified (*Re Robbins, Robbins v Legge [1907] 2 Ch 8*). The testator may attach to the direction to purchase an annuity a prohibition against the annuitant taking a capital sum in lieu, but there is authority to suggest that this is not effective to prevent the capital sum from being taken at the annuitant's option before purchase (*Hunt-Foulston v Furber (1876) 3 Ch D 285*). This should be distinguished from a direction in the will attaching to the annuity that the annuity should cease and the annuitant be required to be assigned to another on a specified event, as this would prevent the annuitant from taking the capital sum in lieu (*Re Draper (1888) 57 LJ Ch 942*).

3.   *Where there is insufficient capital in the estate to provide a fund large enough to generate sufficient income to pay the annuity*

In these circumstances the annuitant can have his interest actuarially valued and that interest settled by a single capital payment (*Re Cox, Public Trustee v Eve [1938] Ch 556*, but see also *Re Hill, Westminster Bank Ltd v Wilson [1944] Ch 270* on the practical circumstances where a court would not apply this general rule).

4.   *Under the rule in Saunders v Vautier (1841) 4 Beav 115*

Where, if the annuitant and the beneficiaries entitled to the remainder after the annuity are all ascertained and sui juris, they may collectively agree on a division of the fund and direct the trustee to distribute it in that way.

5.   *A court application under the Variation of Trusts Act 1958*

If the beneficiaries are not all ascertained and sui juris, a court application is possible where the sums involved are sufficiently large to warrant the costs of such an exercise.

Taxation issues

Inheritance tax

2.22   An annuity is the right to receive an income stream and, whilst a general legacy, it is the underlying capital value from which the income is generated that is subject to inheritance tax.

Where an annuity is given 'free of tax' or 'subject to tax', depending upon the context this may be a reference to income tax (which will be considered later), rather than inheritance tax.

Where there is a direction to apply a particular sum (or fund) in the purchase of an annuity, the provisions of section 211 IHTA 1984 will need to be considered.

Section 211 provides that inheritance tax on UK assets is a testamentary expense. In the absence of a contrary intention in the will, residue will bear the tax on prior gifts to the extent that they are to be satisfied out of UK assets. There is no need for the will to provide that any such gift is 'free of tax'. The fact that a will directs that some gifts are 'free of tax' but is silent on others does not cause those other gifts to be subject to tax – clear words imposing a charge to tax must be used if the residuary estate is to be relieved of the liability.

The words 'free of tax' will only relieve the gift of UK inheritance tax, and not of any similar tax payable in a foreign country in respect of any part of the fund out of which the gift is to be satisfied. More particular words are necessary in such instance, specifically directing that the gift is free of all taxes and duties whatsoever (there are many forms of words that may be used and each situation will need to be considered on its own merits).

If the annuity is payable out of a fund comprised of foreign assets, in the absence of specific directions the sum to be set aside will be reduced both by the foreign taxes relating to that fund and the proportionate part of the UK inheritance tax.

Capital gains tax

2.23   Where the annuity is charged upon a particular fund, any assets appropriated to that fund will be acquired by the trustee(s) as 'legatee' at the date of death value (TCGA 1992, s 62(4)).

The trustee(s) will be assessable to capital gains tax upon the net gains (if any) arising in the fund out of which the annuity is payable, whether or not it is set aside from the remainder of the estate.

Income tax

2.24   In the absence of any direction to the contrary:

- the annuity begins immediately after the death of the testator;

- payments are made in arrears; and

- the first payment is due upon the expiry of the executor's year (per Lord Eldon in *Gibson v Bott (1802) 7 Ves 89*).

Annuity payments are made net of tax at the basic rate, and the annuitant is entitled to receive a certificate of deduction of tax. Payments are due upon the anniversary of the death of the testator unless the will directs otherwise, in which case the instalments of the annuity are payable on the dates set down in the will.

Whilst the annuity is taxable as the income of the annuitant upon the due date of payment, if the income of the fund is insufficient to satisfy any particular payment, the annuitant's income for that year is reduced accordingly. If the deficiency is subsequently satisfied, the sum then paid is treated as income of the year of receipt.

Where the will directs that any shortfall in the income is to be made up out of capital, such capital sum applied is after deduction of tax at the basic rate (*Brodies' Trustees v IRC (1933) 17 TC 432*).

Whilst the stated amount of the annuity is usually the amount payable before the deduction of tax at the basic rate, the will may direct that the annuity is 'free of income tax', or 'after deduction of tax at the basic rate'.

In the first instance, the amount paid to the annuitant is the stated sum, which is grossed up at the basic rate for income tax purposes. If the annuitant is entitled to a refund of tax, due to his personal income together with the annuity not exceeding the lower rate tax band, he must account to the trustees for the proportionate part of any refund of tax obtained in respect of the annuity paid to him in that tax year (*Re Pettit, Le Fevre v Pettit [1922] 2 Ch 765*).

Where the terms of the will direct the payment of a specified sum 'after deduction of tax at the basic rate', any repayment of tax obtained by the annuitant is due wholly to him and no part of it may be claimed by the trustee(s) (*Re Jones, Jones v Jones [1933] Ch 842*).

Where the LPR purchases the annuity, the whole of the payments to the annuitant are subject to tax at the basic rate (ICTA 1988, s 657(2)(c)). However, if the annuitant has a right to call for the value of the annuity to be paid to him, instead of the LPR applying it in the purchase of an annuity, the sum paid by the executor to the annuitant will be received by the annuitant as capital, not income. If the annuitant then purchases the annuity, only a part of the regular payment will be income, and thus subject to the deduction of tax at the basic rate; the remainder will be capital, and free from tax (ICTA 1988, s 656).

Statutory legacies

2.25   Statutory legacy is the term applied to the statutory provision made for a surviving spouse, prior to the statutory gift of residue, on the intestacy of the other spouse (Administration of Estates Act 1925, s 46). The amount of the statutory legacy is adjusted from time to time by statutory instrument. Such adjustments are not retrospective in effect and therefore when examining questions of intestacy it is important to ensure that the relevant statutory instrument is applied. The last such adjustment was in 1993 (Family Provision (Intestate Succession) Order 1993 (SI 1993/2906)). The surviving spouse's statutory legacy is on one of two amounts:

(a)   Where there are surviving issue of the intestate, the spouse's statutory legacy is an absolute gift of the personal chattels, £125,000 (free of duties and costs), together with interest thereon from the date of death to payment of 6% simple per annum (Intestate Succession (Interest and Capitalisation) Order 1977 (SI 1977/1491) amended by Intestate Succession (Interest and Capitalisation) Order 1977 (Amendment) Order 1983 (SI 1983/1374)).

(b)   Where there are no surviving issue of the intestate (but there is a parent, sibling of the whole blood or their issue), the spouse's statutory legacy is an absolute gift of the personal chattels, £200,000 (free of duties and costs), together with interest thereon from the date of death to payment of 6% simple per annum (Intestate Succession (Interest and Capitalisation) Order 1977 (SI 1977/1491) amended by Intestate Succession (Interest and Capitalisation) Amendment Order 1983 (SI 1983/1374)).

NB Where there are no surviving issue or parents, or no siblings of the whole blood or their issue, there would be no statutory legacy for the surviving spouse as they would take the entire estate of the intestate spouse.

Taxation issues

Inheritance tax

2.26   As a gift to the spouse of the intestate, the legacy will usually be exempt from inheritance tax (IHTA 1984, s 18(1)), except where, immediately before the death, the intestate, but not the surviving spouse, was domiciled within the UK. In this latter instance, any transfer to the spouse is exempt only up to the sum of £55,000 (IHTA 1984, s 18(2)).

Where the statutory legacy to a non-UK domiciled spouse exceeds the combined total of the reduced exemption and the balance of any inheritance tax nil rate band available upon the death of the intestate, the amount of that excess is 'grossed up' and inheritance tax is payable out of residue upon the gross amount.

Capital gains tax

2.27   The satisfaction of the statutory legacy in cash does not give rise to any capital gains tax issues.

If the spouse receives assets, these will normally be appropriated to him/her at the value as at the date of appropriation (*Re Charteris, Charteris v Biddulph [1917] 2 Ch 379*). Provided that the value appropriated does not exceed the value of the legacy, the spouse will be deemed to acquire the assets at the date of death value, as 'legatee' under section 62(4) TCGA 1992.

Income tax

2.28   Interest is payable to the spouse without the deduction of tax (ICTA 1988, ss 348, 349), even though it may be payable out of taxed income.

There is an exception, though, where the interest is due to a person 'whose place of abode is outside of the United Kingdom' (ICTA 1988, s 349(2)). In such instances, interest is paid after deduction of tax at the 'rate applicable to savings' (20% in the tax year 2002–03). The LPR must account to the Inland Revenue for the tax deducted (ICTA 1988, s 350) and provide the legatee with a tax deduction certificate.

Interest is treated as income of the spouse in the year of receipt, irrespective of the period during which it might have accrued.

Interest paid on legacies is not allowable as a deduction against the income of the LPR for taxation purposes. However, it is deductible when computing the residuary estate income in the hands of those beneficiaries entitled (ICTA 1988, s 697(1)).

Stamp duty

2.29   Where the transfer or conveyance by which title to any asset appropriated in satisfaction of a statutory legacy is vested in the name of the spouse, or his/her nominee, it will be exempt from stamp duty if it is endorsed with the relevant certificate under category C of the Schedule to the Stamp Duty (Exempt Instruments) Regulations 1987 (SI 1987/516).

If the transfer or conveyance does not carry the appropriate certificate, it should be submitted to the Stamp Office for adjudication and will be subject to stamp at the fixed rate of £5.

Residuary legacies

2.30   Residue is that part of an estate which remains after the payment of:

- all debts due at death;

- taxes;

- prior legacies (i.e. all other legacies that are not expressed as residuary legacies);

- estate administration costs;

and if the payment of these items exhausts the estate the residuary legatees will receive nothing.

Generally residuary gifts in wills are easily identified in that they are clearly expressed as gifts of residue or shares of a residuary fund. Greater difficulty will arise where residue is ill-defined. It should also be noted that whereas shares of residue are conventionally expressed as percentages of fractions of the residue of the estate, it is sometimes the case that some parts of the residuary gift may be expressed in fixed amounts.

The value of gifts of residue will be eroded by falls in value of the estate, for example by depreciation in assets, debts, gifts etc. Equally, it will be enhanced by increases in value in the estate. For this reason, it is important for testators to keep the terms of the will under review where their wills contain substantial legacies, as the ratio between the value of the specific gifts and the residuary gifts can alter swiftly with changes to the estate. For similar reasons it is important for testators to understand the extent to which additional burdens placed on residue (through the burden of inheritance tax being placed on residue, for example) reduce the amount that the residuary legatees receive.

Income

2.31   The residuary income is the balance of the estate income after all outgoings and other liabilities properly payable out of income have been satisfied (this will include interest paid on both inheritance tax and legacies as well as other payments which are generally accepted to be of an income nature, together with those general administration costs of the estate that relate to income). The beneficiaries are entitled to such income in proportion to their rights to share in the capital of the residuary estate (clearly, if there is a life interest, it is the life tenant who is entitled to the appropriate share of the income, not the remaindermen of that share).

Where the beneficiaries are absolutely entitled to residue, regard is rarely given to the possibility of an apportionment of income over the date of the deceased's death. As the eventual destination of the income will be the same, such an apportionment is generally seen as unnecessary. In such cases, the tax certificates issued to the beneficiaries at the end of the day will normally reflect all the income received by the LPRs, less the permitted deductions.

However, where beneficiaries have a limited interest in residue, the effect of apportionment is to convert income accruing up to the date of death into capital in the hands of the LPR. In such cases, the income of the beneficiary with only a limited interest in residue may appear to be less than that of a beneficiary with an absolute interest in an equivalent share of the estate.

Most modern wills contain an express direction that no apportionment shall be made. By such a will, if any beneficiary is entitled only to income, the relevant proportion of any income receipt (or expenditure incurred) after the date of the testator's death will 'belong' to that beneficiary. Care must be taken, however, as the form of wording of such clauses may vary. Some direct the benefit of the income stream (or liabilities) by reference to the due date of payment, others to the date of receipt. Whilst the former is clear, the latter may be uncertain – is a dividend 'received' when the dividend cheque appears on the proverbial doormat; when the executor pays it into the estate bank account; or when the cheque is eventually debited to the drawer's account?

One might look to the rules for the making of a gift, where the relevant date is the date that the cheque is debited to the donor's account, on the basis that payment could be stopped at any point up until then. A cheque is not an assignment of any money standing to the credit of the drawer's account (*Hopkinson v Forster (1874) LR 19 Eq 74*), so that no 'debt' arises until the cheque is presented for payment at the drawer's bankers (*Schroeder v Central Bank of London (1876) 24 WR 710*). However, the payment of a dividend is a contractual matter, once the dividend has been declared, and so would the paying company have any right to stop the cheque? Reliance upon the date that dividends etc are 'received' may therefore give rise to debate. It is unfortunate that what would normally be a 'simplifying' clause should introduce uncertainty.

Taxation issues

Inheritance tax

2.32   The residuary estate will bear the inheritance tax due upon all prior legacies and/or devises, to the extent that such gifts are not specifically charged with the payment of tax (IHTA 1984, s 211). Where prior legacies and devises do not bear their own tax, the tax is usually a general charge on the residuary estate before division, so that even those shares of residue given to exempt beneficiaries (e.g. the surviving spouse or charities) will bear a proportionate part of the tax on such gifts. Whilst it is open to the testator to direct that the tax on such gifts is to be paid out of a particular part of his estate, this happens only rarely in practice. The residuary beneficiaries will be liable for the tax in the ratio that the value of their respective interests have to each other. Where part of residue is given to trustees (whether for an interest in possession or a discretionary trust), it is the trustees' 'share' that will bear the tax.

Where residue is given wholly to an exempt beneficiary, whilst no inheritance tax will be payable on that residue, it will still be liable for the inheritance tax on any prior gifts not bearing their own tax.

If residue is given to a number of beneficiaries, some of whom are exempt, and the others non-exempt, the extent to which inheritance tax will be assessable upon, and payable out of, individual shares of residue will be dependent upon the precise wording of the will.

The traditional 'gross division' view is that the provisions of section 41 IHTA 1984 require that the value of the residuary estate is notionally divided between the exempt and non-exempt beneficiaries, in proportion to their stated interests. The value of the non-exempt share(s) is then brought into the calculation of the inheritance tax charge and the tax due on the residuary gifts charged proportionately between the non-exempt shares of residue only.

This traditional view was brought into question by the courts in 1994 (*Re Benham's Will Trusts [1995] STC 210*), when it was held that the division of the residuary estate took place only after inheritance tax had been paid. This resulted in both a significant increase in the charge to inheritance tax, and the need for a very complicated model for calculating the tax charge, even in the most straightforward of estates (for such purposes were computers invented!).

The application of section 41 and the decision in *Re Benham's* were reviewed by the court in 1999 (*Re Ratcliffe, Holmes v McMullan [1999] STC 262*), and it was held that the traditional view of section 41 applied, notwithstanding the decision in *Re Benham's*, as that decision did not set down a principle and, therefore, need not be followed.

In writing of the 1999 decision in *The TACT Review (The Quarterly Journal of The Association of Corporate Trustees, October 1999)* 'Benham's Will Trusts – RIP', Brian Walsh of Campbell Hooper, the solicitors who represented the charities in that case, observed:

> 'In effect, Mr Justice Blackburne's decision overrules *Re Benham* although the decisions are both at the same level and decided in courts of equal standing, it is settled law that: "where there are two conflicting decisions, the latter decision is preferred, if it is reached after full consideration of the earlier decision . . .".'

If, in an estate, there is any doubt that residue should be divided between exempt and non-exempt beneficiaries other than on the 'gross division' basis, the LPR would be well advised to take formal legal advice.

Capital gains tax

2.33   In the year of death, and in each of the following two tax years, the LPR has a capital gains tax annual allowance equal to that for an individual (TCGA 1992, s 3(7)) (2003–04 – £7,900) . After the expiry of this period, the LPR's annual allowance ceases. They are also entitled to 'taper relief', the qualifying period of ownership starting on the date of death. LPRs are assessable to capital gains tax at the rate of 34%, to the extent that net gains exceed the available allowance. If disposals by the LPR give rise to a loss for capital gains tax purposes, normally this may only be set against gains of the LPR realised in the tax year in which the loss arose, and in subsequent years. The loss cannot be passed on to the beneficiaries.

Accordingly, when considering the sale of assets, the LPR may need to review whether they should be made by him in his capacity as LPR, or if they should be made on behalf of the beneficiaries (see CHAPTER 12, for consideration of the factors relevant to the appropriation of assets to beneficiaries). If sales are made by the LPR after appropriation to a residuary beneficiary, the sale will be made as 'bare trustee' for that beneficiary and no part of the gains (or any losses) will be attributable to the estate for capital gains tax purposes.

When assets are appropriated to, or otherwise transferred to, the residuary legatee there is normally no disposal by the LPR. The beneficiary will be deemed to acquire those assets at the date of death value as legatee (TCGA 1992, s 62(4)).

There will be occasions where a residuary beneficiary will introduce cash into the estate so as to avoid the need to sell particular assets, with a view to those assets being transferred to him in specie at the end of the administration period. This most frequently occurs where he wants to keep the house, which would otherwise need to be sold to discharge the liabilities of the estate, whether such liabilities are outstanding debts, administration expenses, inheritance tax or prior legacies.

Where a beneficiary introduces cash to enable the liabilities of the estate to be discharged and, as a consequence thereof, for land (such as the deceased's house) to be appropriated to him, whilst the transaction is characterised as a sale (*Passant v Jackson [1986] STC 164*, per Slade LJ at 240G), it would appear to be settled law that the beneficiary will acquire the property as 'legatee' under section 62(4) TCGA 1992 (*Passant v Jackson*). The amount paid into the estate cannot be used to reduce any gain upon the eventual sale of the property by the beneficiary, although it is treated as 'consideration' for stamp duty purposes (*Passant v Jackson*), so that ad valorem duty is payable upon the amount of such moneys introduced.

Where the beneficiary introduces cash to enable investments to be transferred to him in specie, this is a sale by the LPR to the beneficiary, to the extent of the moneys paid in. As a sale, the LPR will be assessable for any gain arising on the disposal, so that he may need to carefully consider which investments will be 'purchased' by the beneficiary. If it is possible to 'cherry pick' the investments to be 'purchased', there might be merit in selecting those which give rise to the least gain within any capital gains tax allowance available to the LPR (taking account also of any other disposals the LPR may have made, or might make, during the same tax year). The moneys introduced will be treated as consideration for stamp duty, so that ad valorem duty will be payable on the transfers to the beneficiary, or his nominee.

It should be noted that 'private residence relief' (TCGA 1992, s 222) is not available to the LPR in respect of the deceased's home following the death. However, if it is appropriated to a beneficiary who occupies it, that beneficiary may be able to claim such relief for his own period of occupancy, back-dated to the date of death.

Income tax

2.34   Until such time as an appropriation is made in favour of a beneficiary, he only has a chose in action for the due administration of the estate (as confirmed by the House of Lords in *Marshall (Inspector of Taxes) v Kerr [1995] 1 AC 148*). This chose in action represents the beneficiary's (remaining) interest in the estate at any particular point in time. The chose in action is a capital asset, and its value is reduced by the amount of any distribution made to the beneficiary out of the estate, whether such distribution is made in cash or any other form.

The implications of a beneficiary's chose in action were considered by the courts as long ago as 1921 (*Barnardo's Homes v Special Income Tax Comrs [1921] 2 AC 1*). Dr Barnardo's Homes, a charity, submitted a claim to the Inland Revenue for a refund of tax suffered on the income in the hands of the executor of an estate of which it was a beneficiary. The court held that any distribution the charity received from the executor could only be capital, reflecting the nature of its right for the due administration of the estate. Accordingly, it could not claim a refund of tax suffered on the income within the estate. This was, however, a pyrrhic victory for the Inland Revenue. The corollary of the charity not being able to claim the payment of tax suffered in the estate was that those beneficiaries who would otherwise be liable to tax at higher rates on the income from an estate would escape paying the additional tax charge.

The outcome of the *Barnardo's* case is that the residuary beneficiaries are deemed to receive the estate income. The present statutory provisions are in Part XVI ICTA 1988 (ss 695–701). (These provisions were amended by the Finance Act 1995 to assist beneficiaries in complying with the statutory time limits for the lodgement of returns under self assessment; and by the Finance (No 2) Act 1997 to take account of the new regime for the taxation of dividends under Schedule F, effective from 5 April 1999.)

Legislation sets out a different treatment for those beneficiaries with an absolute interest in residue, to those with only a limited interest (e.g. a life interest). These are considered separately below (the position considered is that which applies from 6 April 1999 – the income tax treatment for tax years ending before 6 April 1999 is outside the scope of this work).

Where there are a number of income sources in an estate, subject to tax at differing rates, e.g. basic rate, lower rate, or the Schedule F rate (dividends), it may be beneficial for any allowable deductions to first be applied against the non-repayable Schedule F income; then the income taxed at the lower rate and, lastly, against income taxed at the basic rate. This way, if the beneficiary pays tax other than at the basic or higher rate, he should be able to maximise any potential refund claim.

When issuing the beneficiary with a tax certificate, the LPR is required to 'gross up' the income deemed to have been received by the beneficiary. The certificate must identify the extent to which income was subject to tax at the basic rate, the lower rate, and the Schedule F rate. It is usually beneficial to allocate the income firstly to the basic rate, then to the lower rate and, lastly, to the Schedule F rate. The amount for each tax rate will be limited to the individual beneficiary's proportionate share of:

- the cumulative aggregated income entitlement for the tax year (absolute beneficiaries) (for an explanation of the term 'absolute beneficiaries' and the manner in which it is applied, see 2.35 below), or

- the cumulative income of the estate less the amount of any such income vouched to the beneficiary in previous years, if any (limited interest),

for each of the individual tax rates.

Beneficiary with absolute interest in residue

2.35   To identify the beneficiary's tax position in any tax year, it is necessary to consider two basic points:

1.   what, if anything, has been distributed to them on account of their interest in the estate, and

2.   what is the residual amount of the LPR's cumulative income balance at the end of the tax year?

Under the first point, it should be noted that any distribution to the beneficiary is to be taken into account when considering his income tax position. (Whilst ICTA 1988, s 696(3) refers to the payment of any sum to the beneficiary, ICTA 1988, s 701(12) directs that the payment of any sum under s 696(3) includes an appropriation of assets to the beneficiary, not just payments in cash, or in the nature of cash.) Accordingly, the transfer of, say, the deceased's motor car, or other chattel, to a residuary beneficiary may result in that beneficiary being deemed to have received income from the estate. The release of a debt could also be treated as an income receipt. Other than in the year in which the administration of the estate is completed (see below), the residuary beneficiary is only deemed to have received income if he has actually received benefit from the estate. Such deemed income cannot exceed the value of those distributions.

Having established the limits on the maximum amount of estate income that the residuary beneficiary may be deemed to have received, what is the mechanism applied to identify the actual amount of income deemed to have been paid to that beneficiary?

In the first tax year (i.e. in the tax year in which death occurs), the net income of the LPR is established (this is the amount of income due and payable to the estate, less allowable deductions). From this amount is deducted those expenses and liabilities as permitted under section 697 ICTA 1988, to determine the residuary income of the estate. Such deductions include annual interest, annuity payments, interest on legacies and any management expenses properly payable out of income (to the extent that they have not already been deducted in ascertaining the net income of the estate). The resulting amount is the aggregated income entitlement (AIE) for the estate (if the AIE is a negative amount, the unutilised loss is carried forward to the following year).

Having established the AIE, the beneficiaries are deemed to have received income from the estate of an amount equal to the lesser of:

•   the total of any distributions made to each of them in that tax year, and

•   their proportionate share of the AIE.

If the full amount of a beneficiary's share of the AIE has not been distributed to them, the excess is carried forward and added to that beneficiary's AIE for the next tax year.

If, at the end of the administration of the estate, there is any unutilised balance of AIE, such balance is treated as having been paid to the beneficiary immediately before the end of the administration period (ICTA 1988, s 696(5)).

The above explanation might, perhaps, be helped by an example.

Death: Tax Year 1

Administration completed: Tax Year 3

Residue: to two individuals, in equal shares

Net income of the estate, less permitted deductions:	Tax Year 1: £1,000
	Tax Year 2: £3,500
	Tax Year 3: £2,500

Distributions:

Tax Year	Beneficiary 1	Beneficiary 2
1	£800	Nil
2	£100,000	£100,000
3	£1,000	£1,800

Calculation of beneficiaries' income under section 696:

Tax Year			Beneficiary 1	Beneficiary 2
1	AIE for tax year 1	£1,000	£500	£500
	Less distributions	£500	£500*	Nil
	Carry forward	£500	Nil	£500
2	AIE for tax year 2	£3,500	£1,750	£1,750
	Cumulative AIE	£4,000	£1,750	£2,250
	Less distributions	£4,000	£1,750*	£2,250*
	Carry forward	Nil	Nil	Nil
3	AIE for tax year 3	£2,500	£1,250	£1,250
	Less distributions	£2,250	£1,000*	£1,250
	Unutilised at completion of administration	£250	£250**	Nil

* This is the amount of income deemed to have been received by the beneficiary, being the lesser of the total distribution made to him in the tax year and his proportionate share of the cumulative AIE.

** This amount is deemed to have been paid to the beneficiary immediately before the end of the administration period.

If a beneficiary dies during the course of the administration of the estate, the AIE is 'ruled off' as at the date of his death. To the extent that his proportionate share of the AIE at that date attaches to distributions made during his lifetime, it is deemed to be his income and is included in the tax settlement to the date of his death. Any unutilised balance of the AIE will attach to future distributions to the deceased beneficiary's LPRs or, if the unadministered interest in the estate is assented to those entitled to that beneficiary's estate, to those beneficiaries (ICTA 1988, s 698(2)).

Beneficiary with a limited interest

2.36   The beneficiary is deemed to have received a payment of income equal to the aggregate amount of the distributions, if any, made to him during any tax year during the administration of the estate. The amount of the distributions is 'grossed up' at the appropriate tax rates (depending upon the source of the income out of which it is deemed to have been paid, i.e. basic rate, lower rate or Schedule F rate) and is treated as income of the tax year in which it is paid.

At the end of the administration period, the beneficiary is deemed to have been paid any outstanding balance due to him in that tax year, irrespective of whether or not it is actually paid over to him (ICTA 1988, s 695(3)). Unlike the pre-1995 regime, there is no requirement to re-allocate the income on a day-to-day basis throughout the entire period of the administration.

Stamp duty

2.37   Other than where assets are appropriated to a beneficiary who has introduced cash to satisfy any liabilities of the estate (including the satisfaction of prior legacies), transfers to beneficiaries are exempt from stamp duty under the Stamp Duty (Exempt Instruments) Regulations 1987 (SI 1987/516).

The transfer or conveyance by which title to the asset is vested in the name of the residuary beneficiary, or his nominee, should be endorsed with the relevant certificate referring to category E of the Schedule to the 1987 Regulations.

If the transfer or conveyance does not carry the appropriate certificate, it should be submitted to the Stamp Office for adjudication and will be subject to stamp duty at the fixed rate of £5.

Legacies to executors

2.38   Legacies that are given to those who are appointed executors of the will require special consideration. The points considered below regarding executors do not arise if the legacy given to the executor is a residuary legacy (*Griffiths v Pruen (1840) 11 Sim 202*). The prime importance of this issue is that the executor who renounces, or otherwise fails to act as executor, will not receive his legacy unless he can show that the legacy does not attach to that office.

A legacy given to an executor is presumed to be given to him as executor and the burden is placed on him to show that there is something within the gift, or the other circumstances of the will, that rebuts this presumption (*Harrison v Rowley (1798) 4 Ves 212; Stackpoole v Howell (1807) 13 Ves 417*). This presumption is rebutted if it is established (usually from the terms of the gift) that it was not given to the executor in that capacity. Thus, words which can indicate that the legacy is given as, and designated, as:

- a remembrance (*Bubb v Yelverton (1871) LR 13 Eq 131*),

- a mark of esteem (*Burgess v Burgess (1844) 1 Coll 367*),

- to a friend (*Re Denby (1861) 3 De GF & J 350*),

- through love and affection or to a relative (*Compton v Bloxham (1845) 2 Coll 201*),

tend against the gift attaching to the office of executor. In the case of a solicitor appointed as executor where the will contained a professional charging clause as well as a personal legacy, it was held that the legacy was to reward the solicitor for work and responsibility as executor which was not covered by the charging clause (*Re Parry, Dalton v Cooke [1969] 2 All ER 512*). The reform by Part V Trustee Act 2000 would now make the inclusion of a charging clause in favour of the professional acting as executor unnecessary, but it is suggested the same position would pertain after this Act, as the statutory power would be considered to replace the express charging clause.

In order to receive his legacy (one which has attached to his office) the executor must:

(a)   prove the will, or

(b)   take steps, short of proving the will, which show an unequivocal intention to act.

Whilst (a) is essentially a question of fact, proving the will must be done with the intention of performing the administration. To prove the will and take no further steps in the administration does not entitle the executor to his legacy (this is wonderfully illustrated by *Harford v Browning (1787) 1 Cox Eq Cas 302* where the executor eloped with and married the testator's daughter (and heiress), but apart from taking the grant took no action in the estate) unless the reason for taking further action is the death of the executor (*Hollingworth v Grasett (1845) 15 Sim 52*). In order to take his legacy, it is not necessary that the executor should carry out all of the administration; it is possible that he can still take his legacy if, having initially reserved power, he subsequently takes a grant (*Angermann v Ford (1861) 29 Beav 349*).

The position in (b) is less clear cut. It has been held that where an executor has died, prior to obtaining a grant, that his estate would nonetheless receive his legacy where he had arranged for the funeral (*Harrison v Rowley (1798) 4 Ves 212*) or, when out of the country, has given a power of attorney to another to obtain a grant (*Lewis v Matthews (1869) LR 8 Eq 277*). However, where the executor may be willing to act, but is prevented from doing so by age or illness this is insufficient to permit him to claim his legacy (*Re Hawkins Trusts (1864) 33 Beav 570*).

Interest

2.39   In the absence of any indication in the will that the legacy is not given to the executor in that capacity, or of any direction as to the payment of interest upon the legacy, the executor is entitled to receive interest from the date upon which the legacy becomes due (*Angermann v Ford (1861) 29 Beav 349*). Where the executor takes up his duties shortly after the death, it may be convenient to take the date of death as the appropriate date.

Unless the will specifies a particular rate, interest is payable at 6% simple (Rules of the Supreme Court (Amendment No 2) Order 1983, SI 1983/1181), even if the residuary estate has been producing income at a higher rate (*Re Campbell, Campbell v Campbell [1893] 3 Ch 468*).

If the executor is a minor as at the date of death, the legacy cannot be 'due' during his minority. Interest will not start to run until he takes a grant.

The interest will accrue on a daily basis, on the amount of the legacy that remains outstanding. When any distribution is made in part satisfaction of the legacy, it is first applied to discharge the interest accrued to that date, and any surplus used to reduce the outstanding balance of the legacy (*Re Morley's Estate, Hollenden v Morley [1937] 3 All ER 204*).

If the legacy is given to the executor, other than in that capacity, the rules for interest on general legacies will apply.

If the legacy to the executor is a specific legacy, or devise, there is no difference in the entitlement to the income produced by the subject matter of the gift, and the executor's entitlement will be as described in 2.3 above.

Taxation issues

Inheritance tax

2.40   Section 211 IHTA 1984 provides that inheritance tax on UK assets is a testamentary expense. In the absence of a contrary intention in the will, residue will bear the tax on prior legacies and devises to the extent that they are comprised of UK assets. There is no need for the will to provide that any such gift is 'free of tax'. The fact that a will might state that some gifts are 'free of tax' but is silent on others, does not cause those other gifts to be subject to tax – clear words imposing a charge to tax must be used if the residuary estate is to be relieved of the liability.

The words 'free of tax' will only relieve the gift of UK inheritance tax, but not of any similar tax payable in a foreign country in respect of any part of the fund from which the legacy is to be satisfied. More particular words are necessary in such instance, specifically directing that the gift is free of all taxes and duties whatsoever (there are many forms of words that may be used and each situation will need to be considered on its own merits).

Capital gains tax

2.41   The satisfaction of a general legacy in cash does not give rise to any capital gains tax issues.

The statutory power of appropriation under section 41 Administration of Estates Act 1925 does not permit an LPR to appropriate assets to himself, other than cash or the equivalent of cash (*Kane v Radley-Kane [1999] Ch 274*).

If the executor wishes to appropriate assets to himself, he may only do so under a specific power within the will, or with the consent of all the beneficiaries, if such appropriation is not to be voidable.

In those rare situations where the executor may be able validly to appropriate assets to himself, these will normally be appropriated to him at the value as at the date of appropriation (*Re Charteris, Charteris v Biddulph [1917] 2 Ch 379*). Provided that the value appropriated does not exceed the value of the legacy, the executor will be deemed to acquire the assets at the date of death value, as 'legatee' under section 62(4) TCGA 1992.

If the gift to the executor is a specific legacy or devise, the capital gains tax position will be as described in 2.5.

Income tax

2.42   Interest is payable to the legatee without the deduction of tax (ICTA 1988, ss 348, 349), even though it may be payable out of taxed income.

There is an exception, though, where the interest is due to a person 'whose place of abode is outside of the United Kingdom' (ICTA 1988, s 349(2)). In such instances, interest is paid after deduction of tax at the 'rate applicable to savings' (20% in the tax year 2002–03). The LPR must account to the Inland Revenue for the tax deducted (ICTA 1988, s 350) and provide the legatee with a tax deduction certificate.

In the hands of the legatee, the interest is treated as income of the year of receipt, irrespective of the period during which it might have accrued.

Any interest paid on legacies is not allowable as a deduction against the income of the LPR for taxation purposes. However, it is deductible when computing the residuary estate income in the hands of those beneficiaries entitled (ICTA 1988, s 697(1)).

If the gift to the executor is a specific legacy or devise, the income tax position will be as described in 2.6 above.

Stamp duty

2.43   As identified above, the circumstances in which an executor may appropriate assets other than cash, or the equivalent of cash, in satisfaction of his legacy will be rare. However, where this is permitted, the transfer or conveyance by which title to any asset appropriated in satisfaction of such a legacy is vested in the name of the executor, or his nominee, will be exempt from stamp duty if it is endorsed with the relevant certificate referring to category D of the Schedule to the Stamp Duty (Exempt Instruments) Regulations 1987 (SI 1987/516).

If the transfer or conveyance does not carry the appropriate certificate, it should be submitted to the Stamp Office for adjudication and will be subject to stamp duty at the fixed rate of £5.

If the gift to the executor is a specific legacy or devise, the stamp duty position will be as described in **2.7** above.

Legacies for monuments or tombs

2.44   A legacy for the purpose of a maintaining or repairing a monument or tomb is not a charitable legacy unless it is part of the fabric of a church and, therefore, potentially void for remoteness unless the expenditure will all be made within the perpetuity period (*Re Martin, Barclays Bank v Board of Governors of St Bartholomew's Hospital [1952] WN 339*). Where the monument or tomb is part of the fabric of the church the purpose is charitable as would be a straightforward gift for the maintenance of the church (*Re Ross [1964] Qd R 132*).

A gift for a sum of money to be expended on erecting a tomb or monument is again not charitable but it is a valid direction to the personal representative which the personal representative can insist on carrying out, although there is no beneficiary who can compel him to do so (*Mellick v President of the Asylum (1821) Jac 180*).

Legacies for animals

2.45   Legacies for the maintenance or upkeep of particular animals are not charitable. Such legacies have in the past been found to be valid although without a beneficiary to enforce them (*Pettinghall v Pettinghall (1842) 11 LJ Ch 176* and *Re Dean, Cooper-Dean v Stevens (1889) 41 Ch D 552*: both have been criticised and are now of slightly dubious authority). Such trusts should be distributable within the permitted perpetuity period, which in this case is twenty-one years (for perpetuity purposes the animal(s) in question could not be taken as the life in being, which must be human; *Re Kelly [1932] IR 255*).

Legacies of human bodies (or parts thereof) and their disposal

2.46   The right to dispose of the body by funeral is the executor's and this cannot be overridden by the terms of the will (*Williams v Williams (1882) 20 Ch D 659*). Therefore legacies in the proper sense of the word cannot be created by will for a body or its parts. The costs of the executor meeting these wishes is borne by the estate. As such costs are paid in preference to the legacies the costs must be reasonable and appropriate to the testator's station in life and wishes.

The law does not recognise any ownership of a corpse (it is possible for ownership of parts to exist, but as this is after the application of skill, this can only arise after death and disposal for medical research; *Dobson v North Tyneside Health Authority [1997] 1 WLR 596*; *R v Kelly [1999] QB 621*) although as well as the right to dispose of the body by funeral, the executor may also dispose of it for anatomical examination and research (see Anatomy Act 1984 generally and section 4 of that Act for conditions for disposal by the executor). Use of body parts for therapeutic purposes may also be authorised by the executor (Human Tissue Act 1961 and Corneal Tissue Act 1986).

Chapter 3

Settled legacies

Introduction

3.1   In this section, we consider the principal features of settled legacies, and the reasons for (and advantages of) their use in wills.

Description

What is a settled legacy?

3.2   In lieu of an outright gift, a testator may consider it preferable to declare that a particular gift should be held upon trust. The effect of this is that the named beneficiaries may only receive income, while the capital is preserved for others, or for the same beneficiaries absolutely upon some future specified date or event (such as when they attain a particular age or marry).

Why do testators use them?

3.3   Settled legacies may be appropriate or advantageous where, for example:

- The testator wants to provide an income for one or more persons (but to preserve the capital for others);

- The testator wishes to protect a person, either from himself or from others;

- The testator wishes to take advantage of whatever tax rules may be in force at his death, so as to maximise the benefit to his family;

- The gift is for beneficiaries who may be under 18 (or sometimes, under 25) at the death of the testator, or disabled; and/or

- The testator wishes to create a flexible discretionary gift to take account of the needs of his family after the date of his death.

When trusts are not appropriate

3.4   A settled legacy is not always appropriate, however. In some cases, there may be good reasons why one should not be used. This will sometimes be the case where a testator is a foreign national, since the laws of the jurisdiction to which he is subject may prohibit the creation of trusts by nationals/citizens of that state (as in Monaco, for example), or may not recognise trusts and may treat the legacy as a beneficial gift to the trustees, sometimes with harmful tax consequences (as in France, for example).

A further point to consider is whether the creation of a trust will infringe the testator's obligations to maintain his spouse, children and other dependants. Under the Inheritance (Provision for Family and Dependants) Act 1975 (IPFDA 1975), a UK domiciled deceased is required to have made 'reasonable financial provision' (s 2(1)) for:

- his surviving spouse;

- any non-remarried former spouse and, since 1 January 1996, any unmarried cohabitee of the deceased;

- his children and any other person treated by the deceased as a child of the family; and

- any other dependant of the deceased.

The standard of provision for a surviving spouse (or non-remarried former spouse if the death occurs within a short period after the separation or divorce) is higher than that for the other classes of applicant. Analogous to the position on divorce, what is required is more than mere maintenance, and the court has a broad discretion to determine what is reasonable (see, for example, *Re Coventry [1980] Ch 461*). Conversely, the other classes of applicant can expect more than is required to keep them 'just above the breadline', but not to have every conceivable need or contingency provided for – in short, there is a subjective assessment of what is reasonable in all the circumstances (*Re Coventry*).

The court's role is not to 'interfere with an estate merely because it would have been reasonable for the deceased to have made provision for the claimant. It is necessary to show that the *lack* of provision was *unreasonable*' (*Cameron v Treasury Solicitor [1997] 1 FCR 188*). By extension, even where provision has been made, it is suggested that it is open to the court to find that the manner in which provision has been made is unreasonable. If a testator left only a life interest to a spouse whose entitlement on divorce would have included an outright sum, it is possible that the court might regard this as unreasonable in all the circumstances. Such an application was refused in a case where the widow had a life interest in the matrimonial home and in a sum of money (*Re Clarke [1991] Fam Law 64*), and an appeal was refused in another case where the wife's first application resulted in an award of a life interest in the whole estate (*Davis v Lush*, (15 January 1991, unreported)). Both these cases, however, pre-date the important House of Lords decision of *White v White ([2001] 1 All ER 1, HL*) which altered the presumptions behind the division of assets on divorce. Whereas previously, the aim of asset allocation was to provide for the needs of the wife (assuming she was non-earning), since *White* the court generally begins with a presumption in favour of equal division, and (put crudely) works backwards. By extension, this is now likely to affect the question of whether an interest in a trust is sufficient for IPFDA 1975 purposes.

Although the quantum of a gift in trust could be insufficient for other claimants, it seems relatively unlikely that the fact of such a claimant (i.e. other than a spouse) only having a life interest would be found unreasonable, since the testator's obligation is only to maintain him, and he would be receiving income. However, if the testator included the claimant only as a discretionary beneficiary, it is possible that the court would act to enlarge the claimant's interest.

Different kinds of trusts

3.5   The terms of the trust will, clearly, depend upon what the testator wishes to achieve. The examples which follow are among the most common types of trust.

Simple life interest trust for beneficiary

3.6   The most basic type of trust, which can be used for settled legacies as easily as for inter vivos settlements, is a fixed interest trust such as a life interest: 'to A for life and then to B'. It is suggested, however, that it is relatively unusual for testators to create simple settled legacies (as opposed to settling upon trust the whole of, or shares in, the residuary estate). It is perhaps more common for the testator to make an outright gift by will, or to settle a legacy in the context of a protective trust, accumulation and maintenance trust or (for details of each of which, see 3.7, 3.9, 3.10 below). In a will where a simple settled legacy is used, it might take a similar form to the following.

Example

'I give to my trustees the sum of [£] [free of tax] to hold the same upon trust to pay the income thereof to my son Albert for life, and subject thereto to hold the same upon trust as to both income and capital for such of Albert's children as survive him [and attain the age of [18/21]], and if more than one in equal shares absolutely. I declare that the administrative provisions contained in [*clauses/schedule*] shall apply to the trusts created by this clause.'

An alternative form of simple life interest is provided by Parliament. Section 179 Law of Property Act 1925 gives power to the Lord Chancellor from time to time to publish forms which a testator may incorporate into his will, either expressly or by implication. The only forms currently in existence are the Statutory Will Forms 1925 (SR&O 1925/780). Part II of the Schedule to that statutory instrument contains the forms which must be incorporated by express wording, of which Form 7 is a settled legacy. This provides a gift to A for life, with power for A to declare by his own will which of his children (or remoter issue) should receive the capital, and in default of such selection to A's children equally. Thus, a testator need not set out in full the terms of a simple settled legacy, but may incorporate Form 7.

Example

'I give to my trustees the sum of £100,000 [free of tax] to hold upon trust for my daughter Brenda and I expressly declare that Form 7 of the Statutory Will Forms 1925 is hereby incorporated into this Will and shall apply to this legacy [subject to the amendments contained in sub-clause [*next sub-clause*]] and I declare that the trustees of this legacy shall have the further administrative powers contained in [*clauses/schedule*].'

Protective trusts

3.7   Protective trusts can be used to protect a vulnerable legatee from his own spending habits or the influence of others. These trusts are arguably less common nowadays, but historically were frequently used to protect heiresses from gold-digging suitors, or to prevent spendthrifts from gambling (or drinking) their entire fortune. Testators wishing to protect the interests of legatees can use the protective trust mechanism, either for residuary gifts or for pecuniary legacies (see also CHAPTER 8 at 8.7 regarding the effect of these trusts). The trusts can be drafted separately if desired, but are also found in statutory form in section 33 Trustee Act 1925, and can be expressly incorporated into the will as follows.

Example

'I give the sum of £[ ] to my Trustees to hold upon protective trusts for my daughter Caroline during her life, remainder to such of her children as survive her and if more than one in equal shares absolutely. I declare that the provisions of section 33 Trustee Act 1925 shall have effect in relation to the trusts created by this clause [subject to the following modifications: (a) my Trustees shall have power at any time or times to pay the whole or any part or parts of the capital to Caroline absolutely or for her benefit; and (b) the administrative provisions contained in [*clause/schedule*] shall apply to the trusts created by this clause].'

The effect of this gift is that the legatee is entitled to an interest in possession in the income of the fund until (if ever) she becomes bankrupt or attempts to sell, mortgage or assign her interest in the fund. At that time, her interest is forfeited and the trust becomes a discretionary trust for the benefit of the legatee and her family (including her spouse and children). The forfeiture takes effect from the date of the relevant event, and not from the date (if later) of a bankruptcy order being made or a payment becoming due to the purported assignee (*Montefiore v Guedalla [1901] 1 Ch 435*). Note that there is no automatic power under section 33 for the trustees to appoint capital to the named beneficiary, so this should be incorporated if it is intended that the trustees should have that facility.

Simple trust for beneficiary/ies on attaining age

3.8   Frequently, the testator will wish to leave a sum of money by way of legacy to a beneficiary (or class of beneficiaries) who is (or are) currently unborn or minor. Since the recipient might still be a minor (or a class might not yet have closed to unborns) at the date of the testator's death, it is necessary to make provision for gifts to be dealt with appropriately:

- under English law, certain kinds of assets, such as real property in the UK, and shares, cannot be held by persons under 18 and (by virtue of Administration of Estates Act 1925, s 42(1)) the executors may appoint separate trustees to hold assets in which a minor is interested, if the will does not already make provision for trustees. Such assets must be held in trust until the child's 18th birthday (or the later date specified in the will); and

- a practical problem arises in relation to property of other kinds (such as cash), since a minor cannot give a good receipt to the executors for capital received (although he can for income, seemingly). It is common practice to include a clause entitling the trustees to rely on a receipt given by the child's parent or guardian on his behalf, or the child himself if he is at least 16.

In many cases, however, the testator may wish any minor beneficiaries to take at an age equal to or later than 18, in which case a simple trust is created as follows:

Example

'I give the sum of £[ ] to my trustees to hold upon trust for such of my children as attain the age of 21 [or marry under that age], and if more than one in equal shares absolutely.'

The testator may, however, wish to provide for later-born beneficiaries as well. A gift along the following lines is appropriate:

Example

'I give the sum of £[ ] to my trustees to hold upon trust for such of my grandchildren as survive the Relevant Date and attain the age of [18] and if more than one in equal shares absolutely. In this clause, the "Relevant Date" shall mean the later to occur of (a) my death and (b) the death of that grandchild's parent, being a child of mine.'

In both of the above examples, the statutory powers of maintenance and advancement (Trustee Act 1925, ss 31, 32) will automatically apply to permit income and capital of each child's presumptive share to be advanced to them, or applied for their benefit, before they attain the appropriate age. The powers may be extended (or excluded) in the usual way, so as to permit the whole of capital to be appointed to the child (or none), and to defer the age at which he becomes entitled to an interest in possession in the income of his presumptive share (which otherwise occurs at 18).

3.9   *Settled legacies*

Accumulation & maintenance trusts for children/grandchildren

3.9   There are special provisions under section 71 Inheritance Tax Act 1984 to govern accumulation and maintenance trusts ('A&M trusts'). An A&M trust is one where:

- one or more beneficiaries must become entitled to an interest in possession at an age not exceeding 25;

- before that time, the assets are to be held upon discretionary trusts, the income to be applied for the education, maintenance or benefit of the beneficiaries, or accumulated;

- if the trust is to endure for more than 25 years, all the beneficiaries must have a common grandparent.

Whilst an A&M trust would appear to differ little from an ordinary discretionary trust, the advantage of an A&M trust is that it is not subject to the ten-yearly charge to inheritance tax, and there is no exit charge when a beneficiary becomes entitled to an interest in possession (or becomes absolutely entitled). Accordingly, A&M trusts are a popular mechanism – both inter vivos and on death – for creating a flexible trust for children or grandchildren.

Nil-rate band discretionary trust

3.10   A common tax planning tool is the 'nil-rate band discretionary trust'. Discussion in detail of inheritance tax is beyond the scope of this work, but in broad terms, relief from inheritance tax is organised in three principal categories:

- gifts which are excluded from the charge to inheritance tax if made to a qualifying recipient, e.g. gifts to a UK domiciled spouse, or gifts to charity;

- assets which qualify for relief from inheritance tax in their own right, e.g. business property, agricultural property, and heritage assets which are eligible for conditional exemption;

- the nil-rate band, being that part of the testator's estate on which inheritance tax is not charged (currently £250,000).

It is frequently the testator's primary wish to ensure that his spouse is adequately looked after if she survives the testator. However, provided that there are sufficient assets, it seems prudent to make use of the nil-rate band in every case, so as to reduce the overall level of taxation of the combined estates of the testator and his spouse. By making use of the nil-rate band of the first spouse to die, this may save up to £100,000 tax (at present rates) on the death of the second spouse (£250,000 x 40%).

In larger estates, there may be clear capacity in the estate to make outright gifts out of the nil-rate band, for example to the testator's children. Commonly, however, there is not (at the date of making the will) sufficient certainty as to the future needs of the surviving spouse or children, or indeed as to what the testator's assets may be at his death. In such cases, a nil-rate band discretionary trust can provide flexibility, by leaving the relevant sum upon trust for a class of beneficiaries including the testator's spouse, children and grandchildren (and possibly others). These funds can then be applied as appropriate, depending on the circumstances of the family at the date of the testator's death. As with all discretionary trusts, the testator should leave a letter of wishes giving guidance to the trustees.

A typical form of nil-rate band discretionary trust is as follows:

Example

'[1.1] If my [husband/wife] survives me, I give to my Trustees to be held upon the trusts set out in clause [1.3] the cash sum which is equal to the maximum amount which, in the circumstances prevailing at my death, is chargeable to inheritance tax at 0% in accordance with Schedule 1[The interpretation clauses of the will should already provide for re-enactment, amendment or other changes to the Act; if not, specific provision should be made here.] Inheritance Tax Act 1984 (in this clause, 'the Act') (the 'Nil-Rate Amount').

[1.2] In calculating the Nil-Rate Amount, there shall be excluded:

[1.2.1] the value of all property which is excluded property by virtue of sections 6 and 48 of the Act;

[1.2.2] the value of all property which qualifies for business property relief under chapter 1 of part V of the Act, or which qualifies for agricultural property relief under chapter 2 of that part of the Act; and

[1.2.3] the value of all property in which I am deemed to have reserved a benefit for the purposes of section 102 and Schedule 20 Finance Act 1986.

[1.3] My Trustees shall hold the Nil-Rate Amount upon the following trusts:

[1.3.1] My Trustees shall have power to pay, transfer or apply the whole or any part or parts of the capital at any time or times before the Vesting Day [assuming the definition is contained elsewhere in the will] to, or for the benefit of, such one or more of the Beneficiaries [assuming the definition is contained elsewhere in the will], and if more than one, in such shares and in such manner as my Trustees may in their absolute discretion think fit;

[1.3.2] Subject to any exercise of the power in clause [1.3.1], my Trustees shall have power to pay, transfer or apply the income to, or for the benefit of, such one or more of the Beneficiaries, and if more than one, in such shares and in such manner as my Trustees may in their absolute discretion think fit, and in default of such determination my Trustees shall:

(i) during the period of 21 years (less one day) following the date of my death, accumulate the income and treat the same as an accretion to the capital, and thereafter

(ii) divide the income equally between all the Beneficiaries for the time being living; and

[1.3.3] Subject to sub-clauses [1.3.1 and 1.3.2], on the Vesting Day my Trustees shall hold the Nil-Rate Amount as to both income and capital upon trust for such one or more of the Beneficiaries, and if more than one in such shares, as my Trustees shall in their absolute discretion think fit and in default of such determination in equal shares absolutely.'

Trusts for charity

3.11   The testator may wish to make provision for a sum of money to be held upon trusts for charitable purposes. This can be dealt with in the following way:

Example

'I give the sum of £[ ] to my trustees to hold the same upon trust as to both income and capital for such purpose or purposes, being exclusively charitable under English law, as my trustees may in their absolute discretion determine [within [*number*] months of my death] and in default of such determination to pay the same to the Royal Society of . . .and the National Institute of . . .in equal shares absolutely.'

It is sensible for the testator to leave a letter of wishes to give guidance to the executors as to what he has in mind in making a general charitable legacy of this kind.

Two-year discretionary trust of chattels

3.12   A testator wishing to make gifts of chattels will frequently leave *all* the chattels to one beneficiary, coupled with a precatory wish that the beneficiary should distribute the chattels in accordance with any letter of wishes the testator might leave. The vulnerability of such a legacy will be apparent, and in cases where the chattels are particularly valuable, it may be more appropriate to charge the trustees with the responsibility of distributing them, as in the example which follows. Note, however, that this trust can only be effective for inheritance tax purposes whilst section 144 Inheritance Tax Act 1984 remains in force, and for a maximum period of two years after the testator's death.

Example

'I give all my personal chattels to my Trustees to hold the same as to capital and (if any) income upon the following trusts:

(a)   during the period of two years (less one day) after the date of my death, my Trustees shall have power to give all or any of the chattels to such person or persons (whether or not a Beneficiary, but not a Trustee who is not also a Beneficiary) as my Trustees may in their absolute discretion think fit;

(b)   in exercising their discretion, I ask my Trustees (but without imposing any binding trust or obligation upon them) to have regard to any note of my wishes which may come to their attention at any time before the end of the period referred to in (a) above;

(c)   subject to any exercise of my Trustees' discretion, at the end of the period referred to in (a), to hold the chattels and (if any) the income produced thereby as an accretion to my residuary estate; and

(d)   my Trustees shall have all the powers of a beneficial owner in relation to the chattels pending their disposal.'

Disabled trusts

3.13   A testator may wish to leave a gift for a disabled person upon trust to provide for his needs, rather than giving it to him outright. Section 89 Inheritance Tax Act 1984 contains special tax rules for trusts for the benefit of disabled persons, i.e. someone who is (under Mental Health Act 1983) incapable, by reason of mental disorder, of managing his own affairs, or someone who is in receipt of a disability living allowance or attendance allowance (or their equivalents), where the 'care' component is at the middle or higher rate. A disabled trust is typically drafted as a discretionary trust for the benefit of the disabled person, and may include a power of appointment/advancement, but whatever its terms, it is treated (by virtue of section 89) as if it were an interest in possession trust.

Different rules apply for capital gains tax purposes. If the criteria set out in Schedule 1 Taxation of Chargeable Gains Act 1992 are met, the entirety of the individual annual capital gains tax allowance is available to the trustees (rather than, as in other trusts, only half). In order to qualify, the terms of the trust must require that, during the life of the disabled person:

•   at least half the capital which is applied shall be applied for the benefit of the disabled person; and

•   the disabled person must be entitled to receive not less than half of the income of the trust (or it may be provided that no income can be applied for the benefit of any other person – which would not prohibit accumulation).

Clearly, these rules are conflicting and a trust may not necessarily qualify as both an inheritance tax disabled trust and a capital gains tax disabled trust. Careful advice is needed (both for testators and for trustees).

Features

Identity of trustees of settled legacies

3.14   The trustees of the settled legacy may, but need not, be the same persons as the executors of the will. If they are different, it is necessary to consider whether the will provides appropriate protection and benefits for the legacy trustees. They should have the benefit of the same exculpation provisions and charging clauses as the executors (but may need special administrative powers, see 3.17 below).

The powers and duties of trustees of settled legacies

3.15   The trustees of a settled legacy, like any other trustees, have a range of duties, powers and discretions.

Duties of the trustees

3.16   Above all, the main duty of all trustees, in the words of Millett LJ in *Armitage v Nurse [1998] Ch 241*, is to fulfil the 'irreducible core of obligations' owed by every trustee to his beneficiaries, which principally comprises a duty to act honestly. Other principal duties include:

- the statutory duty to 'exercise such care and skill as is reasonable in the circumstances' (Trustee Act 2000, s 1(1)) in relation to many activities undertaken as trustees, in accordance with the terms of Trustee Act 2000;

- a duty to provide accounts and other information (see 3.18 below); and

- a duty to distribute the trust assets in the right shares to the right people (see CHAPTER 12).

Powers of the trustees

3.17   Similarly, the trustees of a settled legacy, as is the case with every kind of trust, need to have a range of powers to administer the trust assets during the life of the trust. If there are other trusts in the will, the administrative provisions can be incorporated by express reference into the trusts applicable to the settled legacy.

Occasionally, a testator may choose not to set out in full all the necessary administrative clauses relating to trusts, and may instead incorporate some of the Statutory Will Forms 1925 or the STEP standard provisions. These standard forms contain very standard administrative provisions, and may be incorporated as follows:

Example

'The Standard Provisions of the Society of Trust and Estate Practitioners (1st Edition) shall apply to the trusts created by this [clause/Will] [subject to the following amendments . . . *specify*].'

In view of the likely scale of a settled legacy, proportionate to any trusts of residue, and the nature of the assets held, it may be appropriate to consider excluding, reducing or even extending some of the trustees' duties, and perhaps also their powers. For example, in the case of a trust of chattels, it may be appropriate to limit the power of sale and to exclude the duty to consider alternative investments (so as to avoid any need to consider sale), to modify the duties and powers relating to insurance (which may be disproportionately expensive), and to extend the duty to take professional advice if the assets include historic or delicate items.

The rights of beneficiaries of settled legacies

3.18   The rights of beneficiaries to information and accounts in respect of settled legacies are important and often the cause of friction between the trustees and beneficiaries. These issues are dealt with in CHAPTER 6.

Chapter 4

Vesting and class closing

Introduction

General

4.1   The trustees have a duty to ensure that they pay any legacy over at the right time, in the correct shares, to the proper person or persons. This creates certain overriding obligations on the part of the trustees. Before a gift of a legacy can be paid over to the beneficiary or beneficiaries by the trustees of a will, the trustees must be satisfied that:

(a)   they have correctly identified the beneficiary, or class of beneficiaries, capable of benefiting and the nature of his/their interests in the legacy fund (discretionary or fixed interest) (see 4.13 *et seq* below);

(b)   where the legacy is to be shared by reference to membership of a class, the class has closed to future members (see 4.13 *et seq* below);

(c)   the proposed payee(s) has/have fulfilled all the conditions attaching to the legacy, i.e. the gift has *vested* (see 4.9–4.12 below); and

(d)   when payment is made, the trustees will have discharged all their obligations.

Discharge of the trustees' obligations

4.2   As discussed throughout this chapter, the trustees must be sure that they have correctly identified the beneficiaries to whom distribution of the funds must be made. However, at the time for making payment, the trustees must be certain that their obligations as trustees will be fully discharged, and this in practical terms means:

(a)   making positive identification of payee(s); and

(b)   dividing the assets correctly between them, if there is more than one.

Identification of payee(s)

4.3   The trustees, having identified the persons who can benefit (see 4.13 below), and having reached the moment when one or more persons are to be paid (see 4.9 below), must ensure that they are paying funds to the right person. If the trustees pay funds to the wrong person, they will be personally liable to make good the loss, unless there was a material fact of which the trustees were unaware, such as (for example) the beneficiary having assigned his interest to a third party (*Leslie v Baillie (1843) 2 Y & C Ch Cas 91*). The trustees in such a situation may be able to recover the money from the payee if it was paid to him under a mistake of fact, but not where there was a mistake of law (*Agip (Africa) Ltd v Jackson [1991] Ch 547*).

Quite apart from the question of identifying the beneficial class, therefore, trustees are obliged to ascertain the identity of the actual individuals to whom funds are being paid over and must (if necessary) obtain proof of their entitle-ment, in the form of passports, or other forms of identification. (Note that a birth certificate by itself is not conclusive proof of identity, given the ease of obtaining copy certificates.)

It follows that the trustees must apply to the court if they have doubts as to the identity of any person, or the propriety of making any payment (*Talbot v Earl of Radnor (1834) 3 My & K 252; National Trustees Co of Australasia Ltd v General Finance Co of Australasia Ltd [1905] AC 373, PC*).

If the trustees have identified the extent of a class of beneficiaries, but know that one or more members of the class are missing, they should apply to court for a Benjamin order, a procedure by which they are authorised to distribute to the other beneficiaries on the assumption that the missing beneficiary has died (*Re Benjamin [1902] 1 Ch 723*). This procedure may also be used if the existence of other members of the class is uncertain, e.g. in cases where it is not known whether a deceased person had any illegitimate children who might be entitled to a share of the estate. In cases where there are other kinds of uncertainty, the trustees may apply more generally for the directions of the court as to how to proceed.

More generally, section 27 Trustee Act 1925 offers some statutory protection to trustees. A trustee may advertise in the London Gazette his intention to distrib-ute the trust assets and, provided that he then deals with all those claims of which he is already aware, and those of creditors or potential beneficiaries who respond to the advertisement, he is protected from liability to claimants who come forward at a later date (see, for example, *Re Aldhous [1955] 2 All ER 80*).

As a last resort, section 63 Trustee Act 1925 contains power for trustees to pay the trust assets into court if they are unable to get a valid discharge (because of the legal incapacity of a beneficiary or uncertainty as to identification), or have some insoluble doubt on a point of law, or if a claim is threatened. However, a trustee who pays funds into court through an excess of caution may be person-ally liable for the costs of all parties in getting the funds paid out again. It is suggested that payment into court will rarely be the only sensible option (*Re Davies' Trusts (1914) 59 Sol Jo 234*). As noted in the preceding paragraphs, there are usually alternative steps available to the trustees, and it will frequently be open to the trustees to issue proceedings for the determination of any uncertain matter, or to apply for directions as to how to proceed further.

Correct division of the assets

4.4   The trustees are required to pay the correct sum to each beneficiary and, in order to be fully discharged from their obligations to each beneficiary, the trustees must take into account the matters discussed below.

(i) Hotchpot

4.5   The prospective recipient must bring into account ('hotchpot') any previous advances of capital made out of his share of the legacy fund. This can be calculated in several ways:

- section 32 Trustee Act 1925 provides for the advance to be brought into account at its cash value as at the date it was paid away (*Re Gollins Declaration of Trust [1969] 3 All ER 1591*);

- over a longer period, a distribution which was substantial when made may appear less valuable in relation to the trust fund on division. Commonly, interest is applied, or the value of the original distribution is multiplied by the Retail Price Index (as recommended in the Law Reform Committee's 23rd Report Cmnd 8733 at para 4.43); or

- occasionally, it may be appropriate to treat the earlier distributions as a percentage of the total fund at the date of distribution (*Re Leigh's Settlement Trusts [1981] CLY 2453*). This produces entirely different results depending upon whether the trust fund has grown, or suffered a loss in value, in the interim.

Example

A testator leaves a sum of money on trust for his four children, Annabel, Boris, Charles and Denise. On 1 March 1990 the trustees appropriated investments then worth £80,000 to C in partial satisfaction of his pre-sumptive 25% interest – the trust fund was worth £400,000. By the date of division on 1 May 2002, the trust fund is worth £900,000.

On a strict division, C would receive a further £165,000 (i.e. 25% of (£900,000+80,000), less what he has already had). A, B and D each receive £245,000.

Applying the Retail Price Index, C's earlier distribution is deemed to be worth £116,080, so he receives a further £137,940 (i.e. 25% of (£900,000+116,080), less the sum already deemed received). A, B and D each take £254,020.

Application of the rule in *Re Leigh's Settlement Trusts* would result in C being treated as having received 80% of his share in March 1990. Thus he is now entitled to a further £56,250 (£900,000 = 320 shares, of which Charles is entitled to 20, having already taken 80 shares in 1990). A, B and

D each take £281,250 (i.e. 100 shares each). (If, at the date of distribution, the trust fund had fallen in value, this method would be unfairly advantageous for C.)

(ii) Difficulty of division

4.6   Depending on the kinds of assets held in the legacy fund, the trustees might find it is impossible or inequitable to divide one particular asset into shares, or there may be other special restrictions or practical difficulties in division of the trust fund. Such assets include:

- land, and interests in land (*Re Marshall, Marshall v Marshall [1914] 1 Ch 192*; *Stephenson v Barclays Bank Trust Co Ltd [1975] 1 WLR 882*; *Crowe v Appleby [1975] 1 WLR 1539*), including mortgages secured on land (*Re Marshall; Crowe v Appleby*);

- sometimes, shares in private companies (*Re Sandeman's Will Trusts [1937] 1 All ER 368*; *Stephenson v Barclays Bank Trust Co Ltd [1975] 1 WLR 882*). If division would cause a trust's shareholding to cease to be a majority holding, to the detriment of all beneficiaries equally, it will not be prevented (*Re Weiner [1956] 1 WLR 579*), but where strict division would result in one beneficiary becoming the majority shareholder, and therefore would be more valuable to him than to any other beneficiary, sale of the entire holding (and division of the cash proceeds) may be ordered (*Lloyds Bank v Duker [1987] 1 WLR 1324*);

- special assets such as certain kinds of contract may be incapable of being divided, and/or may be expressly non-assignable (*Don King Productions Inc v Warren [2000] Ch 291, CA*; *Rodway v Landy [2001] EWCA CIV 471, [2001] Ch 703*); and

- chattels.

It is suggested that it may be relatively unusual to find such a difficulty in the context of a legacy fund (as opposed to trusts of residue), but it might occur where, for example, the testator leaves a house upon trust to provide a residence for a dependent relative for life, remainder to the testator's children who attain 25; or where the testator leaves shares in a family business upon trust; or a trust of chattels with a direction that, in default of appointment, they be divided equally.

Where a legacy fund comprises such assets, the trustees will retain their powers of sale and other administrative powers over the assets in question, until all the beneficiaries' interests have vested and they can agree the division among themselves, or until the asset in issue is converted (by sale or otherwise) into divisible property of which each beneficiary whose interest has vested absolutely can take his proper share.

(iii) The trustees' lien for costs and expenses

4.7   Trustees are personally liable for the trust's dealings with third parties, but are entitled to reimburse themselves from the trust fund, provided that they are not already liable to make good a loss they have caused to the trust fund (Trustee Act 1925, s 30, and see for example *Re Earl of Winchilsea's Policy Trusts (1888) 39 Ch D 168*).

The trustees cannot be required to part with the trust assets if that would leave them exposed to the risk of having to bear the trust's debts personally. Ordinarily, the trustees are not entitled to demand, but frequently may receive, an indemnity from the recipient beneficiary that he will bear a pro rata share of any unexpected liabilities. However, where there is a known or contingent liability, the trustees may be entitled to retain the assets of the trust undistributed (*X v A [2000] 1 All ER 490*).

It follows that the beneficiaries cannot, when their interests vest absolutely, take the assets free of the liability, so as to leave the trustee exposed to a risk. By extension, no single beneficiary whose interest had vested could demand his share free of the risk borne by the other beneficiaries whose prospective shares remain in the trust.

It may be, therefore, that even when one or more beneficiaries are absolutely entitled to the capital of the legacy fund (or shares in it), it is proper for the trustees to retain part or all of the sum otherwise due to be paid. This is appropriate where there is a known or contingent liability (such as, in *X v A*, the risk of a claim being made under the Environmental Protection Act 1990, Part IIA, for an unlimited sum for the cleaning up of land held in the trust, which was known to be contaminated land). A prudent trustee who has complied with his duty to maintain proper records and accounts should always be able to identify whether there are, or are not, contingent risks associated with the trust or its assets. It is not sufficient for the trustees to say that a sum should be retained against the mere possibility that some currently unknown claim might in future come to light.

Vesting and class closing affected by substitution

4.8   Section 33 Wills Act 1837 provides automatic substitution of the children of an intended legatee who has died, in some circumstances. Provided the legacy is for a named child or remoter descendant of the testator, then if the intended legatee predeceases the testator, leaving children of his own who are living at the testator's death, those children take by substitution. Note that this does not apply if the intended legatee survives the testator but fails to satisfy a condition or contingency (e.g. a particular age). In such cases, section 33 is of no assistance.

In the case of gifts to a class of children (or remoter descendants of the testator), then if a member of the class predeceases the testator, leaving children of his own who are living at the testator's death, then those children take by substitution the share of the gift which their parent would have taken (Wills Act 1837, s 33(2)). Again, if a member of the class survives the testator but dies (leaving children) before fulfilling a condition such as the attainment of a specified age, then the statutory substitution does not apply.

In order to overcome the difficulties and inconsistencies caused by the application of section 33, very frequently the testator will expressly exclude or extend the substitution provisions. Commonly, therefore, a testator will provide that a gift should be substituted in favour of the surviving children or a legatee who either predeceases the testator or survives him but fails to attain the specified age (or other condition). It is suggested that this produces a fairer result. Amendment of the application of section 33 is also sometimes made where the testator does not intend substitution to take place in favour of illegitimate children. Section 33 expressly provides that no distinction is to be drawn between legitimate and illegitimate children, but a testator may include wording in the will so as to exclude illegitimate children from all or any of the provisions of his will, including substitution provisions.

Vesting

Definition of 'vesting'

4.9   Vesting has two separate meanings:

- vesting in interest (when a beneficiary's interest in the capital is no longer dependent upon any uncertainty); and

- vesting in possession, sometimes called 'vesting absolutely' (when the beneficiary becomes absolutely entitled to receive the capital).

In the case of legacies, the two occasions often occur together, such as in the case of a gift to the testator's children who survive him and attain 25 – the gift does not vest until they attain 25, but they become entitled to immediate payment at that time. The two occasions of vesting may be separated, if:

- there are successive interests, e.g. where there is a gift to A for life and then to B. B's interest is vested (because A will certainly die one day) but is not absolute; or

- clear words are used in the will, such as where a testator makes a gift to be shared between his children living at his death, provided that the capital shall not be given to them until the age of 25. In this case, each child's interest vests in interest if he survives the testator, and vests absolutely at 25.

In the remainder of this chapter, references to 'vesting' are to the time of absolute vesting, when payment must be made by the trustees.

The date for making payment

4.10   It is important to identify the true vesting date, i.e. the date upon which payment must be made. Gifts may fall into three categories:

- gifts which vest on a clearly identifiable date, for example a simple legacy to 'my nephew if he shall survive me', or 'to Mary for life and then to her son Peter'. If the legatee survives the relevant date, payment is to be made at once (assuming that he is over 18, or his parent/guardian can give a valid receipt);

- gifts which vest in possession, but where payment is delayed, e.g. where a testator leaves a legacy for V absolutely, to accumulate the income until V attains 25, and then to transfer the capital to V. The legacy will become payable on V's 25th birthday, to him if he is living, or to his executors if he has died (this was the position in the well-known case of *Saunders v Vautier (1841) 4 Beav 115*, as to which see further 4.11 below); and

- gifts which are subject to a true condition precedent, such as gifts to 'my children living at my death who attain the age of 25'. The gift is not payable until the 25th birthday of each child, and the fund is shared among all those who attain the specified age (taking no account of those who die under that age).

As a practical matter, the gift cannot vest earlier than the date of the testator's death, so (irrespective of the date of the will) a gift to be divided among 'my children now living' must mean (in accordance with Wills Act 1837, s 24) the testator's children living in the moment of his death. Such a gift might exclude any children born after the date of the will, if a very clear intention is shown. However, a gift can vest earlier than the death of another person who survives the testator, so that a gift to 'my wife for life, then to my children living at my death' would be shared among the children's estates if one or more of them predeceased the testator's widow.

Early payment

4.11   Early payment of a gift may on occasion be demanded by the beneficiaries, under what is known as 'the rule in *Saunders v Vautier*', in cases such as the following:

- where there is a true condition precedent ('to my children who survive me and attain 25') and not all members of the class have yet reached it, the beneficiaries who have fulfilled the condition can demand payment of their share;

- if the testator merely intends payment to be delayed ('to my daughter Kate on her 25th birthday'), the legatee may be able to claim payment as soon as he/she attains 18; or

- when it is clear that the class has closed ('to my children' – the testator has died), if all the members of the class are over 18, they may override any other conditions attaching to the gift and take equal shares of the fund. (See 4.13 *et seq* below as to class closing.)

The rule is derived from the case of *Saunders v Vautier (1841) 4 Beav 115*, where the testator had left certain shares upon trust to accumulate the income until V should attain 25, and then to transfer them to V or his executors absolutely. On attaining the age of 21 (at that time the age of majority), V claimed that the shares should be transferred to him immediately, because they were held upon trust for his benefit alone (or his estate if he died before reaching 25), and the continued accumulation (or not) of the income could only be for his benefit. It was held that a beneficiary who has an absolute interest in capital is entitled to call for the transfer of the trust assets to himself as soon as he is competent to give a valid discharge, i.e. attains his majority and has full capacity.

This rule has more than one result, however. By extension, any beneficiary who is sui juris and absolutely entitled to capital is entitled to call for the assets representing that capital to be transferred to him. There are two main ways where this may happen.

Partition and termination

4.12   It may happen in relation to part only of a legacy fund, when one beneficiary fulfils a condition, so that his share vests, but there are other beneficiaries whose interests have not yet vested because they have not yet fulfilled the condition (for example, because some, but not all, of the beneficiaries have attained 18).

All the beneficiaries acting jointly can choose to call for immediate payment of the legacy fund to them (even against its express terms, e.g. where a sum is to be held on discretionary trusts). It can only occur where *all* those who could possibly become entitled to an interest in the trust are alive, over 18 and mentally capable, and where all agree that the trust should come to an end. (This is what is commonly known as an application of 'the rule in *Saunders v Vautier*', although as can be seen, that is an unnecessarily restrictive view of the precedent provided by that case.)

As noted, the broad rule is that a beneficiary who has an absolute and vested interest in possession in the trust is entitled to have the trust property transferred to him. He must have attained the age of majority, or have married under that age (*Re Somech [1957] Ch 165*, and Law of Property Act 1925, s 21). Where his is only one of several prospective interests, he can call for an equal (or *aliquot*) share of each of the trust assets, whether or not all the interests in the trust have then vested, but provided that the class of beneficiaries has closed (*Re Marshall, Marshall v Marshall [1914] 1 Ch 192*; *Re Sandeman's Will Trusts [1937] 1 All ER 368*; *Stephenson v Barclays Bank Trust Co Ltd [1975] 1 WLR 882*). This right is subject to certain legal and practical limitations to ensure that the trustees can distribute the assets free of any continuing obligation, as discussed in 4.2 above.

Class closing

Description of class gifts

4.13 Frequently, a legacy will be given to a class of individuals who are named or described in the will. Receipt of a share of the legacy fund is therefore conditional upon membership of a particular class on a particular date. The date may be:

- expressly or impliedly defined by simple reference to the date of the testator's death ('to such of my children as survive me'); or

- defined by reference to an uncertain future event or series of events ('to such of my grandchildren as survive the later of (a) my death and (b) the death of their parent being a child of mine, and attain the age of 18').

As noted throughout this chapter, correct identification of the class is necessary before any payment can be made out of the legacy fund held by the trustees.

Identifying the class

4.14 Different rules apply to the identification of classes of beneficiaries of:

- a fixed interest gift ('to such of my children who survive me, and if more than one in equal shares'); and

- a discretionary gift ('upon trust for such one or more of the employees of J Smith & Co, and if more than one in such shares, as my trustees may in their absolute discretion determine . . .').

In the former case, correct identification is necessary in order to ensure that the appropriate share of the money is paid to each member of the class. On the other hand, the trustees of a discretionary trust (or discretionary power of appointment) have a duty to ensure that they give consideration to the whole class, before deciding to which of them to pay a share of the money. Failure to identify and consider the whole class may mean that the process by which the decision is made – and therefore the exercise of the trustees' discretion itself – is void. Frequently, the default provisions for a discretionary trust are that the fund should be divided among the members equally, and it is important for this reason also that the trustees should be able to determine the members of the class.

Some issues are common to the correct determination of both kinds of class – principally, the interpretation of certain phrases used by testators to describe the beneficiaries. These are considered further in CHAPTER 5. Otherwise, the basic rules relating to identification of the class are as follows.

Discretionary class

4.15 Membership of a class of beneficiaries of a discretionary trust has been described as a question, which must be answerable in relation to any person in the world with the answer 'is' or 'is not' [a member of the class] (*Re Gestetner Settlement [1953] Ch 672*; *Re Gulbenkian's Settlements [1970] AC 508, HL*; *McPhail v Doulton [1971] AC 424, HL*).

If the testator has set out too large a class, the whole gift may be void for administrative unworkability, since it would be either impossible or dispropor- tionately expensive or time-consuming for the trustees to attempt to give effect to it (*Morice v Bishop of Durham (1805) 10 Ves 522*; *R v District Auditor, No 3 Audit District of West Yorkshire Metropolitan County Council, ex p West York- shire Metropolitan County Council [1986] RVR 24*). Similarly, if the testator's wishes appear intentionally perverse, the gift can be declared void for capri- ciousness (*Re Manisty's Settlement [1974] Ch 17*). A legacy to be applied at the trustees' discretion among a class consisting of 'the residents of Greater Lon- don', for example, might be either unworkable or capricious, or both.

Fixed interest trusts

4.16   In fixed interest trusts, for obvious reasons, there is a strict need to ensure that every member of the class can be identified by name. The trustees must be able to draw up a list of all the members of the class of beneficiaries interested in the capital of the trust at the relevant date before distribution can occur (*IRC v Broadway Cottages Trust [1955] Ch 20*).

In cases where one or more members of the class may be missing, or their existence is uncertain, the trustees should apply to court for directions and/or for a Benjamin order under which they are authorised to distribute to the surviving beneficiaries on the assumption that the missing beneficiary has died (*Re Benjamin [1902] 1 Ch 723*).

Interpretation of words and phrases

4.17   In seeking to establish the extent of a class, interpretation of certain words will be crucial. Whilst a detailed discussion of interpretation is beyond the scope of this book, a summary of some common and particularly significant terms is to be found in CHAPTER 5.

When does the class close?

4.18   The relevance of class closing is that it begins to define the persons to whom (or among whom) payment must ultimately be made by the trustees in accordance with the terms of the trust. There are several different ways in which a class may close:

(a)   The wording of the trust may make it clear when the class is to close. This may have one of two effects, so:

    (i)   the closing of the class itself gives rise to a requirement to pay over the money. For example, in a gift 'to my brothers and sisters living at my death in equal shares', the class closes on the testator's death, even though others could in theory join the class; or

(ii) the trust may continue until some later condition is satisfied (or not) in relation to each member of the class, e.g. where there is a specified age that each member of a class must attain, such as 'to my grandchildren living at my death who attain the age of 18' – the class closes on the testator's death, and the ultimate recipients are those who additionally succeed in fulfilling the age condition; or

(b) The gift may be open-ended, which enables other people to join the class after the death of the testator. Again, there are two sub-categories:

(i) there may be a condition to be fulfilled ('to my grandchildren who attain the age of 18'), so the ultimate recipients are those among the class who go on to fulfil the specified condition; or

(ii) there may be no subsequent condition ('to my nephews and nieces').

In relation to open-ended gifts, it will be important to identify the relevant date for closure of the class to new membership. There are various rules by which the date for class closure may be determined, which are set out below.

The rule in Andrews v Partington

4.19   Generally, unless the testator shows a clear contrary intention, the rule in *Andrews v Partington (1791) 3 Bro CC 401* will operate to close a class when the first possible person to satisfy a condition does so (such as, for example, where a gift is conditional upon a class of children attaining 21, in 4.18(b)(i) above). Note that this rule may even apply to close the class at the testator's death, if a member of the class has already fulfilled the condition at the testator's death, thus excluding all after-borns.

This rule does not necessarily apply in cases where birth itself is the criterion, such as in 4.18(b)(ii) above ('to my nephews and nieces'). It may apply if there are members of the class living at the testator's death (*Hill v Chapman (1791) 1 Ves 405*), but if there is any evidence that the testator's intention was to benefit all who fit the description (whenever born), or if there are no members living at the testator's death, then all members whenever born can join the class (*Blech v Blech [2002] WTLR 483* – a gift to '*my grandchildren*' was held to be a gift in favour of all grandchildren of the testator, whenever born, as there was no clear evidence that the testator intended only to refer to the grandchildren living at his death).

Presumption in favour of further children

4.20   Where there is no age or event condition to be met which would enable *Andrews v Partington* to apply, and the only criterion for class membership is birth, the position may be unsatisfactory, with the class remaining open for many years against the possibility that further children could be born who would join the class. No general presumption has ever been made that a woman was past the age of child-bearing, merely for the purposes of enabling a class of beneficiaries to close (see, for example, *Berry v Geen [1938] 2 All ER 362*; *Re Whichelow [1953] 2 All ER 1558*, and the recent case of *Figg v Clarke [1997] STC 247*, confirming that these rules still apply).

The trustees may, in any particular case, apply to the court for leave to distribute, on the footing that (in the circumstances of that case) it is to be assumed that a particular woman would have no further children (*Re Pettifor's Will Trusts [1966] Ch 257*). The age after which such leave would be granted is generally thought to be about 54, and in *Pettifor* it was suggested that, as regards a woman of 70 or older, such an application might even be 'an unnecessary waste of money'. Applications should always be made where the woman is between 55 and 70. Clearly, however, the likelihood of such an application being successful should not be assumed, particularly since, in modern times, the court also needs to weigh up the availability of fertility treatments (see CHAPTER 5 for the meaning of 'children') in determining whether or not, in the case before it, the trustees are authorised to distribute.

Perpetuity problems

4.21   It is clear that, if the common law position stood alone, trusts could potentially last longer than 80 years, or a life in being plus 21 years. There is therefore statutory assistance to save class gifts in cases where the cause of failure would be the legal fiction of the presumed continued fertility of a woman. For deaths after 15 July 1964, section 2 Perpetuities and Accumulations Act 1964 operates to deem a woman unable to have children after the age of 55. This continues to apply notwithstanding the increasing availability and success of fertility treatments (see CHAPTER 5 as to the interpretation of 'children').

Note, however, that this statutory presumption only applies for the purposes of perpetuity. If there is no realistic prospect that the gift will fail, the 1964 Act does not help to close the class early (for example, if the gift is to grandchildren, the life in being is that of their parent, and the class may remain open, without risk to the validity of the gift, until the death of the last survivor of the testator's children).

Chapter 5

General principles of construction

5.1 Whilst it is not intended that this book should deal in detail with construction of wills, some of the general principles that are applied to legacies need to be considered for an understanding of what happens when bequests are drafted less than perfectly.

Principles of construction

5.2 The court's function is to interpret what is written in the will and it is not part of this function 'to improve upon or perfect testamentary dispositions' (Jenkins LJ in *Re Bailey [1951] Ch 407* at 421). This may well mean that the interpretation put on words used by the testator is not that which the testator intended, but this is, in a sense, the penalty for mistakes, ambiguities or obscure words. In seeking the intention of the testator a court will, in general, only look at the words actually used. It will construe them as far as possible in the light of the whole document, but it will not seek to supply additional words or to replace wrong words with right ones if the original is capable of being understood (*National Society for the Prevention of Cruelty to Children v Scottish National Society for the Prevention of Cruelty to Children [1915] AC 207*, where extrinsic evidence, had it been admissible, would have shown that it was most unlikely indeed that the former charity was meant, but there was no ambiguity in the will itself which might have permitted extrinsic evidence to correct this).

The use of the whole document to explain a particular word or phrase is a key principle.

Words are initially given what the court takes to be their ordinary grammatical sense (*Grey v Pearson (1857) 6 HL Cas 61*) in the context in which they are used in the will (*Re Rowland [1963] Ch 1*). It is possible that the meaning of a word or phrase has changed between the time of the will and when the court is called upon to construe it and in these circumstances the meaning must be that of the time when it was used, i.e. the date of the will (*Perrin v Morgan [1943] AC 399*).

Words and phrases often have more than one meaning and, where they do, no presumption exists as to one meaning rather than another. The court considers them in the context of the will as a whole and may, if there is ambiguity, resort to some extrinsic evidence.

As part of the process of construing a word in the light of the will as a whole, it may become apparent to the court that the ordinary meaning of a word has been rejected by the testator in favour of another meaning. The ordinary meaning can therefore be rejected by the court if it is satisfied that the testator in effect set up and used his own dictionary within the will ('the dictionary principle'). That is to say that the terms of the will provide evidence as to how the testator meant to use the word or words in question (*Re Davidson [1949] Ch 670*). The clearest example of this is where the testator actually includes a definition clause within his will defining the meaning of certain words or phrases used. In attempting to construe a will, the court will examine whether or not the testator has supplied his own dictionary in this sense, before resorting to other principles of construction (*Perrin v Morgan [1943] AC 399*).

Unless a word's meaning is capable of being redefined in this way, and in the absence of any other evidence in the will, the court will apply the ordinary meaning even if this results in an eccentric or capricious construction:

> '... a testator is entitled to be capricious or eccentric in his (will) if he chooses ... and the fact that the terms of his will, when interpreted according to their ordinary and apparent meaning, may produce odd results is not alone a ground for construing his language in some other sense which it is less apt to bear: nor is the fact that he may have failed to think out how the scheme of his will might operate in all possible or probable circumstances, for to infer from the fact that the language may not appropriately fit all the possible or probable circumstances that the testator used such language in some sense other than its natural meaning assumes that the testator did the very thing which it seems he failed to do, namely, consider the appropriateness of his will to all possible or probable contingencies. One likely explanation may be that he meant his words to bear their normal meaning and failed to appreciate the consequences.' (*Re James's Will Trusts [1962] Ch 226*, Buckley J at *234*).

In contrast, if there are two or more ordinary meanings the court may prefer the meaning which makes more sense or gives a less capricious result (*Abbott v Middleton (1858) 7 HL Cas 68*).

As a corollary to the principle that words should in general be given their ordinary meaning, words and phrases that have specific legal meanings will usually be given those meanings. Like the ordinary meaning, this may be rebutted either by the dictionary principle or if some secondary meaning makes more sense in the overall context of the will. Examples of technical expressions misused by testators could be 'personal estate' or 'realty'.

Admissible evidence for construction of terms of a will

Grant of representation

5.3   The starting point is that the terms of the will as shown in the copy will attached to the grant of representation are conclusive of the terms of the will. A court will not look at the wording of the original if it varies from that of the grant, unless there has been a separate successful application to the court to amend the wording of the probate. The court may look at the layout of the words in the original will if this throws more light on the meaning. A photocopy will annexed to the grant makes this problem less of an issue than when wills were copied by hand or re-typed, but there will still be occasions where looking at the original can be of use, particular where the copy will attached to the grant is not a photocopy (for example where grant has been obtained to a fiat copy – i.e. a re-typed copy will submitted to the court where the terms of the original have been amended post-execution and the amendments are invalid and are deleted so that the original terms are admitted to probate).

Meaning of words

5.4   In order to determine the meaning of the words in a will, a court is entitled to consult extraneous sources that can throw light on the usage of words or phrases at particular times (such as dictionaries, published books, newspapers etc and Acts of Parliament as well as previous judgments of the court). Expert evidence as to the meaning of foreign words or symbols may be obtained, as it may be where a word or phrase has a special meaning in a trade, profession or even geographical locality.

The armchair principle

5.5

> 'You may place yourself, so to speak, in the (testator's) armchair, and to consider the circumstances by which he was surrounded when he made his will to assist you in arriving at his intention.' (James LJ in *Boyes v Cook (1880) 14 Ch D 53 at 56*).

> 'The justification for the armchair principle is that the court infers that the testator had his own surrounding circumstances in mind when he made his will and used the words in his will with reference to those circumstances.' (*Theobald on Wills*, 16th edition Sweet & Maxwell 17-38).

Caution is needed however with this principle in that, although the court may use the circumstances to shed light on the testator's circumstances, it will not permit a court to change or substitute words, nor will it permit a court to give a meaning to a word which that word is not plainly capable of having.

The golden rule

5.6   The court will always endeavour to construe the terms of a will in a way which will not only give a sensible conclusion (given the other tools available to it) but will also avoid an intestacy or partial intestacy: *Re Harrison, Turner v Hellard (1885) 30 Ch D 390* where Esher MR memorably observed (at 393):

> 'Where a testator has executed a will in solemn form you must assume that he did not intend to make it a solemn farce – that he did not intend to die

intestate when he had gone through the form of making a will. You ought, if possible, to read the will so as to lead to a testacy, not an intestacy.'

Inconsistent clauses

5.7   As a general rule, if two parts of a will are inconsistent between themselves then the latter part has been held to prevail. This rule applies to gifts within the same instrument. Where the inconsistency is between a gift in the will and a gift in a codicil, the codicil gift will prevail on the ground that it has revoked the earlier bequest (*Re Stoodley, Hooson v Locock [1916] 1 Ch 242*). The same rule will apply to inconsistencies within the same gift, such as where the words and figures are different ('one thousand pounds (£2,000)') (*Re Hammond, Hammond v Treharne [1938] 3 All ER 308*). This is on the fairly artificial basis that it has been found that the latter part was said to be the last expression of wish (*Paramour v Yardley (1579) 2 Plowd 539; Ulrich v Litchfield (1742) 2 Atk 372; Re Potter's Will Trusts [1944] Ch 70* where Lord Greene MR (at 77) calls it 'this rule of despair'). As a consequence, despite this being a rule of some antiquity, courts have been apparently eager to relax its rigour.

By applying the usual approach to construction, that of construing in the context of the whole will, a court may not necessarily find that the later clause will prevail (*Re Bywater, Bywater v Clarke (1881) 18 Ch D 17*). A similar application of the golden rule (see 5.6 above) is to be preferred in order to prevent the latter expression from giving rise to an intestacy or partial intestacy (*Piper v Piper (1886) 5 NZLR 135*).

Where a gift of the same thing is given inconsistently to two (or possibly more) beneficiaries in the same will they may both take the gift. How they take the gift depends upon the nature of the property and the type of bequest. The court has variously awarded the property as joint tenants, tenants in common, life tenants in succession or divided the property between the competing bequests: *Re Alexander's Will Trusts, Courtauld-Thomson v Tilney [1948] 2 All ER 111*.

A different approach may be taken by the court to inconsistent gifts of residue, where it has been found that the former gift should prevail: *Re Spencer (1886) 54 LT 597; Re Gare [1952] Ch 80*.

Ejusdem generis ('of the same kind or nature')

5.8   Where particular words are followed by general words, the scope of the general words is limited to the same kind of things as the particular words. This rule of construction is applied much more widely to documents and statutes and is not limited to wills. It is, however, of frequent application to wills particularly in construing gifts of specific items or classes of items: *Re Miller, Daniel v Daniel (1889) 61 LT 365*, where gifts of wine books and plate were followed by a gift of all of the rest of the 'furniture and effects at my residence'. 'Effects' was limited and could not include anything which fell outside of the scope of the preceding words i.e. wine books plate and furniture.

Falsa demonstratio non nocet cum de corpore constat

5.9   More usually known as the 'falsa demonstratio' principle, it means that a false description does not vitiate a document. Thus if part of a description is true and part is false and the true part describes the subject with sufficient certainty, then the untrue element will be rejected or ignored. Like ejusdem generis (see 5.8 above) this is a general rule of construction in legal documents, which, although not limited to wills, is of great use as an aid to construction.

This rule applies to descriptions both of beneficiaries and property. A gift to 'my wife Caroline' was looked at in the light of all surrounding circumstances. The testator had a wife called Mary but lived with a woman called Caroline (they had gone through an invalid marriage ceremony) and the word wife was ignored in favour of the accurate description Caroline (*Pratt v Mathew (1856) 22 Beav 328*).

Rectification

5.10   Although not strictly speaking an issue of construction, the terms used in a will can be altered by the court to reflect the testator's intentions if it can be shown either that the terms used in the will fail to reflect the intentions of the testator because of clerical error, or that the draftsman failed to understand the testator's instructions (Administration of Justice Act 1982, s 20). A clerical error refers to the nature of the error, not to the person who made it, and so it is possible for such an error to be made in a homemade will (but there may be difficulties here with showing what the testator's intentions were) (*Re Williams [1985] 1 WLR 905*). Clerical errors will usually be errors of omission, but they can arise through the failure to understand words or to confuse them. A clerical error is not the deliberate, but mistaken, use of a phrase or precedent which does not in fact have the desired effect (*Wordingham v Royal Exchange Trust Company Ltd [1992] 3 All ER 204; Re Segelman [1996] Ch 171*).

Any application for rectification in this way must be made within six months of a grant of representation being issued, although it is at the discretion of the court to admit later applications where it believes that it is reasonable to do so.

From the above more general points on construction it is possible to look in more detail at the construction of gifts to persons and gifts of property, which are probably the most frequent cause of difficulty.

Gifts to persons

5.11   In many wills persons are identified only by their relationship to the testator (e.g. 'my wife' or 'my son') and mostly this does not create difficulties, notwithstanding that it is good practice to more exactly identify the person intended.

As a general principle the person who meets the description used in the will at the date of the will is the person intended by the testator. (This is of course the opposite to section 24 Wills Act 1837 which provides for descriptions of property to speak from death in the absence of a contrary intention. Section 24 does not apply to beneficiaries.) Thus where a gift by will was made to 'Lord Sherborne' and between the date of the will and the testator's death Lord Sherborne died, the legacy failed. This was notwithstanding that Lord Sherborne's son succeeded him, taking the same title (*Re Whorwood, Ogle v Lord Sherborne (1887) 34 Ch D 446*; also *Amyot v Dwarris [1904] AC 268* where a gift to 'the eldest son of my sister Frances' failed when the eldest son at the date of the will predeceased the testator, despite there being another son). This general rule may be amended where the will is republished by codicil, thus where the codicil referred to a gift to A's wife and the wife at the time of death was not the same as at the date of the will, the later wife took. This may well depend, however, upon the testator being aware of the relevant facts (*Re Hardyman, Teesdale v McClintock [1925] Ch 287*).

Greater difficulties arise if there is no person meeting the description at the date of the will. It is possible that the gift may be saved by the court treating the gift as being one to the first person after the date of the will to meet the description (*Radford v Willis (1871) 7 Ch App 7*), or it may be that the context may be found to indicate that the description is to be at the date of death (*Re Daniels, London City and Midland Executor and Trustee Co Ltd v Daniels (1918) 87 LJ Ch 661*). Difficulty has been encountered with the first person to meet the description taking the gift where that person subsequently loses the description. A gift to the wife of a grandson, where the grandson was not married at the time of the will, was found to be a gift to his wife who he married later. She kept this gift notwithstanding that she was no longer married to the grandson at the time of death and he had remarried (*Re Hickman, Hickman v Hickman [1948] Ch 624*).

Describing relations by their relationship to the testator is less often encountered today, as good practice is to use more full names and less ambiguous descriptions. Since the Family Law Reform Act 1969 and the re-enactment and widening of those provisions in the Law Reform Act 1987, illegitimate relations will rank equally with legitimate (as do adopted children of the testator) and this has removed one of the issues that caused difficulties in the past with descriptions of children.

One of the commonly encountered issues with the description of relatives is the confusion between relatives by blood and relatives by marriage (more correctly known as relatives by affinity). Relatives by blood are preferred in descriptions to relatives by marriage, although in the absence of any relatives by blood, those by marriage may take (as indeed they would if there was any intention on the face of the will that they should) (*Frogley v Phillips (1861) 3 De GF & J 466*). In general usage 'aunt', 'uncle', 'cousin', 'nephew' and 'niece' are descriptions that often contain confusion between relationship by blood or marriage (and indeed by half blood as well). It is difficult to suggest that there is any general principle in the various cases where this issue has been examined by the court.

Child/children

Adopted

5.12   The treatment of adopted children under wills (and intestacies) is contained in section 39 *et seq* Adoption Act 1976 (for deaths on or after 1 January 1976). If the child has been adopted by both spouses to a marriage, he is treated as if he was a legitimate child of that marriage (whatever his date of birth), and if he was adopted by only one of them, he is treated as if he was a legitimate child of a former marriage of that person (whether or not the adopter has ever previously been married, and not so as to impute the child to be a child of any particular marriage). An adopted child is not, following his adoption, treated as ever having been the child of any person other than the adoptive parent(s), but this does not affect any vested or contingent interest he had prior to his adoption (s 42).

Illegitimate

5.13   For legacies contained in any will or codicil made after 1 January 1970, every reference to a child will include illegitimate children, unless the testator shows a contrary intention (Family Law Reform Act 1969, s 15(1)), subject to some exceptions (and a notable doubt over whether illegitimate children of illegitimate children were included). References to children in testamentary instruments made after 4 April 1988, are now to be construed without regard for the question of whether or not the parents of the person at issue were ever married (Family Law Reform Act 1987, ss 1, 19), although again, the testator may exclude illegitimate children if he wishes. Note that neither of the Family Law Reform Acts affects gifts which are intended to devolve with a title or other dignity.

Legitimated

5.14   Illegitimate children are legitimated by the subsequent marriage of their parents, provided that the marriage has taken place since 1976 (Legitimacy Act 1976). The predecessor legislation (Legitimacy Acts 1926 and 1959) did not necessarily operate to legitimise children if one, or both, of the parents were, at the time of their birth, married to someone else, and if a child had not been legitimated by the time of the testator's death, it could not benefit from a gift to his parents' 'children'. Children can also be legitimated by paternal recognition, by adoption, or by some other conduct.

Assisted reproduction

5.15   Increasingly, fertility and reproductive treatments such as in vitro fertilisation, artificial insemination, sperm or egg donation, and surrogate motherhood, are commonly used.

A child born as a result of sperm donation prior to 4 April 1988 was apparently illegitimate (as regards the mother's husband), but after that date (by virtue of Family Law Reform Act 1987, s 27) is treated as the child of the mother's husband, provided that he consented to the use of the sperm donation. If he did not so consent in relation to a child born before 1 August 1991, paternity may rest with the sperm donor.

For children conceived as a result of treatment on or after 1 August 1991, the child of an assisted reproductive technique involving implantation, insemination or donation is for all purposes the child of the mother and father to whom it is born (Human Fertilisation and Embryology Act 1990, ss 27–29).

Where, following the birth of a child resulting from implantation and/or donation treatments, the child is adopted, it is treated as being the child only of its adoptive parents (s 27(2)). This would appear to cover surrogacy arrangements. However, surrogacy itself has no real recognition under English law (and payment is not permitted) and thus the legal parentage of the child, before birth or pending adoption, could rest with the surrogate mother and her husband under section 27(1). The Court has power to make a 'parental order' under section 30, so as to declare the parents of the child to be both spouses in a marriage where the sperm and/or eggs of the spouses have been used to create an embryo which has been carried by a woman other than the wife. Payment, however, must not have been made.

'Family' and other terms

5.16   Where a testator provides a legacy for his 'family' this is usually construed as meaning children, but if there are no children or a broader intention is shown by the testator, it may mean the statutory next of kin, or any blood relation of the deceased (see, for example, *Re Barlow's Will Trust [1979] 1 WLR 278*).

Other, similar words such as 'relations' are usually interpreted as referring to the individuals who would be entitled on the testator's intestacy, but 'next of kin' does not necessarily include all those who would take on an intestacy and may be limited to his immediate descendants and parents or other forebears. In drafting, therefore, it is preferable to avoid such uncertain terms.

'Friends'

5.17   A gift to each of the testator's friends, or a class gift to be divided among his friends, may not necessarily fail for uncertainty. It is for each potential claimant to show that he/she qualifies as a 'friend' of the deceased, which usually requires evidence of a longstanding social relationship (*Re Gulbenkian's Settlements [1970] AC 508; Re Barlow's Will Trust [1979] 1 WLR 278*).

Issue

5.18 'Issue' in pure legal terms means children, grandchildren, and every degree of remoter descendant, although it has been accepted that, in the language of those other than lawyers, it probably commonly means only children and would not include grandchildren or any remoter class (*Re Linklater's Estate (1967) 66 DLR (2d) 30*). In cases where there is a gift to a person 'and his issue' it has been construed as a gift only to children (*Thompson v Simpson (1841) 1 Dr & War 459*). The rule is not absolute, and the express or implied intentions of the testator can, as in any other gift, be deduced from the will.

Gifts of property

5.19 Unless there is a contrary intention in a will, references to property are to be construed as at the date of death of the testator (Wills Act 1837, s 24). This statutory rule, whilst fairly simply stated, causes much difficulty in practice, particularly with specific gifts.

The word 'my', which usually attaches to specific gifts, may be a sufficient contrary intention to convert the description from being one at the date of death (as statute would provide) to one at the date of the will, the theory being that use of 'my' indicates a specific item of property being contemplated by the testator which he owned. The court has accepted this approach (*Re Fowler, Fowler v Wittingham (1915) 139 LT Jo 183*), but even where there was a stronger direction ('which I now possess') the court has not limited the gift to that at the date of the will but has included within it after-acquired elements of property (*Wagstaff v Wagstaff (1869) LR 8 Eq 229; Hepburn v Skirving (1858) 32 LTOS 26*). It is suggested that in practice the court has wide powers of construction for such gifts. In practical terms, the possible doubt that 'my car' could be either the car at the date of will or the car owned at the date of death is avoided with the more direct addition of a description of the car for that owned at the date of the will, or the use of 'such car as I may own at the date of my death' where that is intended.

Conditions

5.20 A testator may attempt to attach conditions to legacies and the implications of these and the difficulties of how they are construed need to be considered. However, it should be observed at the outset that this is a subject both of much complexity and technical analysis of the terms of the gift. The validity of conditions will also depend upon the lawful nature of the condition that the legatee is required to meet as conditions that are illegal or contrary to public policy will not be upheld. The points below are therefore only a very general outline.

Condition not to dispute

5.21   Such directions can be valid (*Cooke v Turner (1846) 15 M & W 727*; *Re Nathan, Nathan v Leonard [2002] WTLR 1061*), where they are imposed so as not to dispute the terms of a will. However, in practice they are of little consequence if the testator attempts to use them to bequeath a legacy that would be smaller than the award that a beneficiary would be likely to obtain under an Inheritance (Provision for Family and Dependants) Act 1975 claim, as of course the testator cannot remove an individual's right to make such a claim. A condition will not be valid if the condition not to dispute is not limited to the interest given but extends to the assets and liabilities of the estate generally (*Rhodes v Muswell Hill Land Co (1861) 29 B 560*).

Condition as to residence

5.22   These conditions may be valid if drafted with sufficient certainty to be construed properly (*Re Gape [1952] Ch 743*). However, terms such as 'reside' and 'residence' and 'occupy' are difficult to construe and serve to underline the difficulty of accurate and certain drafting of these conditions.

Names and Arms clauses

5.23   These clauses, much beloved of Victorian and early twentieth century wills, can be valid, although they are much less seen in practice today. There is far less importance attached to family names and coats of arms.

Effect of valid and invalid conditions

5.24   A difficult point of construction in conditions is the determination of whether a condition is regarded as a condition precedent or a condition subsequent. The effect of the condition being void or not being met may be different between the two types. Broadly speaking a condition precedent is required to be complied with before the gift will vest and a condition subsequent is to be complied with after vesting. The court will, in questions of doubt, lean towards finding a condition to be a condition subsequent. A condition precedent could be a gift to a person provided they have not taken up permanent residence in a specific country. The gift vests if the legatee meets the condition, and the condition has no effect if there is a future change of mind by the legatee. A condition subsequent could be a gift valid until marriage.

Chapter 6

Beneficiaries' rights

Administration and trusteeship

6.1   The extent of the rights conferred by law on a beneficiary or legatee depends upon the capacity in which the personal representatives hold the assets constituting the deceased's estate. Whilst an administrator or executor holds the net estate for the benefit of the beneficiaries under the will or intestacy during the period of administration of the estate (and accordingly is in a fiduciary position), he does not do so as trustee.

The question of precisely when a personal representative becomes a trustee is therefore one of crucial importance, but is one to which there is no single, clear answer. Often it will be answered by the execution of an assent by the personal representative. An assent has been defined in the following terms:

> 'An assent is an acknowledgement by a personal representative that an asset is no longer required for the payment of the debts, funeral expenses or general pecuniary legacies'. (Williams Mortimer & Sunnucks: *Executors, Administrators and Probate* (16th edition, Sweet & Maxwell) at para 78-01, citing the authority of *Kemp v IRC [1905] 1 KB 581*).

Accordingly, after an assent the assets in question, not being required for the payment of the matters set out in the definition above, are owned beneficially by the beneficiaries in such shares as specified by the will or the rules governing intestacy. If the assent is in favour of a person other than the beneficiary or beneficiaries entitled to the property (including, for example, the personal representative himself) that person will hold the property upon trust for the beneficial owners. (Where land forms part of the estate and is to be held upon trust by the representatives for the beneficiaries, it is necessary for the representatives to execute an assent in favour of themselves: *Re King's Will Trusts [1964] Ch 542*.)

The position is not, however, as straightforward as simply waiting for an assent to be made by the personal representatives, as whilst an assent is clearly sufficient to make the legal owner of the property a trustee of it, it is not a necessary condition of such trusteeship (*Re Cockburn [1957] Ch 438*). The administration of the estate is complete when all the debts and expenses have been paid and the residue ascertained (*Re Ponder [1921] 2 Ch 59*). Thereafter, the assets of the estate are no longer required for any purpose other than payment to the beneficiaries entitled to them and, accordingly, those beneficiaries are able to assert beneficial ownership of the net estate held by the personal representatives. In such circumstances the personal representatives hold the estate on trust for the beneficiaries (*Re Cockburn*; *Re King's Will Trusts*). An assent is merely an acknowledgement of the fact that an asset is no longer required by the personal representatives in order to meet expenses, but it is the fact that the asset is no longer required that gives rise to the trust in favour of the beneficial owners. This is reflected to some extent by sections 33 and 39 Administration of Estates Act 1925, which provide that in cases of intestacy, administrators are in the position of trustees when distribution of the estate is postponed by reason of the minority of certain beneficiaries or the existence of life interests.

In addition, where the will makes specific provision for the personal representatives to become trustees at a prescribed time, they will become trustees in accordance with that direction.

Rights to property

6.2   During the administration of the estate, the beneficiary does not have any equitable proprietary interest in the property contained in the estate. This must be contrasted with the position of a beneficiary under a trust who is the equitable owner (or one of a number of equitable owners) of the trust property. The extensive rights of a beneficiary under a trust derive from his ownership of the trust property, and therefore the absence of such ownership during administration means that the rights of beneficiaries are of a very different nature.

After completion of the administration of the estate, the personal representative holds the estate upon trust for the beneficiaries entitled under the terms of the will or under the intestacy rules (*Re Ponder [1921] 2 Ch 59*). The duties of a trustee to his beneficiaries differ from those owed by a personal representative in certain significant ways. Accordingly the corresponding various rights of the beneficiary/legatee arising after the personal representative becomes trustee differ from those rights subsisting during the course of administration.

The trustee is the legal owner of the property that he holds on trust for the beneficiary. A beneficiary is the beneficial owner (or one of a number of beneficial owners) of the trust property, and therefore the rights conferred upon him derive from that ownership. The first (and perhaps most fundamental) of these is the right to call for the trust property to be conveyed to him, and thereby put an end to the trust.

A sole beneficiary under a trust who is of sound mind and full age and capacity is entitled to call for the property to be transferred to him or at his direction, putting an end to the trust (under the rule in *Saunders v Vautier (1841) 4 Beav 115*). Where there is more than one beneficiary, it is necessary for them to act unanimously. If they do so, they may compel the trustees to convey the property to them in the same manner as a sole beneficiary (*Anson v Potter (1879) 13 Ch D 141*).

The right to due administration

6.3   During administration beneficiaries have no equitable proprietary interest in the estate. Instead they have a chose in action: the right to have the estate duly administered in accordance with the will or intestacy rules, depending on which applies. During this period the personal representatives do not hold the assets beneficially: they are said to hold it 'in auter droit'. The right to due administration is the primary right of the beneficiaries during the period of administration. Essentially the other rights conferred on a beneficiary during administration are subsidiary to the basic right to due administration and serve the purpose of enabling the beneficiary to ascertain whether the estate is being duly administered, and, if not, to take steps to remedy any default on the part of the personal representatives.

The right to information

6.4   Perhaps the most important subsidiary right to the right to due administration is the right of a beneficiary under a will or intestacy to be given information concerning the administration of the estate. As a matter of logic, it follows that in order for a beneficiary to ensure that an estate in which he is interested is being administered properly and in accordance with the will or intestacy rules, he must be in possession of the information (a) that he is entitled under the terms of the will or intestacy; and (b) as to how the administration is being carried out by the personal representative.

Whereas a trustee is under a positive duty to inform the beneficiaries of the existence of a trust under which they are entitled and also their respective interests thereunder (*Hawkesley v May [1956] 1 QB 304*), the law imposes no corresponding duty upon personal representatives (*Re Lewis [1904] 2 Ch 656*). The reason for the distinction is that a trust deed is a private document, the contents of which are unlikely to be known to the beneficiary unless disclosed to him by the trustee (*Hawksley v May*). A will, on the other hand, is a public document that may be inspected at the Principal Probate Registry, and therefore anyone is able to ascertain whether they are named as a beneficiary in a will. Similarly, it would seem to follow that the rules of intestacy are imposed by statute and a beneficiary's entitlement under the intestacy will be known to him once it has been established that there is no will (again, by reference to the public records) and letters of administration have been granted accordingly.

Even though there is no strict legal duty on a personal representative to inform the beneficiaries of their entitlements under a will or intestacy, as a matter of practice it is common for personal representatives to seek out and inform the beneficiaries of their entitlements at an early stage. This is a prudent step for representatives to take, as it can often facilitate the administration of the estates, and by doing so within two years of the death of the deceased it enables the beneficiaries to decide whether to vary their entitlements under the will or intestacy and take advantage of relief from inheritance tax and capital gains tax on such a variation or disclaimer (under section 142 Inheritance Tax Act 1984 and section 62 Taxation of Chargeable Gains Act 1992 respectively; see CHAPTER 7 in relation to the variation of legacies).

Having established that they are entitled under the will or intestacy, beneficiaries are entitled to be provided with information about the personal representative's conduct of the administration of the estate. This is achieved through the provision of an account and inventory. A personal representative is under a duty to maintain proper accounts, and a beneficiary has the right to inspect those accounts (*Re Tillott [1892] 1 Ch 86*). This right is enshrined in statute, in section 25 of the Administration of Estates Act 1925 which provides as follows:

'25. The personal representative of a deceased person shall be under a duty to –

(a)   collect and get in the real and personal estate of the deceased person and administer it according to law;

(b)   when required to do so by the court, exhibit on oath in the court a full inventory of the estate and when required render an account of the administration of the estate to the court;

(c)   when required to do so by the High Court, deliver up the grant of probate or administration to that court.'

Where a personal representative fails to provide on request an account and inventory to a beneficiary, the beneficiary may apply to the court for an order compelling the representative to produce the requisite account and inventory, in compliance with his duty under section 25(b). An application may be made in one of two ways: either to the Chancery Division of the High Court, under CPR Part 64 (as to which see below), or on application to the Family Division. The latter is a cheaper alternative to bringing an administration claim in the Chancery Division of the High Court, and is appropriate where there are no other issues to be determined by the court. The Chancery Division is the forum for all other matters in relation to the administration of trusts and estates (CPR 64.1(3)), and has jurisdiction to make a wider range of orders.

An application to the Family Division must be supported by written evidence in the form of an affidavit or witness statement setting out such details of the estate as are known to the beneficiary (such as the approximate value of the estate, the date of the deceased's death and the date of the grant) and the applicant's interest in the estate. The applicant need not establish any maladministration or misapplication of assets on the part of the representative in order to obtain an order, which provided the formalities are complied with, should be granted as a matter of course. If the representative fails to comply with the order, the beneficiary can either seek to commit the representative for contempt of court, or alternatively use the failure as a basis for seeking administration of the estate by the court (as to which see 6.6 below) or the removal/replacement of the representative (under Administration of Justice Act 1985, s 50; see 6.7 below).

The costs of *preparing* accounts are proper expenses of the administration, but if the beneficiaries are forced to make an application to the court for production of the accounts, they may recover the costs of the application (as opposed to the cost of preparing the accounts) from the representative personally, in accordance with the general legal principles on costs.

Section 25 of the Administration of Justice Act 1925 is not the only basis on which a beneficiary may obtain an account from the representatives. The duty to account is one of the most basic duties of a trustee or representative. It provides not only a means of obtaining information about the administration of the trust or estate, but a mechanism by which the beneficiary can obtain redress for maladministration or misappropriation on the part of the trustee or representative.

The High Court has inherent jurisdiction in relation to the administration and execution of estates and trusts. The relevant rules governing the court's procedures in this regard are contained in CPR 64 (introduced with effect from 1 December 2002; the previous provisions were contained in CPR Sch 1, RSC Ord 85). Under CPR 64.2(c), the court is able to make any order that it could make if the trust or estate in question were being administered or executed under the direction of the court. (In the High Court, such claims must be brought in the Chancery Division (CPR 64.1(3).) If the value of the trust or estate in question does not exceed £30,000, the county court has jurisdiction to deal with applications for the administration of the estate of a deceased person or the execution of a trust by virtue of section 23 County Courts Act 1984.) That therefore includes an order for the provision of proper accounts (which under PD 64 para 3.2, is listed as one of the orders the court may make in the course of administration or execution).

An application under CPR 64 must be made to the Chancery Division of the High Court (unless the value of the estate is less than £30,000, in which case the county court has jurisdiction pursuant to section 23 County Courts Act 1984), and be made using the Part 8 claims procedure (CPR 64.3; the relevant court form is N208 which may be downloaded in Adobe Acrobat (.pdf) format from www.courtservice.gov.uk). The claim form should be supported by evidence in the form of a witness statement or affidavit (PD 8A para 5.1), setting out the details of the estate. The parties to the claim under CPR 64 should all be trustees or representatives, and all persons with an interest in or claim against the estate or trust whom it is appropriate to make parties having regard to the nature of the order sought (CPR 64.4(1)). In the case of a claim for an account, the appropriate parties will therefore be the trustees but not all of the beneficiaries, unless an account is to be sought on the footing of wilful default (as to which see below) in which case it will be appropriate to join as parties all beneficiaries likely to be affected by the taking of the account, unless a representation order (under CPR 19.6) is obtained.

There are two different forms of account that may be brought by the beneficiary in the circumstances being considered here:

(a)   a common account; and

(b)   an account on the footing of wilful default.

A common account is the form of account to which the beneficiary is entitled as of right (*Re Wells [1962] 1 WLR 874*): there is no need to establish any wrongdoing on the part of the representative or trustee, but on such a basis the representative or trustee is only required to account for the moneys he has actually received, not that which he ought to have received. An account on the footing of wilful default, on the other hand, requires the beneficiary to plead and prove at least one instance of wilful default. Wilful default in this context does not mean a deliberate breach of duty on the part of the representative or trustee; rather it means a wrongful omission (see *Bartlett v Barclays Bank [1980] Ch 515*). This therefore includes instances of devastavit (i.e. waste on the part of the representatives) during the course of administration, or other failures to comply with the duty of due administration, and in the case of trustees, breach of trust such as a failure to invest the trust fund. Where wilful default is established, the court may order an enquiry into the general administration of the estate or trust by ordering a general account on the footing of wilful default. It will do so where it considers that the conduct of the representative or trustee as established gives rise to a reasonable inference that other breaches of duty have been committed.

When an account has been taken, the beneficiary is then able to surcharge or falsify the account, requiring the representative or trustee to make good the loss caused by his default. Surcharging is the act of requiring the representative or trustee to add in amounts that should be, but are not, contained in the account. For example, where a trustee fails to invest the trust fund, he may be surcharged with the income that would have been earned had he fulfilled his duty to invest. Falsification on the other hand involves the deletion of items of disbursement from the account, such as an improper expense or investment. Where the account is falsified, the expenditure is disallowed, and the representative or trustee is required to account on the footing that the wrongful expenditure had never been incurred.

Following the taking of an account (and the making of the requisite adjustments in order to rectify any maladministration or misapplication) an order for payment may be made. This is likely to be appropriate more often in the case of a straightforward administration where the representatives are simply required to pay out the various legacies to the beneficiaries. Where the will creates a trust with trustees other than the personal representatives, an order may be obtained vesting the property in the trustees, or requiring the representatives to execute an assent in favour of the will trustees.

Other rights to information

6.5   In addition to the right to an account and inventory, a beneficiary is entitled to have access to other information concerning the administration. In cases involving trusts arising out of a will (or intestacy), issues in relation to disclosure of the document creating the trust will not arise, as the will is a public document, and the rules of intestacy are a matter of public knowledge. Where the provisions of the will have been varied posthumously by the execution of a deed of variation, it would seem to follow as a matter of logic that the deed should be treated as the trust instrument. However, when the trust has been fully constituted post-administration, there are likely to be a number of documents produced in relation to the trust of which beneficiaries will wish to procure disclosure. Beneficiaries are entitled to inspect 'trust documents', and to obtain copies of them at their own expense. The first question that must be answered is that of 'what are "trust documents"?' That question was largely answered by the court in the case of *Re Londonderry [1965] Ch 918*, in which it was held that essentially, trust documents are those created at the expense of the trust fund. Therefore where the trustees have taken legal advice and obtained counsel's opinion as to the construction of the will, the beneficiaries are entitled to see that opinion. The basis for disclosure is that a beneficiary, as equitable owner, is entitled to inspect his own property.

Due to the absence of such property rights during the course of administration (see 6.2 above), the beneficiaries' right to inspect documents during administration does not have its basis in equitable ownership. Nevertheless it has been established that such beneficiaries have the right to inspect title deeds of properties forming part of the estate (*Gough v Offley (1852) 5 De G & Sm 653*), *and in principle are entitled to see all documents forming part of the estate, and paid for out of the estate.*

The rule is not, however, absolute. There are examples of instances in which beneficiaries are not entitled to inspect documents relating to the administration of the trust (it would seem to follow that the restrictions imposed by law in relation to beneficiaries under a trust must apply also to beneficiaries during the administration of an estate).

Firstly (and perhaps most importantly) beneficiaries are not entitled to inspect documents concerning the exercise by trustees of their discretions. The basis for this is that trustees are not required to give reasons for their decisions (*Re Londonderry*). Therefore, where a legacy creates a discretionary trust, a beneficiary is not entitled to documents recording the trustees' deliberations, and those recording the reasons for their decisions. However, if the trustees have received written legal advice as to the scope of their discretion, and/or how they should exercise their discretion in any given case, the beneficiary is entitled to inspect such advice. Further, whilst beneficiaries are entitled to access to the minutes of trustees' meetings, they are not entitled to the agenda of those meetings (*Hartigan v Rydge (1992) 29 NSWLR 405*).

Secondly, beneficiaries are not entitled to see correspondence between the trustees, and between the trustees and other beneficiaries (*Re Londonderry*).

Thirdly, certain documents may attract specific rights to confidentiality. In *Hartigan v Rydge* one of the judges (Mahoney JA) held that disclosure of the settlor's letter of wishes could be refused on the basis that it had been expressed to be confidential (this principle was accepted in the Jersey case of *Re Rabaiotti's Settlements [2000] WTLR 953* at *967*). Further, there may be documents in relation to which the trustees owe a duty of confidentiality to a third party. If that is so, the trustees are bound not to breach that duty through disclosure to a beneficiary. Confidentiality may also be asserted as a ground for withholding information where the beneficiaries seeking disclosure are engaged in hostile litigation against the trustees in a capacity other than as beneficiaries under the trust (*Rouse v 100F Australia Trustees [2000] WTLR 111*).

In determining whether in any given circumstances disclosure of the classes of documents should be required to be disclosed by the trustees, Commonwealth courts have applied a general test of whether ordering disclosure is in the interests of the beneficiaries as a whole (*Re Rabaiotti's Settlements*; *Rouse v 100F Australia Trustees*). If a beneficiary can prove that disclosure is in the interests of the beneficiaries as a whole (and not just in his own interests) he should be able to obtain disclosure. It remains to be seen whether this principle will be accepted by the English courts as a general one which overrides the more rigid approach of *Re Londonderry*.

Letters of wishes cause perhaps the greatest controversy. It is now a common practice for a testator (or a settlor inter vivos) to create a discretionary trust, and provide by way of a separate document details of how he desires the discretion conferred to be exercised. Understandably, beneficiaries are often keen to have sight of such documents in order to see whether (and to what extent) trustees have complied with the wishes of the person who created the trust. In relation to inter vivos trusts it may be argued that the letter of wishes is in fact mandatory, and forms part of the trust itself (rather than a mere expression of wishes) justifying a slavish obedience to its terms by the trustees. However, in cases involving wills, such an argument is more difficult given the likelihood that requisite formalities of the Wills Act 1837 will not have been complied with, thereby preventing the letter from being treated as a codicil. In such cases, trustees who merely follow the terms of the letter of wishes may be accused of putting an excessive degree of weight on the testator's letter, and failing to exercise their own discretion properly (effectively an application of the principle in *Re Hastings-Bass [1975] Ch 25*).

Right to administration by the court

6.6   CPR 64.2(b) enables a beneficiary to apply to the Chancery Division of the High Court (or the county court if the value of the estate or trust in question is less than £30,000: County Courts Act 1984, s 23) for an order that the administration of the estate of a deceased person, or the execution of a trust be carried out under the direction of the court. The effect of an order for general administration is that the entirety of the administration of the estate is brought under the court's control. The making of an order of administration will require the personal representatives or trustees to seek the direction of the court as to how they should exercise their powers in the future (*Re Furness [1943] Ch 415*; alternatively, the court may even remove them from office) and may require the payment into court of all money assets forming part of the trust or estate. In addition they will invariably be required by the court to provide a full account of the administration to date. When the administration is carried out under the court's control, it remains incumbent on the personal representatives or trustees to be proactive, and make applications to the court for the requisite directions, as the court will do very little (if anything) of its own motion.

A claim for administration is brought by way of a Part 8 Claim (CPR 64.3) and must be supported by written evidence in the form of a witness statement or affidavit (CPR 8.5(1)). The parties will be all of the representatives or trustees, and all beneficiaries unless a representation order under CPR 19.6 is obtained.

Claims for administration are not encountered in practice as often as used to be the case, and indeed are now relatively rare. Indeed, CPR 64 PD 3.1 now provides that the court will only make an administration order if it considers that the issues between the parties cannot properly be resolved in any other way, thereby making it essentially a remedy of last resort. Historically, as a matter of practice, it was necessary for trustees seeking the guidance of the court to seek administration of the trust. However, CPR 64.2(b) provides that the court may make an order directing any act to be done which the court could order to be done if the estate or trust in question were being administered or executed under the direction of the court.

Right to remove or replace personal representatives

6.7   Where beneficiaries are dissatisfied with the conduct of the administration of the estate under which they are entitled, an alternative remedy to administration by the court is that of removal or replacement of the representative. Beneficiaries may seek the removal of the representatives under section 50 Administration of Justice Act 1985, which gives the court (being the High Court) the power to terminate the appointment of one or more representative, and/or to appoint a new representative in their place. It should be noted that whilst seeking removal or replacement of a representative may be an effective way of remedying poor administration on the part of the representative, it is not necessary to establish any wrongdoing on the part of the representative in order to have him removed. Orders for removal and/or replacement may be made in circumstances where, for example, the relationship between the representative and his fellow representatives (or the beneficiaries) is such that it hinders the administration of the estate, or simply because the beneficiaries have lost confidence in the representative. Of course, where wrongdoing can be proved, it is more likely that a beneficiary will obtain an order for removal, but against that must be weighed the greater likelihood that the proceedings will be contested, and the inevitable increase in costs and delay.

The procedure for seeking the removal or replacement of a personal representative is now governed by CPR 57, the former provisions of which were contained in RSC Ord 85. An application for removal or replacement may be made to the Chancery Division of the High Court by way of a Part 8 Claim, or where there are existing proceedings, by way of an application under CPR 23. Both forms of application must have exhibited a sealed or certified copy of the grant of probate or letters of administration (the original must be produced at the hearing so that if an order is made, the grant may be sent to the Principal Registry of the Family Division for the appropriate endorsement to be made), supported by written evidence containing the following information:

(a)   brief details of the property comprised in the estate together with an approximate estimate of its capital value and the income received;

(b)   brief details of the liabilities of the estate;

(c)   the names and addresses of the people in possession of the documents relating to the estate;

(d)   the names and addresses of the beneficiaries and details of their respective interests in the estate; and

(e)   the name, address and occupation of any proposed substitute personal representative.

Where it is sought to appoint a replacement representative, the application must also be supported by the signed consent of the proposed replacement (where the proposed replacement is either a corporation or the Public Trustee, the consent should be sealed), together with a witness statement or affidavit as to the fitness of the proposed replacement (PD 57 para 13.2).

The parties to an application for removal and/or replacement should be all of the personal representatives (CPR 57.13(3)), together with all beneficiaries who have not provided their written consent to the application for removal.

The right to remove trustees

6.8   Section 50 Administration of Justice Act 1985 provides a means of replacing or removing personal representatives, and does not confer jurisdiction to remove or replace trustees. Beneficiaries under a trust do have a corresponding right to remove or replace trustees. In the case of a comprehensive, well-drafted trust instrument, there may be an express power of removal in specified circumstances. However, in practice such provisions are relatively rare, and recourse must be had to the general rules which are set out below.

Firstly, beneficiaries have the power under section 19 Trusts of Land and Appointment of Trustees Act 1996 to direct a trustee to retire and to appoint a replacement in his stead. The power applies where no person is nominated by the trust instrument (i.e. the will in the case of testamentary trusts) to appoint new trustees, and the beneficiaries under the trust are all of full age and capacity, and (taken together) are absolutely entitled to the trust property. The statutory definition of 'beneficiary' in this context is 'any person who under the trust has an interest in the property subject to the trust (including a person who has such an interest as a trustee or personal representative)' (Trusts of Land and Appointment of Trustees Act 1996, s 22(1)) and therefore is potentially wide. It is unclear whether the term includes beneficiaries under a discretionary trust prior to the exercise of the trustees' discretion in their favour, or to the objects of a fiduciary power, as there has been no reported judicial determination of this question. However, it would seem that as a matter of principle the former category ought to be within the definition of beneficiary, whilst the latter probably is not.

Provided the conditions set out above are satisfied, the beneficiaries may, under section 19(2) either:

(a)   give a written direction to the trustee or trustees to retire from the trust; or

(b)   give a written direction to the trustees or trustee for the time being (or if there are none) to the personal representative of the last person who was a trustee, to appoint by writing as a trustee the person or persons specified in the direction.

Section 19(3) provides that where a trustee has been given a direction under section 19(2)(a), provided that:

(i)   reasonable arrangements have been made for the protection of any rights of his in connection with the trust;

(ii)   after his retirement there will be at least two trustees or a trust corporation to act as trustee; and

(iii)   either another person is to be appointed in replacement of him, or the continuing body consent to his retirement; he is required to exercise a deed declaring his retirement and he is deemed to have retired and be discharged from the trust.

If after a valid direction the trustee fails to exercise the requisite deed, it is open to the beneficiaries to apply to the court for enforcement. Such enforcement might be through an order expressly ordering the removal of the trustee (in the exercise of the court's inherent jurisdiction, as to which see below), or alternatively an order nominating some other person to execute the deed on the trustee's behalf (Supreme Court Act 1981, s 39).

Secondly, under section 36 Trustee Act 1925, where a trustee either remains outside of the UK for a period in excess of 12 months, refuses to act, or is unfit or incapable of doing so, a new trustee may be appointed in replacement of him by the execution of a written document appointing a new trustee (there is no specific requirement in section 36 for the document in question to be a deed, but given the issues concerning the vesting of real property in the new trustee, a deed should always be used). The right of replacement conferred by section 36 is not always conferred on a beneficiary: it vests in the person specified in the instrument creating the trust, and if there is no such person, in the remaining trustees (Trustee Act 1925, s 36(1)). It is, however, open to the beneficiaries to ask the court to exercise that power instead, under section 41 Trustee Act 1925, on the basis that it is 'inexpedient, difficult or impracticable' to do so without the court's assistance.

Thirdly, the High Court has the inherent jurisdiction to remove a trustee. This may need to be invoked where for whatever reason an application under section 41 Trustee Act 1925 is not possible.

Proceedings for removal of a trustee are within the scope of CPR 64.2(1), being an order that the court could make if it were administering the trust (CPR 64.2(c)). Consequently the claim must be brought by use of the Part 8 Claim procedure (CPR 64.3; whilst this part expressly provides that a Part 8 claim must be brought, it would seem logical that if proceedings were already ongoing, the claim for removal could be added to the pre-existing claim by way of an application under CPR 23), supported by written evidence in the form of a witness statement of affidavit (CPR 8.5(1)). All of the trustees should be named as parties (CPR 64.4(1)) together with all beneficiaries interested in the claim (in the case of removal that is all of them), unless a representation order under CPR 19.6 is obtained.

The costs of an application for removal will, in accordance with general principles, be paid by the losing party. However, there may be circumstances where the court considers that the costs should be borne by the trust fund, such as where the trustee required to exercise a deed under section 19 Trusts of Land and Appointment of Trustees Act 1996 has become incapable of doing so, or where the application is essentially by consent but an order of the court is required due to the inapplicability of the statutory mechanisms for removal and/or replacement.

The right to interest on legacies

6.9   Section 44 Administration of Estates Act 1925 provides that a personal representative is entitled to the period of one year (commencing with the date of the grant) for the administration of the estate. This period is commonly referred to as 'the executor's year'). Consequently personal representatives cannot be compelled to distribute the estate before the expiry of the executor's year. This rule applies even where there is express provision in the will for the estate to be distributed at some earlier time, or where a legacy is expressed to be payable at some time before the expiry of the executor's year.

Subject to any contrary direction in the will, all general and demonstrative legacies carry interest at the rate of 6% per annum from the end of the executor's year if they have not been paid by that time. If a legacy is contingent, the right to interest arises only after the conditions have been met, again, subject to any express direction to the contrary in the will and subject to a number of exceptions where the legacy carries interest from the date of death, such as:

(a)   legacies to infant children of the testator where the child is entitled to the legacy at the age of eighteen, or upon marriage at an earlier age, and there is no other provision made in the will for the child;

(b)   a legacy charged on land; and

(c)   a legacy to a child where it can be shown that the testator's intention was that the legacy was for the child's maintenance.

The applicable rate of interest is currently 6% per annum, as established by CPR Sch 1, RSC Ord 44 r 10.

Given the degree of complexity in relation to the rules concerning interest on legacies and the ability of a testator to make express provision in the will, it is advisable for a testator to set out expressly which legacies are to carry interest, and from what point in time.

The right to intermediate income

6.10   The law relating to the right to be paid the income arising on a legacy before it falls into possession is dealt with elsewhere in this book (see CHAPTER 12).

Chapter 7

Variation

Introduction

7.1   This chapter considers the effect that a variation or disclaimer has once it has been made. In considering the making of a variation or disclaimer, reference should be made to other published texts aimed at advising those preparing such documents, etc (e.g. *A Practitioner's Guide to Post-Death Variations*).

Nowadays, when reference is made to variations and disclaimers, thoughts naturally turn to the provisions of section 142 Inheritance Tax Act 1984 (IHTA 1984). However, to consider only this aspect would be to ignore the other forms of variation that exist and which are adopted by practitioners in differing circumstances. The following are the main forms currently in use.

Instruments of variation

7.2   Many instruments of variation are drafted in such a way that they purport to vary the deceased's will or the laws of intestacy applying upon the death of the deceased. However, only a court of law may vary the will of a deceased person. Parliament has sole control over the laws of intestacy. When considering any instrument of variation, it is necessary to look behind the deeming effects of the tax legislation at the true facts of the transaction.

Definition

7.3   An instrument of variation (IoV) is:

'A gift out of an inheritance received by the original beneficiary from a deceased person and to which certain benefits can accrue for inheritance tax and capital gains tax purposes, provided that the appropriate statements, as required by the relevant statutes, are included within the document effecting the gift.'

The expression 'instrument of variation' is usually applied to a document to which the provisions of section 142(1) IHTA 1984 and/or section 62(6) Taxation of Chargeable Gains Act 1992 (TCGA 1992) apply (see APPENDIX 1 for detailed provisions of both IHTA 1984, s 142 and TCGA 1992, s 62).

Whilst it is more usual to refer to a 'deed of variation', this is merely due to the fact that *most* variations are made by deed. A variation does not need to be made by deed – a simple letter (or, perhaps, a series of letters) signed by the appropriate person(s) may suffice (*Crowden v Aldridge [1993] 3 All ER 603*).

The important point is that any such variation is made in writing and signed by those persons entitled to the benefit which is the subject of the variation. That a variation be made in writing is not simply an Inland Revenue requirement as, where the subject of the gift under the variation is an equitable interest (as may often be the case, especially if the estate is still under administration), it may only be assigned by way of a document in writing (Law of Property Act 1925, s 53(1)(c): 'A disposition of an equitable interest or trust subsisting at the time of the disposition, must be in writing signed by the person disposing of the same or his agent thereunto lawfully authorised in writing or by will').

Who can make an instrument of variation?

7.4   An IoV may be made by a beneficiary entitled to benefit upon the death of another:

- under his will;

- under his intestacy (including a partial intestacy if the will does not dispose of the whole of the deceased's estate);

- as surviving owner of property owned by them under a beneficial joint tenancy;

- who has made a valid nomination of certain classes of assets in favour of the beneficiary (most frequently nominations are made over National Savings products; however, nominations may also be made over some life policies and other assets); or

- who has exercised by his will a general power of appointment (but not a special power of appointment) over trust property.

The person making the variation is usually referred to as 'the original beneficiary'. A variation will only affect the original beneficiary's actual interest in the estate. If, for example, he has only a life interest, he cannot (on his own) change the way in which the underlying capital will pass; if he has an interest which is vested, but may be divested if certain events occur (intermediate events), the beneficiary can only give away his interest subject to those intermediate events. Clearly, though, if all the relevant beneficiaries of an estate are able to act together, it is possible for them to re-organise the entirety of their beneficial interests (*Saunders v Vautier (1841) 4 Beav 115*).

In order to make an IoV, the beneficiary(s) must first accept the gift and, having done so, it is not then open to him to disclaim his interest if, for some reason, this should later be considered preferable (in certain circumstances, a partial disclaimer may be possible, see 7.28 below).

The Inland Revenue accept that, if the original beneficiary dies after the deceased, it is possible for the beneficiary's own legal personal representative (LPR) to make a variation of his interest in the original estate. This is frequently referred to as a 'double death' variation and often results in the original beneficiary's interest being 'recycled' to the beneficiaries of his own estate, thus avoiding the potential for double taxation of the interest as it passes through both estates (or to make full use of the remaining balance of the nil rate band in the estate of the first to die). The use of an IoV in these circumstances will often be more beneficial than relying upon section 141 IHTA 1984 (quick succession relief).

Many practitioners consider that it is open to the LPR of a deceased beneficiary who was entitled to an income interest only in the estate of the first to die to enter into a variation to prevent the income interest from aggregating with the value of the deceased beneficiary's estate. The Inland Revenue has rejected this view on the basis that 'in the real world' there is no property that might pass under the variation as the former income interest has been extinguished on the death of the income beneficiary (IR Capital Taxes Newsletter, December 2001 – see APPENDIX 2). However, as at the date of writing, it is understood that the position is the subject of an application to the Special Commissioners. One case has already been considered in Scotland: *Miss Felicity E Soutter's Executry v IRC [2002] WTLR 1207*. The Special Commissioner held that the LPR of Miss Greenlees, who was given only a right to reside in the late Miss Soutter's home (by Miss Soutter's will), could not extinguish that right for inheritance tax purposes by use of the deeming provisions of section 142 IHTA 1984. The Special Commissioner held that the right to reside was extinguished by the death of Miss Greenlees and could not, therefore, be the subject of a variation after her death. Whether or not one accepts that decision, the particular circumstances do not translate readily to a situation where the beneficiary is entitled to receive an income stream. As at the date of his death there is still an entitlement outstanding and due to him, being income received by the LPR (or trustee) but not yet paid to him. In that instance, there will be an 'asset' upon which the variation may 'bite' – the unpaid income. Alternatively, there is the income already paid to him, which could be redirected to another party.)

Date from which an instrument of variation is effective

7.5   An IoV is effective from its own date (*Waddington v O'Callaghan (1931) 16 TC 187*), unless by the terms of the instrument a contingency or condition is imposed. Where a contingency or condition is imposed, if it is not, or cannot be, complied with within the period of two years after the date of death of the person, the dispositions of whose estate are being varied, it is likely that the variation will fall outside of section 142(1) IHTA 1984 and section 62(6) TCGA 1992. It is also possible that, if such condition or contingency is considered by the Inland Revenue to import 'consideration' into the transaction, the variation may well fall foul of section 142(3) IHTA 1984.

Often an IoV will include a statement to the effect that the variation is effective 'from the date of this instrument' or 'from the date of death of the deceased'.

This does not cause the variation to be effective from the specified date, rather it defines the interest that the new beneficiary(s) under the deed are to take.

Clearly, if an IoV contains a statement that its terms will be effective from a certain date, being after the date of the instrument but within two years of the relevant death, the variation will only take effect on that date, but will be binding upon the original beneficiary once it is completed.

Can an instrument of variation be made once the estate is fully distributed?

7.6   A variation may be made irrespective of whether the estate in question has been fully administered, or the property subject to the variation has been distributed to the beneficiary entitled under the original disposition (IHTA 1984, s 142(6) – see APPENDIX 1).

Where the variation is made over, say, a former beneficial joint tenancy, it does not matter if the LPR has completed the administration of the deceased's estate as the asset subject to the deed has passed outside of the estate subject to the grant. The position is the same for assets passing under a nomination.

Where the estate is still under administration, however, the nature of the variation may differ from that where the administration is complete. This is due to the fact that whilst the estate is in the course of administration, the beneficiary making the variation may only have a right to require the proper administration of the estate (i.e. a chose in action), rather than the right to call for any particular asset.

The position is different when a variation is made over part of the estate which is already in the hands of the original beneficiary (or held upon bare trusts for him), than if the same variation was made in respect of an asset still in the hands of the LPR as LPR. This mostly has implications for the potential taxation consequences, which are discussed at 7.13 *et seq* below.

What can be gifted by an instrument of variation?

7.7   As indicated above, a beneficiary, or group of beneficiaries together, can only gift by IoV an interest inherited upon the relevant death. An interest inherited from settled funds upon the deceased's death is specifically excluded from the provisions of section 142 IHTA 1984, as is the subject of any gift with reservation made by the deceased and subject to section 102 Finance Act 1986 (IHTA 1984, s 142(5)).

If, for example, a beneficiary is gifted the deceased's half share of a property held by the beneficiary and the deceased as tenants in common in equal shares, the beneficiary cannot make a variation of the entire property, even if his original half share was gifted to him by the deceased during his lifetime, but within two years before the date of the purported variation. Whilst the Inland

Revenue might accept the variation was effective for taxation purposes in respect of the inherited share of the property, the other half would be taxable as a personal gift by the beneficiary.

Even though an estate might not be fully administered, it is possible for a beneficiary to make a variation over specific assets in the hands of the LPR. The effects of this will be considered in more detail later.

Most gifts made under an IoV tend to be of cash.

What passes under an instrument of variation?

7.8   As previously stated, the original beneficiary (or beneficiaries) cannot gift by an IoV more than he inherits from the deceased as a result of his death.

Where the subject matter of the IoV ('the gift') includes an interest in the unadministered estate, that part of the gift is a chose in action, being the right to the due administration of the estate. The IoV will be an assignment of the right over that interest, to the extent that it is gifted by the instrument. This is irrespective of whether the gift is of, say, a cash sum or specific item(s), although, with the latter, the new beneficiary (under the IoV) will not become entitled to those assets until the LPR appropriates them.

Clearly, where the LPR is provided with the IoV (or a copy of it) in the above situation, he is on notice of the assignment and should normally account to the new beneficiary for the gift. Where it would be possible for the original beneficiary to satisfy the gift out of assets already distributed from the estate, the LPR might obtain written confirmation from him as to whether the gift, or any part of it, is to be satisfied from those assets already in the beneficiary's possession. Ideally, the IoV might contain a recital to this effect.

If the IoV gifts assets already in the possession of, or under the control of, the original beneficiary, the new beneficiary will be entitled to those assets. This will include assets appropriated by the LPR to the original beneficiary but, as at the date of the IoV, not yet transferred to him or his nominee. In the latter instance, as the LPR is holding as 'bare trustee', he may be advised to obtain written instructions from the original beneficiary to satisfy the gift out of those assets.

The gift of a capital asset under an IoV may also carry with it rights to income or interest, and the nature of such right, and the extent to which it exists, is discussed at 7.10 below.

Whether or not the assets, or interest, gifted by an IoV form a chose in action generally has little direct effect upon the manner in which the gift is satisfied. However, it may impact upon certain taxation aspects, which are discussed at 7.13 *et seq* below.

At this point, it might be noted that, irrespective of the particular wording of a IoV, the effect of it is that the original beneficiary only gifts the interest or assets as stated in the instrument. So if, for example, the sole beneficiary under a will wishes to keep a house or a specific cash sum, but gift the whole of the rest of the estate to another party, the IoV might direct that the entire estate other than the house, or the cash sum, is treated as having been a residuary gift in favour of the new beneficiary. Although some view such an arrangement as creating an intestacy in the assets excluded from the IoV, this cannot be the case without further, more specific, words for, as stated above, in order to make an IoV, the original beneficiary must first accept the benefit. It is then 'his' and cannot be 'undisposed of' by the deceased (even if the deceased died intestate, or only partially intestate).

What is the new beneficiary entitled to?

7.9   This section considers the entitlement of the new beneficiary under the IoV to a capital sum, or capital assets. Entitlement will depend both upon the actual wording of the IoV and the nature of the original beneficiary's interest in the estate.

The right of the new beneficiary to receive income or interest upon the gift is considered in 7.10 below.

Whilst most IoVs are used to create gifts out of the residuary interest, this is not always the case. It is therefore necessary to consider the rights of the original beneficiary before being able to say with any certainty what the new beneficiary should receive. The following is a brief summary of the nature of particular types of legacies (see CHAPTER 2 for more detail).

- *Specific legacy/devise:*

the original beneficiary is entitled to the asset(s) specified in the will.

- *General legacy:*

this is a gift of a cash sum, or of items not owned by the deceased but which are capable of being acquired by the personal representative.

- *Demonstrative legacy/devise:*

the original beneficiary is entitled to the cash gift, to be paid out of the specified asset or fund, although if that asset or fund is insufficient, or no longer exists, it is treated as a general legacy.

- *Annuity:*

the annuitant is generally entitled only to receive a periodic payment, as directed in the will. However, where the will contains a direction for the LPR to purchase the annuity, the annuitant may claim the lump sum.

- *Statutory legacy:*

the personal chattels and cash sum to which the surviving spouse is entitled upon the death of his/her husband/wife, whether intestate, or partially intestate.

- *Residuary estate:*

what is left of the estate after satisfaction of all debts, taxes, prior legacies and devises and the costs and expenses of administering the estate.

- *Settled legacies:*

as a settled legacy is merely a particular version of any of the above forms of legacy, given to trustees, the entitlement of the trustees will be as above.

- *Former joint property:*

where assets are held jointly by persons as beneficial joint tenants, upon the death of any co-owner his entire interest in such assets passes absolutely to the surviving co-owner(s).

- *Nominated assets:*

a nomination is effectively a specific legacy given outside of the will. Where a valid nomination is made, the named beneficiary is entitled to the nominated asset(s) in priority to any gift of those same assets in the will.

- *Exercise of general power of appointment:*

the nature of any interest arising under the exercise of such a power will be in one of the forms above, and the beneficiary's interest will be defined accordingly.

If the gift to the original beneficiary abates, unless the IoV provides otherwise, the gift to the new beneficiary will only be reduced if the inheritance from which it is to be paid is insufficient to satisfy it (clearly, if the gift under the IoV is of a proportionate part of the inheritance, such gift will abate with the inheritance generally).

Whilst an IoV may be used to create new gifts out of the various forms of inheritance, as above, the new gift will invariably fall under one of the following heads:

- *Fixed cash sum:*

the specified amount (if the IoV contains a power to appropriate in satisfaction of the amount due, the cash sum may be satisfied by the transfer of assets up to that value as at the date of appropriation (applying *Re Charteris, Charteris v Biddulph [1917] 2 Ch 379*). The capital gains tax implications of such a situation are considered later, see 7.15 below).

- *Specific assets:*

the assets specified or, if they have been sold or are subject to a binding contract for sale before the date of the instrument, the proceeds of sale of such assets (if the proceeds of sale have been reinvested, the new beneficiary may be able to follow the proceeds and claim an interest in any new asset purchased with them. Any such claim would be dependent upon the precise circumstances of the estate, etc).

- *Residue, or a share of residue:*

the specified share of the estate.

- *New trusts (this applies irrespective of the nature of the trust, which might be the creation of, say, an annuity fund, a life interest or discretionary trust):*

the original beneficiary may take advantage of the inheritance tax provisions of section 142 IHTA 1984 to settle part (or all) of his inheritance in such a way that the deceased is deemed to have been the settlor (although only for inheritance tax purposes). If he does, then the 'new beneficiary' under the IoV will be the trustee(s), and his interest under the instrument will be the same as for any other donee, depending upon the nature of the gift, as above. It is not the nature of the recipient that affects the benefit under the IoV, merely the nature of the gift made.

The new beneficiary's right to income or interest under an IoV

7.10   As discussed above, the original beneficiary making the variation may gift no more than his original entitlement.

Clearly, if the original beneficiary has no right to income or interest, the new beneficiary can have no such entitlement. When deciding upon the new beneficiary's right, it is also necessary to look at both what the original beneficiary was entitled to and the nature of the gift to the new beneficiary.

Whilst inter-related, the individual elements of each are considered separately in view of the potentially large number of combinations that can arise.

The right of the original beneficiary to receive income or interest on his inheritance is briefly summarised below. For a detailed analysis of such rights, see CHAPTER 2.

- *Specific legacy/devise:*

will usually carry the right to income from the date of death of the deceased (see 2.3 above).

- *General legacy:*

such a legacy usually only carries the right to income or interest from the earlier of the date upon which it is satisfied and the end of the executor's year (see 2.10 above).

- *Demonstrative legacy/devise:*

where the fund still exists, the legacy carries the right to income from the entire fund, in the same proportion that the legacy bears to the fund. In this case, the right to income runs from the date of death. If the legacy exceeds the fund out of which it is payable (including when the fund no longer exists), the excess is treated as a general legacy and carries a right to interest accordingly (see 2.16 above).

- *Annuity:*

runs from the date of death, although the first payment is not due until the end of the executor's year, unless it is directed to be paid, say, monthly or quarterly, when the first payment will be due at the end of the first month, or quarter, respectively (see 2.21 above).

- *Statutory legacy:*

interest at the statutory rate from the date of death – 6% gross (from 1 October 1983 – Intestate Succession (Interest and Capitalisation) Order 1977 (Amendment) Order 1983, SI 1983/1374). (see 2.25 above).

- *Residuary estate:*

carries with it the right to the income from the estate after payment of all liabilities properly chargeable against income.

- *Settled legacies:*

these are merely a particular type of specific, general or demonstrative legacy/devise, and carry the same rights to income or interest as such legacy or devise.

- *Former joint property:*

where there is only one surviving co-owner, the whole of the interest or income produced by the assets; where there is more than one such survivor, they share the interest or income equally.

- *Nominated assets:*

these carry the income rights attaching to the assets nominated and, if part of a fund, in the same proportion that the nominated amount bears to the entire fund.

- *Exercise of general power of appointment:*

the right to receive income or interest will be defined by the clause under which the power of appointment is exercised and will fall within one of the above categories.

Type of new 'legacy' (where the new beneficiary is entitled to interest or income, the date from which this will run is discussed at 7.11 below):

- *Fixed cash amount:*

these are frequently described within an IoV as 'pecuniary legacies', perpetuating the myth that an IoV changes the will (or the laws of intestacy) after the testator's death.

A gift under an IoV is a lifetime gift by the original beneficiary (see 7.3 above) and the general rules applicable to such gifts apply. The donee under an IoV is in the same position as the donee of an inter vivos gift of cash – he is not entitled to interest unless the IoV specifically provides for it.

If this were not the case, how, for example, are the rules applied where an IoV creating cash gifts is made more than a year after death? From what date would interest run?

Further, if fixed sum gifts are made under an IoV following an intestate death, especially where the IoV creates a 'notional will', on what basis can the rules for general legacies be invoked where the only applicable rules are the laws of intestacy? As stated above, an IoV cannot change the facts, it is merely deemed to have certain consequences for certain taxation purposes (see 7.2 above).

If the gift under the IoV is paid by the original beneficiary, perhaps after he has received his inheritance, will the new beneficiary demand interest on the cash gift?

If the original beneficiary is a general legatee and, by IoV, gifts the full amount of his legacy, then the benefit passing under the IoV may include any right to interest (although it should be borne in mind that the interest on a general legacy is deemed to be a separate gift – *Dewar v IRC [1935] 2 KB 351*, in which Maugham LJ said: 'I conceive that there is no doubt that in the case of pecuniary legacies the legatee is entitled to disclaim part or the legacy if he likes, and to disclaim in particular the interest on the legacy, being a pecuniary legacy, if he so wishes.'). Of course, if such original beneficiary does not also gift the right to interest on his legacy, and payment is made by the LPR to the new beneficiary (after the first anniversary of death), the LPR will still need to account to the original beneficiary for the interest, but might not be able to recover the payment from the new beneficiary.

Where the cash gift is given out of a share of residue, some consider that the rules of pecuniary legacies will apply, whilst others view the 'legacy' to be a share of residue defined by reference to the cash sum, thus carrying with it the right to a proportionate part of the residuary income. However, there would appear to be no reason to deviate from the general proposition, above, that the donee is not entitled to interest unless the IoV specifically provides for it.

The same position applies where cash sums are given by the IoV out of other assets inherited upon the death of the deceased person.

More often than not, the original beneficiary intends only to gift the sum stated in the IoV.

If the original gift is a general legacy of, say, shares, and, by IoV, the original beneficiary gifts the right to receive some (or all) of those shares to another, the same position will apply. The original beneficiary's right to interest or income does not run until either the gift is satisfied or the first anniversary of the death of the deceased, whichever occurs first. As a general legacy, any interest arising before it is satisfied is a separate legacy (*Dewar v IRC*). In this context, it must be remembered that the right of the beneficiary (whether original or new) is not to any shares matching the description in the will/IoV, and which the testator may have owned at the date of his death. It is the right to require the LPR to acquire the specified shares for him, or to account to him for a sum equal to the cost of purchasing those shares. Accordingly, until the gift is satisfied, the beneficiary's interest is in a cash sum, not the shares.

- *Specified assets:*

often these are described in an IoV as 'specific legacies' or 'specific devises' although, as above, they can only be gifts made by the original beneficiary and should not be treated as having been made by the deceased other than for the particular purposes provided for by section 142(1) IHTA 1984 and section 62(6) TCGA 1992 (which confer no right to either interest or income).

As identified generally above, the terms of the IoV will define the respective rights of the original beneficiary and the new beneficiary to income on the gifted assets. This is irrespective of whether the assets in question have been appropriated to the original beneficiary, or remain part of the unadministered estate.

If the gift is effective from the date of the instrument, the new beneficiary will be entitled to the equivalent of the income and any other distributions (this will include not only the income but also any capital distributions made in the relevant period) arising from the assets from the date of the instrument to the date of satisfaction of the gift (other than any 'XD' dividends, etc). If the gift is stated to be effective from any other date, the new beneficiary will similarly be entitled to the equivalent of the income and any other distributions since the relevant date. The amount of the dividends and any other distributions will be payable out of the original beneficiary's interest.

- *Residue, or a share of residue:*

the new beneficiary will be entitled to a proportionate share of the residuary income, after payment of all expenditure properly payable out of the income of the estate.

- *Joint property:*

where the IoV creates a gift out of property formerly held by the deceased and the original beneficiary as beneficial joint tenants (whether or not with others), the new beneficiary will be entitled to a proportionate share of the interest or income. (Where the original beneficiary is not the sole surviving joint tenant, if the terms of the IoV are inconsistent with the continuation of the joint tenancy, the effect of the instrument may also be to create an actual severance of the joint tenancy between the surviving co-owners, so that they hold with the new beneficiary as tenants in common.)

- *New trusts:*

the trustees' right to interest or income will be the same as for any other donee, depending upon whether the gift to the trustees is a fixed cash sum, specified assets, a share of the estate or former joint property. It is not the nature of the recipient that affects the right to income or interest, merely the nature of the gift made under the IoV.

When does the new beneficiary's right to interest or income start?

7.11   Once the new beneficiary's right to interest or income has been established, the next question that arises is – 'from what date is it payable?'

If the IoV contains no direction as to when:

•   the new beneficiary's entitlement under the IoV becomes effective, or

•   the date from which any right to interest or income should run,

such right will normally be from the date of the instrument itself (applying *Waddington v O'Callaghan (1931) 16 TC 187*).

The new beneficiary will be entitled only to the appropriate share of the original beneficiary's income from the date of the instrument. The income before that date remains in the original beneficiary's estate as it is not included in the gift. Unless specified within the instrument, there is no apportionment of the income or interest over the date of the IoV (as with an inter vivos gift it is generally accepted that the gift carries with it the right to income which has yet to be paid – despite the fact that it may have accrued before the effective date of the gift. However, this point has yet to be judicially tested).

There may be occasions where the original beneficiary executes the instrument, intending it to be effective immediately, but, for some reason, it is not dated until some time later. The extent of the new beneficiary's entitlement to interest or income in such cases may well depend upon the particular circumstances of the case. If the situation cannot be resolved by negotiation, it may be necessary to seek legal advice in the light of the specific facts that apply.

A number of standard precedents for IoVs include a statement that it varies the dispositions arising upon the death of the deceased either with effect from: 'the date of death of the deceased', or from its own date.

Where the instrument contains such a statement, it is generally accepted that the new beneficiary's right to interest or income runs from the date specified (but see also below).

In the first instance, if the original beneficiary has, say, gifted his share of the residuary estate to the new beneficiary, that new beneficiary should also receive all the interest or income arising on that share of residue to which the original beneficiary would have been entitled (there may be income tax implications if the original beneficiary has already received a distribution on account of the original interest (see 2.35 above).

If, in the same circumstances, the IoV contained a statement that it was effective only from its own date, the rights of the original and new beneficiary would be the same as where the IoV contains no direction, as above.

Where an IoV deals only with a right to income, such as the creation or assignment of an income interest (e.g. such as where the original beneficiary might settle the estate or a part of it upon a third party for life), clearly it gives the new beneficiary a right to receive the income. The date upon which such income entitlement arises will depend upon the wording of the instrument, as above.

In some cases, a gift in an IoV might contain a proviso along the lines of:

"Provided that such gift shall not carry the right to income or interest until it is actually paid".

This is most frequently included where the IoV is used to make a cash gift to the new beneficiary, in which case the new beneficiary receives no interest or income until actual satisfaction of the gift, whether this be by way of payment to, or on behalf of, the new beneficiary, or the sum being set aside out of the estate for him.

On occasion, though, the proviso is also used where a gift of a specified asset is made by the IoV. This case is much the same as for a cash gift, with any interest or income up to the date of satisfaction of the gift being due to the original beneficiary. If the gift is of, say, shares, the new beneficiary will not be entitled to any dividends paid before the date the shares are transferred, or formally appropriated, to him. If the books of the company have closed for payment of a dividend at that time (i.e. the shares would then be quoted 'XD') that dividend is due to the original beneficiary in the same way as if the original beneficiary had personally transferred the shares to the new beneficiary on that date.

In any event, when such proviso is contained within an instrument, it does not appear to detract from the effectiveness of the instrument for the purposes of section 142 IHTA 1984 or section 62(6) TCGA 1992.

What if the effect of the instrument of variation is not what was intended?

7.12   There are many recorded instances of cases where an IoV does not achieve its stated objective, due to a mistake or misunderstanding arising at the time it was prepared (e.g.: *Lake v Lake [1989] STC 865*; *Matthews v Martin [1991] STI 418*). In such cases it is open to the person(s) who made the variation to rectify the dispositions of the original instrument. However, it may be necessary for those who have (erroneously) benefited under the original instrument to be party to the rectification.

It is not open to the original beneficiary, with or without the consent of the beneficiaries entitled under the IoV, merely to make a second IoV to correct the situation (*Re Russell, Russell v IRC [1988] STC 195*).

Whilst it may be relatively straightforward to correct any errors in an IoV as between the beneficiaries, if such rectification has taxation consequences, it may be necessary to satisfy the Inland Revenue as to the nature of the original error and the manner in which it is corrected. The Inland Revenue, like the courts, tends to require substantial evidence to support a claim for rectification.

The Inland Revenue cannot reject rectification of an IoV merely on the grounds that this would give tax benefits to the beneficiaries, whether original or new (in *Re Slocock's Will Trusts [1979] 1 All ER 358*, Graham J held that where a mistake is made in a document legitimately designed to avoid tax, there is no reason why it should not be corrected). However, the Inland Revenue may decline to accept rectification is effective without an order of the court.

Taxation issues of an instrument of variation

7.13 Having considered the dispositive effects of IoVs, it is necessary also to consider the taxation consequences.

An IoV may be made solely to rectify a defect or ambiguity in the will, rather than the beneficiaries going to the cost of an application to court for rectification under section 20 Administration of Justice Act 1982. In such cases the Inland Revenue may accept that the effect of the instrument is merely to set out what the testator intended, so that there are no taxation consequences attaching to it. There may be considerable benefit in approaching the Inland Revenue with a draft of any such deed in the hope that it might be willing to indicate how it will treat such an instrument.

There are four taxes relevant to IoVs in the UK:

- inheritance tax;

- capital gains tax;

- income tax;

- stamp duty.

These shall be considered separately.

The provisions of section 142 IHTA 1984 or section 62(6) TCGA 1992 do not automatically apply to an IoV and there is no reason why, in the appropriate circumstances, only one (or perhaps neither) should apply to a particular IoV. In which case, the dispositions effected by the instrument will be treated as having been made by the original beneficiary, and subjected to the provisions of IHTA 1984 and/or TCGA 1992 accordingly.

Inheritance tax

7.14 In the absence of section 142 IHTA 1984, and its statutory predecessors, any disposition effected by an IoV would be treated as a potentially exempt transfer (PET) or an immediately chargeable transfer by the original beneficiary, unless the gift was otherwise exempt (e.g. it was a gift to the original beneficiary's (UK domiciled) spouse, a charity, qualifying political party or other donee deemed to be exempt for inheritance tax purposes) or was of excluded property (see IHTA 1984, s 48 for definition of 'excluded property').

In order to qualify for relief under section 142, the IoV:

- must be completed within two years of the date of death of the person, the dispositions of whose estate are to be varied; and

- where the variation is made on or after 1 August 2002, the instrument must contain a statement, made by all the relevant persons, to the effect that they intend the provisions of section 142(1) to apply to the variation (IHTA 1984, s 142(2) as amended by Finance Act 2002, s 120(1)).

The 'relevant persons' are:

- the person or persons making the instrument, and

- where the variation results in additional tax being payable, the personal representatives (LPRs).

However, the LPRs may refuse to join in the statement if, as at the date of the IoV, they have no, or insufficient, assets in their hands as LPRs to satisfy the additional tax liability (IHTA 1984, s 142(2A) as inserted by Finance Act 2002, s 120(1)).

NB Where an IoV was dated before 1 August 2002, in order for the provisions of section 142 to apply to the dispositions of that instrument, the parties to it were required to lodge an election to that effect with the Inland Revenue within six months of the date of the instrument. The election could either be contained within the instrument itself, or be a separate document. Failure to lodge the election in time would usually result in the benefit of section 142 being denied to the gift contained within the instrument.

In the event that no statement is incorporated in the IoV (or, for pre August 2002 variations, no valid election is made), as required under section 142(2) (see APPENDIX 1), the dispositions by the IoV will be treated for inheritance tax purposes in the same way as they are treated under general law – as personal gifts by the beneficiary(s) making the instrument. The IoV will have no effect upon the inheritance tax payable as a consequence of the death of the person, the dispositions of whose estate are purported to be varied by the instrument.

There will be particular circumstances where the original beneficiary may be advised not to invoke the provisions of section 142. In such cases the inheritance tax consequences of such an instrument will follow the facts, irrespective of the particular wording of the instrument or if the provisions of section 62(6) TCGA 1992 have been invoked by the instrument.

The fact that the provisions of section 142 might be denied to an IoV for any reason does not cause the gifts made under that instrument to be void or otherwise fail.

Under section 142(3), the giving of 'consideration' for an IoV is fatal to the application of section 142 to the dispositions effected by that instrument. This is so even if the instrument contains an appropriate statement to the effect that the section will apply to its dispositions. However, if the 'consideration' is by way of another variation (or disclaimer) of the dispositions of the same estate, and to which section 142 applies, section 142(3) may not apply. (The author is aware of one case where the beneficiaries of a husband's estate agreed to settle a claim under the Inheritance (Provision for Family and Dependants) Act 1975 by the widow by use of an IoV. The widow died before implementation and her LPR gave an indemnity to the beneficiaries of the husband's estate against any additional inheritance tax that might arise as a result of implementation of the arrangement. The widow's LPR disclosed the existence of the indemnity to the Inland Revenue, which promptly raised assessments on the basis that section 142 could not apply as there was extraneous consideration for the making of the IoV.)

The rest of this section on inheritance tax relates to the situation where the provisions of section 142 apply.

When an IoV invokes the provisions of section 142, it is generally accepted that such relief will apply to all the dispositions made by the instrument. If it is intended that the benefit of section 142 apply only to some parts of the instrument, but not to others, then usually more than one IoV should be made. (There is no doubt that, under the pre-1 August 2002 legislation, an election under section 142(2) was an 'all or nothing' issue. However, it has been suggested that the new section 142(2) might permit a 'mix & match' application of section 142(1) within the same IoV. Until such time as this issue is fully tested with the Inland Revenue (or is subject to judicial consideration), such suggestion should be treated with caution.)

Where a beneficiary enters into an IoV that creates gifts to new beneficiaries which are exempt for inheritance tax purposes (e.g. a charity, or the widow(er) of the deceased), any reduction in inheritance tax will be allocated in accordance with the usual rules for the incidence of such tax. It will not necessarily accrue for the benefit of the beneficiary making the variation (see below for examples). Clearly, though, the instrument might specifically provide for the benefit of the relief to accrue to the beneficiary making the variation (there appears to be no published precedent to cater for such a situation; if the relief is to accrue to the beneficiary making the IoV, it may be necessary for those other beneficiaries who would otherwise benefit under the normal incidence rules to also be party to the instrument).

Example 1

A is given a general legacy of £10,000 'free of tax' under a will. By IoV, he gives half of it to charity. If the estate is taxable, the inheritance tax relief will accrue to the residuary beneficiaries.

Example 2

B is entitled to a one-third share of the residuary estate, the rest of residue passing to other individuals. By IoV, he gives a half share of his residuary interest to charity. The inheritance tax relief accrues to the estate before residue is ascertained and, therefore, before division of the residuary estate.

Example 3

C is a child of the deceased. The deceased and C owned a house as beneficial joint tenants. The residuary estate passes equally to the children of the deceased. By IoV, the child creates a notional severance of the joint tenancy and gives the deceased's nominal half share to the widow. The deceased's former interest in the house is now exempt from inheritance tax, which releases the full benefit of the deceased's nil rate band to reduce the inheritance tax charge on the estate passing under his will.

Where an IoV :

• includes a statement under section 142(2) IHTA 1984, and

• creates an additional inheritance tax liability,

the parties to the variation must, within six months after the date of the instrument, lodge a copy with the Inland Revenue (IR Capital Taxes) and give notice of the amount of the additional tax charge (IHTA 1984, s 218A as inserted by Finance Act 2002, s 120(2)). (See APPENDIX 1). Although lodgement by *any* party to the instrument fulfils the statutory requirement (and discharges the others from their responsibility), a failure to lodge the instrument within the statutory time limit results in *every party* to the instrument being potentially liable to a penalty for late delivery. Section 245(1A) IHTA 1984 (inserted by Finance Act 2002, s 120(3)) (see APPENDIX 1) imposes a penalty of £100 upon each person, plus a further penalty not exceeding £60 a day, from the day after a court or Special Commissioner has 'declared' the parties to have failed in their statutory obligation, until the day before they comply with the statutory obligation.

There is no statutory requirement for a copy IoV to be lodged with the Inland Revenue where the application of section 142 results in a refund of inheritance tax becoming due. However, no refund of tax will be forthcoming until a copy of the deed is lodged with IR Capital Taxes.

Where the provisions of section 142 apply to an IoV, they apply for *all* the purposes of IHTA 1984. This raises a number of apparent anomalies, examples of which are:

• *Gifts with reservation (Finance Act 1986, s 102):*

As, when the provisions of section 142 apply, the deceased is deemed to have made the gift for all purposes of IHTA 1984, if the original beneficiary creates a trust by IoV, and includes himself within the class of beneficiaries, the deeming provisions of section 142 will exclude such reservation of benefit from coming within the scope of section 102 Finance Act 1986.

• *Multiple settlements:*

If any beneficiary creates a trust by IoV, it is deemed to have been created by the deceased upon his death for inheritance tax purposes. If more than one beneficiary creates a trust by IoV upon the death of the same person, those trusts will all be deemed to have been made by the deceased. If any of the trusts are non-interest in possession trusts, subject to the provisions of Part III, Chapter III, IHTA 1984, then they will be 'related' for the purpose of calculating any exit or ten-yearly charge arising in the non-interest in possession trust. This is irrespective of whether any of the beneficiaries who declared the individual trusts had any knowledge of the other trusts being created.

• *Interaction with section 144 IHTA 1984:*

The Inland Revenue has confirmed that following the creation of a discretionary trust by instrument of variation, the provisions of section 144 IHTA 1984 will apply to a distribution out of that trust within two years of the deceased's date of death.

It is also suggested that the Inland Revenue will allow the provisions of section 142 IHTA 1984 to apply to an IoV made over assets distributed from a testamentary discretionary trust, making full use of the provisions of both section 142 and section 144 in the other order. When implementing such an arrangement, though, there must be a danger that the exercise of the trustees', or LPRs' discretion in this manner may be a fraud upon the power. This is especially so if it is known, or might reasonably have been ascertained at the time of the appointment out of the discretionary trust, that a variation was to made in favour of non-objects.

Clearance

Where the LPR has submitted an account to the Inland Revenue, he will normally apply for a formal clearance certificate under section 239 IHTA 1984, so as to protect himself against any further charge to tax that might arise. Such application should include details of any IoV made in respect of the estate in question. If any other party has also lodged an account, or paid inheritance tax on the death of the deceased, they might also consider the need to include in their application for inheritance tax clearance reference to any IoV of which they are aware.

Capital gains tax

7.15   In the absence of section 62(6) TCGA 1992, and its statutory predecessors, any disposition effected by an IoV would be treated as a disposal by the original beneficiary for capital gains tax purposes. This could have a particularly draconian effect if the instrument disposed of an interest in the unadministered estate, being a 'chose in action for the due administration of the estate' (a 'chose in action').

In order to qualify for relief under section 62(6) TCGA 1992 the IoV:

- must be completed within two years of the date of death of the person, the dispositions of whose estate are to be varied, and

- where the variation is made on or after 1 August 2002, the instrument must contain a statement by the persons making it to the effect that section 62(6) will apply to the variation (unlike IHTA 1984, s 142, TCGA 1992, s 62(7) contains no more specific direction as to who should be party to the statement. It would therefore appear that all parties to the instrument, whatever their interests, should join in the making of the statement of intent).

Unlike inheritance tax, there is no requirement to lodge a copy of the deed with the Inland Revenue, irrespective of whether or not the instrument gives rise to a charge to capital gains tax.

NB Where an IoV is dated before 1 August 2002, in order for the provisions of section 62(6) to apply to the dispositions of that instrument, the parties to it were required to lodge an election to that effect with the Inland Revenue within six months of the date of the instrument. The election could either be contained within the instrument itself, or be a separate document. Failure to lodge the election in time would usually result in the benefit of the relief under section 62(6) being denied to the gift(s) contained within the instrument.

When an IoV invokes the provisions of section 62(6), it is generally accepted that such relief will apply to all the dispositions made by the instrument. If it is intended that the benefit of section 62(6) applies only to some parts of the instrument, but not to others, then usually more than one IoV will be made. There is no doubt that, under the pre-1 August 2002 legislation, an election under section 62(7) was an 'all or nothing' issue. However, it has been suggested that the amended section 62(7) might permit a 'mix & match' application of section 62(6) within the same IoV. Until such time as this issue is fully tested with the Inland Revenue (or is subject to judicial consideration), such suggestion should be treated with caution.

If the appropriate statement is included in an IoV, the effect of this is for the dispositions effected by the instrument to be deemed to have been made by the deceased for the limited purposes of section 62 TCGA 1992 only (as confirmed by the House of Lords in *Marshall (Inspector of Taxes) v Kerr [1995] 1 AC 148*).

If the original beneficiary should settle any of his interest then, even if the provisions of section 62(6) apply to the variation, he will be the settlor for the purposes of capital gains tax. Should he have retained a relevant interest, despite the fact that he will not be deemed to be the settlor for inheritance tax purposes, the settlement will be 'settlor assessable' under section 77 TCGA 1992 (where a UK settlement is created) or section 87 TCGA 1992 (where the settlement is off-shore).

In considering the effect of section 62(6) in any specific situation, it is necessary to consider the nature of the asset disposed of by the original beneficiary and the source from which the gift under the IoV is to be satisfied.

As identified above, whilst the original beneficiary's interest remains in the hands of the LPR, as personal representative, the beneficiary has only a chose in action. Irrespective of the nature of his legacy or devise in the estate, and whether it arises under the will or intestacy, until such time as the LPR satisfies the original gift, the beneficiary can only dispose of a chose in action (either in part or in full).

The nature and, in particular, the capital gains tax implications of a chose in action were considered by the House of Lords in *Marshall (Inspector of Taxes) v Kerr*. Their Lordships agreed with the view put forward by the Inland Revenue that:

- a chose in action was acquired by the original beneficiary for no consideration;

- the value of that chose in action represented the extent of the beneficiary's interest in the unadministered estate at any particular point in time (i.e. it is progressively reduced by the value of distributions made to the beneficiary);

- the disposal of a chose in action produces a capital gain equal to its full value at the date of the disposal.

Before the decision in *Marshall v Kerr*, there was considerable debate as to the status of a chose in action for capital gains tax purposes, and some commentators still question whether it is a real issue. However, it is understood that the Inland Revenue continues to take the point that the disposal of a chose in action by a beneficiary may still be assessed to capital gains tax on a gain equal to its full value. Accordingly, even though the making of a cash gift normally has no capital gains tax implications, where such a gift is made by IoV out of the unadministered estate, this is a disposal of a chose in action by the original beneficiary and, potentially, is subject to capital gains tax.

It is therefore important, when the inheritance subject to the variation is an interest under a will or intestacy, to identify the precise status of the original beneficiary's interest at the date of the instrument. This will help identify the principles to be applied.

Where all, or part, of the inheritance (arising under the deceased's will or intestacy) has been transferred to the original beneficiary or his nominee, or has been appropriated to them by the LPR (so that it is held upon bare trusts for the original beneficiary), it will no longer form part of the chose in action. The beneficiary will, by then, have acquired the assets as 'legatee' under section 62(4) TCGA 1992 and their acquisition value will be the same as the LPR's acquisition value. If such assets are then the subject of an IoV to which section 62(6) applies, subject to the following paragraph, the beneficiaries under the variation will be deemed to acquire their interest upon the death of the deceased as 'legatee' under section 62(4) at the LPR's acquisition value. Any interest that the original beneficiary had will therefore be ignored.

Where any asset subject to the variation has been disposed of before the date of the IoV, the provisions of section 62(6) cannot apply to that asset. The effect of this is that capital gains tax will follow the facts. If the asset has been sold by the LPR, then any gain or loss will be assessable upon the LPR. If sold by the original beneficiary any gain or loss will be assessed upon that beneficiary. The provisions of section 62(6) cannot be applied retrospectively to any disposal before the date of the instrument of variation.

In order to clarify the position, as stated above, let us consider the following examples.

Example 1

The IoV creates a cash gift of £10,000 out of the residuary estate, the estate is unadministered.

This is the disposal of a chose in action and a capital gains tax charge may arise. Section 62(6) will relieve the capital gains tax charge.

Example 2

As in Example 1, but the payment is to be made out of moneys already paid to the original beneficiary, or assets which passed to him by survivorship upon the death of the deceased.

No charge to capital gains tax arises, and there is no need for a capital gains tax statement under section 62(7).

Example 3

The IoV creates a gift of specific assets out of a residuary interest; again the estate is unadministered.

This is the disposal of a chose in action and a capital gains tax charge may arise. If section 62(6) applies, there is no disposal by the original beneficiary and the new beneficiary will be deemed to acquire the assets as 'legatee' under section 62(4), once the assets are appropriated to them by the LPR.

Example 4

As in Example 3, but the specific assets have already been appropriated or transferred to the original beneficiary (the outcome will be the same if the assets in question had passed to the original beneficiary by survivorship).

The original beneficiary will make a disposal of the assets for capital gains tax as at the date of the IoV. However, if section 62(6) applies, there is no disposal by the original beneficiary and the new beneficiary will be deemed to acquire the assets as 'legatee' under section 62(4).

Example 5

As in Example 3, but the particular assets were sold before the date of the IoV.

The LPR will have made a capital gains tax disposal as at the date of the sale. The new beneficiary's entitlement will be to the proceeds of sale. Section 62(6) has no application in these circumstances.

Example 6

The IoV creates a gift of cash, which is satisfied by the transfer of, say, shares, some of which were in the estate, but others are transferred from personal holdings of the original beneficiary.

If section 62(6) applies, it will prevent a charge to capital gains tax on the disposal of a chose in action if the estate is not fully administered at the date of the IoV and deem the new beneficiary to acquire the shares from the estate as 'legatee' under section 62(4). However, section 62(6) cannot apply to the shares from the original beneficiary's personal holdings, so he will make a disposal of these for capital gains tax and the new beneficiary will acquire them at the disposal value.

Example 7

The IoV creates a cash gift out of former joint property which passes to the original beneficiary by survivorship.

No charge to capital gains tax arises.

Example 8

Following the death of the surviving spouse, within two years of his/her husband/wife, the LPR executes an IoV, purporting to sever the joint tenancy of the matrimonial home and giving the former interest of the first to die to the beneficiaries of the survivor's estate.

No charge to capital gains tax arises. The beneficiaries take the half share subject to the IoV as 'legatees' under section 62(4) on the second death.

If section 62(6) applies, the new beneficiaries instead take that half share as 'legatees' on the first death for capital gains tax purposes. (NB If the property is occupied between the two dates of death by the second to die, the application of section 62(6) may result in the loss of principal private residence relief under section 222 TCGA 1992. In a rising market, it will also reduce the new beneficiaries' acquisition value for capital gains tax, by bringing the acquisition date forward to the date of the first death.)

In neither case will the outcome affect the fact that the 'unvaried' half share will pass to the beneficiaries on the death of the surviving spouse at the value as at that date of death as 'legatees' under section 62(4) TCGA 1992.

Income tax

7.16   An IoV does not have retrospective effect for income tax purposes – it cannot alter the past (*Waddington v O'Callaghan (1931) 16 TC 187*). In many cases, therefore, both the original beneficiary and the new beneficiary(s) will need to consider the effect of the IoV upon their personal income tax positions.

Where, before the date of an IoV, a distribution has been made to the original beneficiary:

- which is income;

- includes an element of income; or

- is deemed to represent an income receipt in the hands of the beneficiary;

this will be his income for tax purposes even if, under an IoV, he gifts the whole of his inheritance to another party. Such income, or deemed income, will need to be included in any return of income the original beneficiary makes to the Inland Revenue and subjected to tax accordingly – so that if the beneficiary is taxed at a lower rate than that suffered on the income, he may be entitled to a refund of tax, even though he has not retained any right to that income (the converse will apply if the beneficiary is a higher rate tax payer – he will have to pay more tax, even though the income is no longer his).

If a capital gift to the new beneficiary carries no rights to interest or income, or such rights do not arise until the gift is paid, or is otherwise satisfied, the status quo will apply. Any interest or income will be payable to the original beneficiary, who will receive the usual income tax certificate or statement from the LPR. The new beneficiary's personal income tax position will not be affected (other than in respect of any interest or income received on the gift once it is in his hands).

Where the new beneficiary is entitled to interest or income upon the gift, or the gift is a right to interest or income, it is necessary to consider the individual facts of each case. The following are indicative of the income tax implications of particular gifts under an IoV, where the new beneficiary is also given a right to interest or income upon the gift to him under the IoV.

(a)   *Cash gift out of a general legacy:*

As discussed earlier (see 2.10 above) the recipient of a general legacy (whether of cash or other assets) is usually entitled to interest from the earlier of the date the gift is satisfied or the first anniversary of the death of the deceased. Where a gift is made by IoV out of such a bequest, the donee will not be entitled to any income unless specified in the IoV.

The LPR must account to the beneficiary (whether original or new) for the interest without the deduction of tax (Income and Corporation Taxes Act 1988 (ICTA 1988), ss 348, 349; although where the 'place of abode' of the beneficiary is outside of the UK, the LPR is required to deduct tax before payment and account for this to the Inland Revenue). Such interest is taxable in the beneficiary's hands in the year of receipt (*Dewar v IRC (1935) 19 TC 561*), so that if interest is not paid to the original beneficiary, only to the new beneficiary, it is the new beneficiary who will be liable to income tax upon the interest, not the original beneficiary.

NB Where a payment is made on account of a general legacy, it is first applied to discharge any outstanding interest before being applied to reduce the outstanding balance of the legacy: *Re Morley's Estate, Hollenden v Morley [1937] 3 All ER 204*. Accordingly, if any distribution on account is made to the original beneficiary once interest has started to run, he will have received part of that distribution as income for taxation purposes.

(b)   *Cash gift out of a specific legacy/devise or residue:*

The new beneficiary will normally only be entitled to interest or income on such a fixed cash sum if the instrument specifically provides for this. Any such interest, like interest on a general legacy, is payable without the deduction of tax (ICTA 1988, ss 348, 349), even though it may be paid out of taxed income. The interest will be taxable as income in the hands of the new beneficiary.

(c)   *Gift of assets out of a specific legacy/devise:*

As previously identified:

- an IoV is not retrospective for the purposes of income tax, and

- the income received by the LPR on a specific legacy or devise does not 'become' the legatee's/devisee's income until the asset (or the proceeds of sale thereof) is appropriated to the beneficiary.

Accordingly, if any part of the asset is gifted by IoV before the date of such appropriation, the income arising from the assets will remain the income of the original beneficiary, irrespective of whether he receives it or it is gifted to the new beneficiary under the terms of the IoV. The new beneficiary will be deemed to have received only that income on the assets gifted to him from the date of the instrument (or such later date as might be specified). Where the assets are investments quoted 'XD' as at the date of the gift, the dividend will be retained by the original beneficiary and deemed to be a part of their taxable income.

If the IoV is made after the date the asset is appropriated to the original beneficiary, it remains the case that the income up to the date of the instrument is taxable upon the original beneficiary (including 'XD' dividends), and after the date of the deed such asset is taxable as income of the new beneficiary.

(d)   *Gift of a share of residue:*

As identified in CHAPTER 2, a residuary beneficiary absolutely entitled to a share of residue is, for income tax purposes, deemed to have received income from the estate of an amount equal to the lesser of:

- the total of any distributions made to him in that tax year, and

- his proportionate share of the aggregated income entitlement (AIE) for the estate.

Upon the date of the IoV, the AIE of the original beneficiary should effectively be 'ruled off' and from that date should only be increased by the amount of any AIE proportionate to his retained interest in the estate. If he disposes of his entire interest, the balance of the AIE at the date of the IoV will be allocated to the new beneficiary to the extent that it has not been used for distributions already made to the original beneficiary during the tax year. (ICTA 1988, s 698(1A)). If only a part is gifted the new beneficiary will start with a 'Nil' AIE balance.

(e)   *Gift of specified assets out of a share of residue:*

As identified earlier, until assets are appropriated to a residuary beneficiary in satisfaction of his interest in the estate, he has only a chose in action for the due administration of the estate. The IoV cannot, therefore, effect an immediate assignment of anything other than a part of that chose in action. However, as this is not a distribution out of the estate, the new beneficiary's right to the asset specified in the IoV does not crystallise until the LPR appropriates that asset in satisfaction of the donee's interest.

Despite any rights to 'income' on the asset that might be granted by the IoV to the new beneficiary, until such time as the LPR appropriates the asset to them, any income arising will be treated as accruing to the original beneficiary's AIE and deemed to be his income for taxation purposes. The new beneficiary will be assessable for the income payable only after the date of appropriation, following which the LPR will hold the asset for him upon bare trusts until transfer of the legal title to the new beneficiary, or his nominee.

Parent/child settlements

7.17   If a parent makes a gift by IoV in favour of his infant child then, subject to certain exceptions, the income arising on the gift whilst the child is an unmarried minor will be treated as the income of the parent rather than as the income of the child for tax purposes (ICTA 1988, s 660B).

Gift Aid

7.18   Subject to satisfying certain conditions, an individual may gift money or assets to charity under the Gift Aid scheme (Finance Act 1990, s 25), in order to obtain relief from higher rate tax, and to enable the charity receiving the gift to claim a repayment of the tax suffered on the amount of the gift, grossed up at the basic rate.

Where such a gift is made by instrument of variation, however, no relief is available either to the beneficiary making the gift or to the charity (*St Dunstan's v Major (Inspector of Taxes) [1997] STC (SCD) 212*), as the beneficiary will receive a benefit as a result of the application of section 142 IHTA 1984 – a refund of inheritance tax in the estate. (Whilst the membership of various charities carries with it a right to certain benefits, such as free admission to country houses, relief under the Gift Aid scheme is allowed on the membership subscriptions. Although a number of commentators have questioned this apparent anomaly, none have yet sought to test the issue further.)

Stamp duty

7.19   An instrument of variation is subject to stamp duty.

The amount of any duty payable is dependent upon the precise nature of the instrument, as the Stamp Office will 'look through' the deeming provisions for inheritance tax and capital gains tax purposes, to the actual transaction(s) effected. It is therefore necessary to consider the underlying effect of the variation being made by the original beneficiary, not the fiction 'perpetrated' for the purposes of section 142 IHTA 1984 or section 62(6) TCGA 1992.

The following table (first published in the *Trusts and Estates Tax Journal, No 19*, September 2001: 'Back to Basics: Deeds of Variation', by Paul Saunders) sets out the stamp duty implications of the more frequently occurring situations:

Type of Instrument	Stamp Duty Requirements	Stamp Duty on Transfer Documents
1 Creation of settlement	£5 fixed duty (declaration of trust)	£5 fixed duty (a conveyance of any other kind)
2 Compromise of a claim under Inheritance (Provision for Family and Dependants) Act 1975	£5 fixed duty (and must be submitted for adjudication)	£5 fixed duty (a conveyance of any other kind)
3 Creation of limited interest (i.e. contingent or life interest)	£5 fixed duty (declaration of trust)	£5 fixed duty (a conveyance of any other kind)

Type of Instrument	Stamp Duty Requirements	Stamp Duty on Transfer Documents
4 Creation of an absolute interest (including assignment of a limited interest, e.g. a life interest). NB If the new gift is to, say, the executor in trust for another person absolutely, £5 duty may be payable under the heading 'Declaration of trust' and the instrument should be submitted for adjudication	Category L certificate (Schedule to the Stamp Duty (Exempt Instruments) Regulations 1987, SI 1987/516)	£5 fixed duty (a conveyance of any other kind)
5 Division of a trust between income and capital beneficiaries, whether on an actuarial basis, or otherwise	£5 fixed duty (Partition)	*Ad valorem* duty
6 Variation effecting a rearrangement of interests on sale between the original beneficiaries		
(a) without the introduction of outside cash	Category M certificate (Schedule to the Stamp Duty (Exempt Instruments) Regulations 1987, SI 1987/516)	£5 fixed duty (a conveyance of any other kind)
(b) outside cash introduced for the interest acquired NB It is unlikely that any instrument under (b) will fall within the provisions of section 142 IHTA 1984	*Ad valorem* duty	£5 fixed duty (a conveyance of any other kind)

Notes		
	1	In most of the above cases (other than those falling within item 5), the IoV should generally include a certificate under category L of the Schedule to the Stamp Duty (Exempt Instruments) Regulations 1987, SI 1987/516, to cover assets passing under the instrument and which are transferable by delivery (e.g. cash, bank balances or chattels).
	2	Where a required exemption certificate is omitted, the IoV may also be subject to a £5 fixed duty in addition to any duty identified in the first column, above.
	3	If the IoV fails to include the relevant exemption certificate at the time it is completed, this may subsequently be endorsed upon the instrument and signed by the transferor (i.e. the original beneficiary(s)), or his solicitor.
	4	Where an IoV purports to vary the disposition of the estate under more than one of the above heads, it will be subject to the stamping requirements of each function. If *ad valorem* duty is payable, it will be in respect only of the value passing in respect of that specific aspect of the transaction.

Stamp duty is a tax on 'instruments', not transactions. To some extent it is a voluntary tax as there is currently no offence committed by a failure to have an instrument stamped – the penalties regime is triggered by the late submission of a document for stamping.

Why then have a document stamped?

Section 14(4) Stamp Act 1891 provides that, where an instrument is not properly stamped (this may also include where the instrument does not include the proper certificate under the Stamp Duty (Exempt Instruments) Regulations 1985, SI 1985/1688 or the Stamp Duty (Exempt Instruments) Regulations 1987, SI 1987/516, as might be appropriate), it 'shall not, except in criminal proceedings, be given in evidence, or be available for any purposes whatsoever . . .'.

Accordingly, if the necessary stamp duty formalities have not been complied with, a question mark arises over the overall effectiveness of the instrument in question as its terms cannot be enforced (without the necessary formalities being first complied with). Many parties will not act upon an instrument unless it is, or appears on its face to be, correctly stamped (e.g. HM Land Registry or a company registrar).

It should be noted that, at the time of writing, there appears to be a question mark over the appropriate exemption category (as identified in the Schedule to the Stamp Duty (Exempt Instruments) Regulations 1987, SI 1987/516) to be applied to an instrument of variation.

In 1992 the Stamp Office, Compliance and Information Department advised:

'Category "M" applies to deeds of variation or family arrangement which effect a rearrangement of interests upon sale without the introduction of outside cash into the transaction. If outside cash is paid in full, or partial consideration for the interest acquired, the deed remains liable to *ad valorem* conveyance on sale duty.

Category "L" is used where the rearrangements are made without payment of cash between the beneficiaries or where property is gifted to parties who are not beneficiaries. For this reason, it is more usual to see Category "L" in the deed.'

(This interpretation was also confirmed at that time by the then Deputy Director of the Stamp Office.)

Recognised precedents for instruments of variation routinely include a category 'L' certificate.

However, the Stamp Office has recently expressed the view that category 'M' applies to an instrument of variation, although this view is not reflected in the Stamp Taxes Manual current at the date of writing. At the time of writing, the Stamp Office has given no substantive reason for its change of interpretation. Whilst this author considers that the 1992 interpretation remains valid, clearly it will be necessary to monitor developments. Matthew Hutton, in *Stamp Duty: A Practical Guide* (2nd edition, FT Law & Tax), at paragraph 3.3.13, observes 'remember that Category M applies only in relatively limited circumstances'. In the meantime, IoVs might contain a certificate claiming exemption from duty under both categories 'L' and 'M' (which both the Stamp Office and Capital Taxes Office have previously indicated to be acceptable to them).

Foreign taxes

7.20   The 'instrument of variation' discussed in this chapter is a creature of UK legislation.

Whilst other countries may allow those entitled on the death of an individual to enter into arrangements that might have a similar effect for death taxes, inheritance taxes or gift taxes to that of an instrument of variation under UK law, this does not mean that an IoV made in England and Wales will have a similar, let alone the same, effect in that jurisdiction as it has here.

If any of the original beneficiary(s) or the new beneficiary(s) is not resident and domiciled within the UK, he may also need to consider the effect of the tax legislation of the country(s) in which he is resident and/or domiciled. An attempt to avoid or save UK inheritance tax could result in the payment of tax in excess of the potential inheritance tax saving by either the original or new beneficiary in their country of residence. (If the original beneficiary is resident in, say, Belgium, and redirects part of his inheritance to a UK charity, this will result in a refund of UK inheritance tax. However, the gift by the beneficiary may then be subject to gift tax in Belgium at rates of up to 80%.)

A similar problem may arise where assets are situated outside of the UK. However, in these cases it might be possible to avoid such potential difficulties if the assets can be brought into the UK before the IoV is completed. If the asset is immovable property, or cannot otherwise be brought into the UK (e.g. it may a chose in action or rights under a contract governed by foreign law), the only way to 'import' it into the UK might be to sell it and remit the proceeds to this country. Such a step should not be taken lightly and then only under advice from appropriately qualified advisers.

Popular misconceptions

7.21

1.   When a variation is made in respect of assets already distributed by the LPR, the beneficiary must return them to the LPR to distribute in accordance with the IoV.

'No'.

If the assets subject to the IoV are already in the hands of the original beneficiary, it will be for them to give effect to the gifts made by the IoV.

2.   If the variation is deemed to sever an interest in property formerly held by the deceased and another as beneficial joint tenants, the surviving owner must convey it into joint names of themselves and the LPR of the deceased co-owner before it can be dealt with.

'No'.

The alleged severance is a fiction created only for taxation purposes. Once the deceased died, the beneficial joint tenancy ceased to exist and the property vested wholly in the survivor. It must be for the surviving owner to give effect to what is his own instrument.

3.   An IoV varies the terms of the will, so that if any assets are not disposed of by the IoV, the deceased has not fully disposed of his estate and those assets not disposed of pass under the laws of intestacy.

'No'.

The person making the IoV can only do so once he has accepted the inheritance. To the extent that any part of the interest given to him is not disposed of by the IoV, it remains with the original beneficiary.

4.   Where an IoV is made by the LPR of a deceased beneficiary, it removes the inheritance from his estate.

'No'.

Whilst the provisions of section 142 may require that the value of the inheritance be left out of account for inheritance tax purposes, the inheritance forms a part of the deceased beneficiary's estate for all other purposes (except for certain aspects of capital gains tax if the provisions of section 62(6) TCGA 1992 apply).

5.   If there is a trust a variation cannot be made.

Incorrect.

The beneficiaries may, individually, vary their own interest although, if such interest is not a vested interest, the outcome may be uncertain.

Where all the beneficiaries of the trust are ascertainable, sui juris and of age, they may join together to vary the terms of the trust in its entirety (*Saunders v Vautier (1841) 4 Beav 115*).

If some of the beneficiaries are minors, or are yet to be born, a variation may be made, subject to an application to the courts under the Variation of Trusts Act 1958.

Distribution out of discretionary trust within two years

Introduction

7.22   Married couples are encouraged to make full use of the inheritance tax nil rate band available upon the death of the first of them to die, rather than just leave their entire estate to the survivor (thereby forgoing the ability to minimise the potential inheritance tax payable on their combined estates). This is often achieved by including within their wills a 'nil rate band' discretionary trust, the class of beneficiaries of which usually includes the surviving spouse and others they may wish to benefit.

Under these trusts, the executor, whether in his capacity as executor or as trustee, can appoint any form of interest he wishes to any member of the class as he might, in his sole discretion, decide. The main aim of such a trust, other than to try to minimise the overall inheritance tax liability on both spouses' deaths, is to introduce flexibility into the provisions of the will. If the surviving spouse is 'well provided for', the 'nil rate band' could be passed on down the generations (or to other members of a wider class of beneficiaries) without suffering additional inheritance tax en route. However, if the survivor requires additional financial support, the trust fund may provide a 'safety net'.

In some cases, a discretionary trust is incorporated into a will purely to permit flexibility by enabling the executor/trustee to allocate funds amongst the members of the class in the light of their particular needs at that time.

There are a number of different schemes in wills which rely upon the discretionary trust in one guise or another. They build upon the basic principles that apply to such trusts generally. Such specialised schemes are addressed in this section, to the extent that the general rules apply. However, it is not practical to consider them in any detail, bearing in mind that they may be tailored to specific situations and are, in any event, inheritance planning schemes, advice upon which is outside of the scope of this book. Neither is this book concerned with the rights and/or wrongs of the inclusion of such provisions in modern wills.

Whilst the benefit is given to trustees upon trust, in many instances the will directs that the discretion may be exercised by either the executor or the trustee. If the will contains no such direction, the executor, in that capacity, may not validly exercise any of the powers etc given to him as trustee.

Clearly, there may be instances where the circumstances of the estate are such that the executor is not able to constitute the trusts within two years of the testator's death. If the trusts have not been constituted, can the trustee exercise the discretion? This question has particular significance if the trust period is of limited duration, say, 23 months from the date of the testator's death.

It used to be considered that trustees could not exercise their discretion if the trust fund had not been constituted. The Inland Revenue supported such a view. However, in 1990 the courts had to consider a complicated scheme involving short term discretionary trusts under the will of the late tenth Earl Fitzwilliam. Whilst the Revenue's attack on the arrangement was based upon the principles established in *Ramsay (WT) Ltd v IRC [1982] AC 300* (in which the House of Lords held that where there was a preordained series of transactions that had no purpose other than tax mitigation and which, once initiated, would occur according to the preconceived plan, then the series of transactions should be treated as a single composite transaction and taxed accordingly), the scheme included the exercise by the trustees of the discretionary trust of their powers under that trust before the grant application for the will had been submitted, let alone any distribution made to those trustees. The issue was heard by Vinelott J at first instance (*Fitzwilliam (Countess) v IRC [1990] STC 65, Ch D*), who accepted the principle that the trustees could validly exercise their discretion over a chose in action, being their right for the due administration of the estate. This view was not disturbed in the Revenue's subsequent appeals to the Court of Appeal and the House of Lords (*Fitzwilliam (Countess) v IRC [1993] 3 All ER 184, HL*).

The effects of the exercise of the discretion by the executor (where permitted) and by the trustee, both in respect of a chose in action and once the trust has been constituted, are considered under the separate heads, below.

The trustees' entitlement to interest or income on the discretionary trust fund will depend upon the nature of the legacy to them – see also CHAPTER 2. If an appointment is made out of the discretionary trust by the executor, that will be treated as satisfaction, or part satisfaction of the trust legacy for the purposes of ascertaining the amount, if any, of interest or income payable to the trustees.

Inheritance tax

7.23   Where discretionary trusts arise under a will, the gift upon such trusts is subject to inheritance tax, even if the class of beneficiaries includes the testator's spouse and/or other exempt beneficiaries. However, there are certain instances where the discretionary trust is exempt from inheritance tax, so that no inheritance tax charge arises on the death of the testator (e.g. the discretionary trust is wholly charitable, or a qualifying employee trust or maintenance trust). That all the objects of a discretionary trust might be 'exempt' (e.g. the class is the surviving spouse and charities) does not of itself make the trust exempt.

In considering the inheritance tax implications of distributions from testamentary discretionary trusts, only those cases where there is a charge to inheritance tax are considered, even though such charge might be at the nil rate (i.e. the taxable value of the estate passing under the will is within the testator's nil rate band available as at the date of death).

Where any funds cease to be subject to the discretionary trust within two years of the date of death of the testator, the provisions of section 144 IHTA 1984 apply. There is no need to make an election, or include a declaration, or other statement – they apply automatically, so long as the few, basic, conditions are met:

- the property was an asset of the deceased's estate immediately before his death (this will exclude the situation where the testator purports to declare trusts over the property of another in circumstances where the doctrine of election applies);

- it was settled by the deceased's will;

- before the date of any appointment, no interest in possession subsists in the property which is to be appointed (the property to be appointed may be a cash sum, specific assets or a share (or even the whole) of the trust fund);

- a charge to inheritance tax would otherwise arise upon the appointment (even if at the nil rate) under Part III, Chapter III, IHTA 1984 (other than s 64 or 79) (this excludes any accumulation and maintenance trusts created by will, as section 71 IHTA 1984 exempts them from the exit charge under section 65(1) IHTA 1984).

As will be noted from the third bullet point above, the provisions of section 144 do not apply if any interest in possession subsists in the appointed property. On occasion, discretionary trusts are structured in such a way that the default beneficiary(s) have an entitlement to the income as it arises, subject to the trustees appointing such income, or the underlying capital, away from those default beneficiaries. The provisions of section 144 will apply in such circumstances.

The relief is applicable irrespective of the trust period specified in the will (so long as it neither infringes the perpetuity rules to such an extent that the gift is void, nor terminates within three months of the testator's death).

Section 144 also applies where the discretionary trust is created by an instrument of variation, provided the provisions of section 142 apply to that variation so that the trust is deemed to have been created by the deceased for all purposes of IHTA 1984 (this is irrespective of the nature of the beneficial interests in the estate before the variation, as the effect of section 142 is to deem the discretionary trust to have arisen upon the death of the deceased (even if in fact he dies intestate!))

If the LPR or trustee makes an appointment out of the discretionary trust within three months of the death of the testator, relief under section 144 will not be available (*Frankland v IRC [1997] STC 1450, CA*). This is due to the fact that no exit charge to inheritance tax can arise upon a distribution made 'in a quarter beginning with the day on which the settlement commenced' (IHTA 1984, s 65(4)).

Whilst the relief afforded by section 144 applies automatically, clearly where a refund of inheritance tax becomes due to the estate under this section, the LPR must give notice to IR Capital Taxes before that refund can be paid to him.

Capital gains tax

7.24   Where an estate is subject to the payment of inheritance tax, the LPR's acquisition value of any assets for capital gains tax will be the value ascertained for the purposes of inheritance tax (TCGA 1992, s 274). This is a simple and convenient rule.

The testamentary discretionary trust is becoming an increasingly popular inheritance tax planning 'tool'. It is often incorporated into a will with a view to securing the testator's available nil rate inheritance tax band. If no inheritance tax is payable in the estate, though, the value of assets transferred into, or appointed on account of, the discretionary trust will not have been 'ascertained' for capital gains tax purposes. This may be of little concern where assets which may be readily valued are concerned (e.g. cash or quoted securities). However, if the assets subject to the trustees' discretion are not so easily valued, this may give rise to uncertainty in dealings with the trust fund, as the level of any capital gains tax charge may be uncertain until such time as the necessary value can be agreed with the Inland Revenue (it may also give rise to problems in ascertaining the value of such assets for the purposes of appropriation).

The capital gains tax consequences of an appointment out of a testamentary discretionary trust differ depending upon whether it is made by the LPR or the trustees. As stated above, however, the discretion may only be exercised by the LPR if he is authorised to do so by the will.

Exercise of discretion by LPR

7.25   Where the discretion is exercised by the LPR, before the appropriation of assets in satisfaction of the discretionary trust, what is appointed is a chose in action for the due administration of the estate representing the interest appointed to the beneficiary.

When the LPR subsequently appropriates assets, whether cash or investments, these reduce the residual value of the chose in action, so that once the full value of the appointment is satisfied, the chose in action is reduced to nil. To the extent that investments, or other assets subject to capital gains tax are appropriated, there will be no disposal by the LPR for capital gains tax purposes and the beneficiary will receive those assets as 'legatee' at the date of death value for capital gains tax purposes (TCGA 1992, s 62(4)).

If the LPR has made a specific appointment of the assets subsequently appropriated to the beneficiaries, such assets will need to be valued as at the date of the appointment in order to establish the extent to which the discretionary trust remains to be satisfied.

Alternatively, if the LPR has appointed to the beneficiary a cash sum, or a defined fraction of the trust fund, then the assets will need to be valued as at the date of the appropriation for the purposes of the distribution (*Re Charteris, Charteris v Biddulph [1917] 2 Ch 379*).

Exercise of discretion by trustee

7.26   The exercise of the discretion by the trustees in respect of assets appropriated to them in satisfaction of the discretionary trust will result in a deemed disposal of the assets in question under section 71(1) TCGA 1992. Any gain or loss will be assessable upon the trustee and the beneficiary will acquire such assets at the trustee's disposal value.

Subject to compliance with the provisions of either section 165 TCGA 1992 (relief for gifts of business property), or section 260 TCGA 1992 (relief for gifts on which inheritance tax is payable, etc), any gains arsing upon the assets appropriated may be held over. Such gains will crystallise upon the disposal of the asset by the beneficiary, or upon the beneficiary ceasing to reside in the UK for the purposes of capital gains tax. In the latter case, the gain may be assessable upon the trustees if the beneficiary becomes non UK resident within six years of the end of the tax year in which the held over gain arose.

Where the trustees are content to exercise the discretion vested in them whilst the estate is in the process of administration, and before any assets are appropriated to them in satisfaction of the trust legacy (the principle of which appears to have been accepted by each court in *Fitzwilliam (Countess) v IRC (see above)*, the trustees will appoint a chose in action to the beneficiary and, upon the LPR appropriating assets to that beneficiary in satisfaction of that chose in action, the beneficiary will acquire the assets as 'legatee' at the date of death value for capital gains tax purposes.

Income tax

7.27   A distribution out of the discretionary trust within two years of the testator's death does not have any direct effect on the income tax position.

Income received by the LPR on assets to be appropriated to the trustees of the discretionary trust is income of the estate and subject to tax in the LPR's hands as such. This will include any income or interest payable upon those assets up to the date of appropriation (and any dividends on investments quoted 'XD' as at the date of appropriation).

If the income is paid over to the objects of the discretionary trust by the LPR 'in the course of administration', there will be no liability to additional tax upon that income under sections 686 and 687 ICTA 1988. To the extent that income passes through the hands of the trustees, though, it will be subject to such additional tax.

To the extent that distributions made to the objects of the discretionary trust are of an income nature, those beneficiaries are entitled to receive a tax certificate detailing the amount of tax deducted.

Disclaimer

7.28   A disclaimer is an unqualified refusal by the beneficiary to accept the gift made to them. They cannot direct who is to receive it in their stead, so that it passes to the next beneficiary entitled or, if there is no alternative beneficiary, in accordance with the laws of intestacy. Accordingly, the effect of a disclaimer, unless carefully considered, may differ from that expected.

A disclaimer of any interest in advance of the death of the deceased is of no effect (*Smith v Smith [2001] WTLR 1205*).

Once made, a disclaimer can only be withdrawn if no one has altered his position in reliance upon that disclaimer (*Re Cranstoun's Will Trusts, Gibbs v Home of Rest for Horses [1949] 1 All ER 871*).

There is no specific rule as to the format of a disclaimer, which may be made by the conduct of the beneficiary. However, it is generally considered 'good practice' for any disclaimer to be evidenced in writing, preferably by deed. Care should be taken though with regard to the costs of preparing any disclaimer – the disclaimer is the beneficiary's document and the costs are his costs. If such costs are met out of the disclaimed interest, it may be argued that, by doing so, the original beneficiary's refusal of the gift is not 'unqualified' as it has been made on the basis that his costs will be paid out of the fund, or, alternatively, that it is only a partial disclaimer (but see below).

A disclaimer must be made before the beneficiary has received any of the benefit being disclaimed.

The disclaimer of benefit must generally relate to the entirety of a particular gift. If the beneficiary has been given two distinct gifts, he may disclaim one, but accept the other. If both gifts are contained within the same clause, it is a matter of construction as to whether the gift is a single combined gift (so that it is an 'all or nothing' situation), or if it is a series of independent gifts to the same person (so that the beneficiary can 'pick and mix') (*Guthrie v Walrond (1883) 22 Ch D 573*).

Where the beneficiary is given a general legacy, interest on that legacy is a separate gift and may be disclaimed without the beneficiary being required also to disclaim the legacy (*Dewar v IRC [1935] 2 KB 351*) and vice versa.

Whilst the general rule is that no partial disclaimer of a single gift is permissible, this is subject to there being no contrary intention in the will. Accordingly, if the will specifically permits the disclaimer by a beneficiary of only part of a gift, this may validly occur.

The effect of a disclaimer is that the gift is deemed never to have been made.

Where the gift is made by will, if it is a general or specific legacy/devise (or even a demonstrative legacy!) the disclaimer by the beneficiary will invariably result in the gift falling into residue (unless there are particular provisions within the will dealing with the disclaimer of any benefit).

If the gift is one of residue, in the absence of any specific saving provision within the will the effect of the disclaimer is to create a partial intestacy of the testator. This is so, even if the will contains savings provisions in the event that the beneficiary had died before the testator. The effect of such provisions is negated by the fact that the beneficiary survived the testator (where the saving provision includes the 'failure' of the gift to the original beneficiary, this is generally sufficient to save the benefit for the alternative beneficiaries).

Where a partial intestacy arises, and the disclaiming beneficiary would also be entitled under such intestacy, the disclaimer of the original gift is not also a disclaimer of the right to benefit under the intestacy.

If the interest to be disclaimed arises upon the intestacy of the deceased, the effect of a disclaimer of the statutory legacy is the same as for a general legacy under a will – it falls into residue (*Re Scott (deceased), Widdows v Friends of the Clergy Corp [1975] 2 All ER 1033*). If the disclaimer is made in respect of a share of the residuary estate, it is necessary to consider the extent of the class originally entitled. If the sole member, or all the members, of a class disclaim, the benefit will pass to the class next entitled under the intestacy provisions (*Re Scott*). It will not be saved for the children of the disclaiming beneficiary if he is one of a number of members of his class. If the disclaiming beneficiary is the surviving spouse, the children of the intestate will benefit as the class next entitled. Their entitlement is personal to them, not ancillary to the entitlement of their parent, as with the other classes of beneficiary.

A disclaimer may also be made by a life tenant or annuitant. Whilst it may be effective in disposing of the income entitlement under the will, it may not accelerate payment of the capital to the remaindermen. Subject to careful scrutiny of the precise wording of the will, the income arising between the death of the testator and the date the capital eventually vests absolutely might:

- pass under an intestacy, or

- be held upon life interest trusts during the trust period to pay the income to the remaindermen, or such of them as are living at any particular point in time (the proportion of the income due to each potential remainderman may vary as any die, or new ones are born into the class of beneficiaries).

If the interest to be disclaimed is a life interest under a protective trust, the effect of the disclaimer will be to trigger the discretionary trusts (unless the will provides a specific exception in these circumstances, which would be unusual).

Where the gift is of a joint nature, a disclaimer by any of the beneficiaries will cause the gift to vest in the remaining beneficiaries (*Re Schar (deceased), Midland Bank Executor and Trustee Co Ltd v Damer [1951] Ch 280*). It does not destroy the nature of the joint tenancy.

Taxation aspects

Inheritance tax

7.29   The provisions of section 142 IHTA 1984 apply automatically to a disclaimer made within two years of the death of the deceased. To obtain any relief from inheritance tax, whether upon the death of the deceased or upon the eventual death of the disclaimant, it is preferable to evidence the disclaimer in writing. (In the absence of a written document, it may be difficult to persuade the Inland Revenue that the beneficiary effected a disclaimer and not a gift, notwithstanding any circumstantial evidence to support a disclaimer.)

The effect of section 142 is to treat the disclaimed gift as though it had never been made. The estate is therefore subject to inheritance tax on the basis of the beneficial interests that apply post-disclaimer.

If a disclaimer is made more than two years after the death, it would appear that this will be treated as a potentially exempt transfer or an immediately chargeable transfer by the disclaiming beneficiary, unless they are able to rely upon the provisions of section 93 IHTA 1984. However, section 93 applies only to the disclaimer of an interest in settled property, so that it might only be available to a beneficiary with a limited interest.

The effect of a disclaimer upon the disposition of the estate is not dependent upon it being effective under section 142.

Capital gains tax

7.30   As with inheritance tax, the provisions of section 62(6) TGGA 1992 apply automatically to a disclaimer made within two years of the death of the deceased. To avoid the possibility of a capital gains tax charge arising against the disclaiming beneficiary by reason of the disposal of a chose in action, it is preferable to evidence the disclaimer in writing. (In the absence of a written document, it may be difficult to persuade the Inland Revenue that the beneficiary effected a disclaimer and not a gift, notwithstanding any circumstantial evidence to support a disclaimer.)

If the disclaimer is made outside of the two-year period, it will be treated as a disposal by the disclaimant for capital gains tax purposes. There are no capital gains tax provisions similar to section 93 IHTA 1984 that might assist the disclaiming beneficiary.

Income tax

7.31   Where a beneficiary disclaims an interest in residue, he is treated as though his interest never existed, and those entitled as a result of the disclaimer are treated as having been entitled immediately upon the death of the deceased. Both section 695 (limited interest in residue) and section 696 (absolute interests in residue) ICTA 1988 deem the beneficiaries to have received income only where a distribution has been made, so that if they receive no distribution from the estate they cannot be deemed to have received income for the purposes of the taxing statutes. If the disclaimer is effective, they cannot have received any distribution.

In the event that a partial disclaimer is made, as specifically permitted by the will, the position needs more careful consideration.

As identified in CHAPTER 2, a residuary beneficiary absolutely entitled to a share of residue is, for income tax purposes, deemed to have received income from the estate of an amount equal to the lesser of:

- the total of any distributions made to him in that tax year, and

- his proportionate share of the aggregated income entitlement (AIE) for the estate.

With this in mind, where a partial disclaimer is made, the AIE of the original beneficiary should effectively be 'ruled off' as at the date of that disclaimer and, from that date, should only be increased by the amount of any AIE proportionate to his retained interest in the estate. A new AIE 'pot' will be created in respect of that proportionate part of the income of the residuary estate deemed to be the income of the new beneficiary(s).

As has previously been identified elsewhere, interest on a general legacy is taxable in the hands of the beneficiary upon receipt (*Dewar v IRC [1935] 2 KB 351*). Accordingly, if the beneficiary disclaims the legacy the right to income is also extinguished, so that he can receive no interest on the legacy. Similarly, if, as in *Dewar v IRC [1935] 2 KB 351*), the legatee keeps the legacy but disclaims the interest, no charge to income tax arises upon the interest forgone.

Where the interest disposed of is a specific legacy, the effect of the disclaimer would appear to be to leave the liability for income tax on the disclaiming beneficiary up to the date of the disclaimer, notwithstanding that he cannot receive any of the income.

Stamp duty

7.32   No stamp duty is payable upon a disclaimer.

Where assets are appropriated to a beneficiary in respect of any interest that arises as a result of a disclaimer, the transfer or conveyance is subject to stamp duty on the same basis as would have applied if the will, or laws of intestacy as appropriate, had omitted any reference to the interest of the disclaiming beneficiary.

Appendix 1

Key provisions of the Inheritance Tax Act 1984 (ss 142, 144, 218A and 245A)

Section 142 Alteration of dispositions taking effect on death

(1) Where, within the period of two years after a person's death–

  (a) any of the dispositions (whether effected by will, under the law relating to intestacy or otherwise) of the property comprised in his estate immediately before his death are varied; or

  (b) the benefit conferred by any of those dispositions is disclaimed,

by an instrument in writing made by the person or any of the persons who benefit or would benefit under the dispositions, this Act shall apply as if the variation had been effected by the deceased or, as the case may be, the disclaimed benefit had never been conferred

(2) [Subsection (1) above shall not apply to a variation unless the instrument contains a statement, made by the relevant persons, to the effect that they intend the subsection to apply to the variation.

(2A) [For the purposes of subsection (2) above the relevant persons are–

  (a) the person or persons making the instrument, and

  (b) where the variation results in additional tax being payable, the personal representatives.

Personal representatives may decline to make a statement under subsection (2) above only if no, or no sufficient, assets are held by them in that capacity for discharging the additional tax.] (*Inserted by section 120 Finance Act 2002, in relation to instruments made on or after 1 August 2002*)

(3) Subsection (1) above shall not apply to a variation or disclaimer made for any consideration in money or money's worth other than consideration consisting of the making, in respect of another of the dispositions, of a variation or disclaimer to which that subsection applies.

(4) Where a variation to which subsection (1) above applies results in property being held in trust for a person for a period which ends not more than two years after the death, this Act shall apply as if the disposition of the property that takes effect at the end of the period had had effect from the beginning of the period; but this subsection shall not affect the application of this Act in relation to any distribution or application of property occurring before that disposition takes effect.

(5) For the purposes of subsection (1) above the property comprised in a

person's estate includes any excluded property but not any property to which he is treated as entitled by virtue of section 49(1) above [or section 102 of the Finance Act 1986] (*Words inserted by Schedule 19, paragraph 24, Finance Act 1986, with effect from 18 March 1986*)

(6) Subsection (1) above applies whether or not the administration of the estate is complete or the property concerned has been distributed in accordance with the original dispositions.

(7) In the application of subsection (4) above to Scotland, property which is subject to proper liferent shall be deemed to be held in trust for the liferenter.

Section 144 Distribution etc from property settled by will

(1) This section applies where property comprised in a person's estate immediately before his death is settled by will and, within the period of two years after his death and before any interest in possession has subsisted in the property, there occurs–

(a) an event on which tax would (apart from this section) be chargeable under any provision, other than section 64 or 79, of Chapter III of Part III of this Act, or

(b) an event on which tax would be so chargeable but for section 75 or 76 above or paragraph 16(1) of Schedule 4 to this Act.

(2) Where this section applies by virtue of an event within paragraph (a) of subsection (1) above, tax shall not be charged under the provision in question on that event; and in every case in which this section applies in relation to an event, the Act shall have effect as if the will had provided that on the testator's death the property should be held as it is held after the event.

[Section 218A Instruments varying dispositions taking effect on death]

(1) [Where –

(a) an instrument is made varying any of the dispositions of the property comprised in the estate of a deceased person immediately before his death,

(b) the instrument contains a statement under subsection (2) of section 142 above, and

(c) the variation results in additional tax being payable,

the relevant persons (within the meaning of that subsection) shall, within six months after the day on which the instrument is made, deliver a copy of it to the Board and notify them of the amount of the additional tax.

(2) [To the extent that any of the relevant persons comply with the require-

ments of this section, the others are discharged from the duty to comply with them.] *(Inserted by section 120 Finance Act 2002)*

[Section 245A Failure to provide information etc]

(1) . . . ..

(1A) [A person who fails to comply with the requirements of section 218A above shall be liable–

    (a)   to a penalty not exceeding £100; and

    (b)   to a further penalty not exceeding £60 for every day after the day on which the failure has been declared by a court or the Special Commissioners and before the day on which the requirements are complied with.] *(inserted by section 120 Finance Act 2002, in relation to instruments made on or after 1 August 2002)*

(2) . . . ..

(3) . . . ..

(4) A person shall not be liable to a penalty under subsection (1)(b), [(1A)(b),] *(inserted by section 120 Finance Act 2002, in relation to instruments made on or after 1 August 2002)* (2)(b) or (3)(b) above if–

    (a)   . . . ..

    (aa) he complies with the requirements of subsection 218A above] *(inserted by section 120 Finance Act 2002, in relation to instruments made on or after 1 August 2002)*

    (b)   . . . ..

    (c)   . . . ..

before proceedings in which the failure could be declared are commenced.

(5) A person who has a reasonable excuse for failing to make a return or to comply with a notice shall not be liable by reason of that failure to a penalty under this section, unless he fails to make the return or to comply with the notice without unreasonable delay after the excuse has ceased *(inserted by section 108 Finance Act 1999)*

Key provisions of the Taxation of Chargeable Gains Act 1992 (ss 62 and 64)

Section 62: Death: general provisions

(1) For the purposes of this Act the assets of which a deceased person was competent to dispose–

    (a)   shall be deemed to be acquired on his death by the personal representatives or other persons on whom they devolve for a consideration equal to their market value as at the date of death, but

(b)   shall not be deemed to be disposed of by him on his death (whether or not they were the subject of a testamentary disposition).

(2)   . . . ..

(2A)   . . . ..*(Inserted by Schedule 21, paragraph 5, Finance Act 1998, with effect from the tax year 1998/99)*

(2B)   . . . ..*(Inserted by Schedule 21, paragraph 5, Finance Act 1998, with effect from the tax year 1998/99)*

(3)   In relation to property forming part of the estate of a deceased person the personal representative shall for the purposes of this Act be treated as a single and continuing body of persons (distinct from the persons who may from time to time be the personal representatives), and that body shall be treated as having the deceased's residence, ordinary residence and domicile as at the date of death.

(4)   On a person acquiring any asset as legatee (as defined in section 64)–

(a)   no chargeable gain shall accrue to the personal representatives, and

(b)   the legatee shall be treated as if the personal representatives' acquisition of the asset had been his acquisition of it.

(5)   Notwithstanding section 17(1) no chargeable gain shall accrue to any person on his making a disposal by way of donatio mortis causa.

(6)   Subject to subsections (7) and (8) below, where within the period of 2 years after a person's death any of the dispositions (whether affected by will, under the law relating to intestacy or otherwise) of the property of which he was competent to dispose are varied, or the benefit conferred by any of those dispositions is disclaimed, by an instrument in writing made by the persons or any of the persons who benefit or would benefit under the dispositions–

(a)   the variation or disclaimer shall not constitute a disposal for the purposes of this Act, and

(b)   this section shall apply as if the variation had been effected by the deceased or, as the case may be, the disclaimed benefit had never been conferred.

(7)   Subsection (6) above does not apply to a variation [unless the instrument contains a statement by the persons making the instrument to the effect that they intend the subsection to apply to the variation] *(words inserted by section 52 Finance Act 2002, in relation to instruments made on or after 1 August 2002)*

(8)   subsection (6) above does not apply to a variation or disclaimer made for any consideration in money or money's worth other than consideration consisting of the making of a variation or disclaimer in respect of another of the dispositions.

(9)   Subsection (6) above applies whether or not the administration of the estate is complete or the property has been distributed in accordance with the original dispositions.

(10)   In this section references to assets of which a deceased person was competent to dispose are references to assets of the deceased which (otherwise than in right of a power of appointment or of the testamentary power conferred by statute to dispose of entailed interests) he could, if of full age and capacity, have disposed of by his will, assuming that all the assets were situated in England and, if he was not domiciled in the United Kingdom, that he was domiciled in England, and include references to his severable share in any assets to which, immediately before his death, he was beneficially entitled as a joint tenant.

Section 64 Expenses in administration of estates and trusts

(1)   . . . ..

(2)   In this Act, unless the context otherwise requires, "legatee" includes any person taking under a testamentary disposition or on an intestacy or partial intestacy, whether he takes beneficially or as trustee, and a person taking under a donatio mortis causa shall be treated (except for the purposes of section 62) as a legatee and his acquisition as made at the time of the donor's death.

(3)   For the purposes of the definition of "legatee" above, and of any reference in this Act to a person acquiring an asset as "legatee", property taken under a testamentary disposition or on an intestacy or partial intestacy includes any asset appropriated by the personal representatives in or towards satisfaction of a pecuniary legacy or any other interest or share in the property devolving under the disposition or intestacy.

Appendix 2

Extract from Inland Revenue, Capital Taxes: IHT Newsletter, December 2001

Section 142 IHTA 1984 – Deeds of variation and the real world

It is perhaps not immediately obvious that a variation must be implemented in the real world. S.17(a) IHTA expressly provides that a variation or disclaimer to which s.142(1) applies is not a transfer of value, so that the instrument in writing must be more than an empty piece of paper. That provision and s.142, in previous incarnations were, in effect a form of relief from double charges under the CTT regime. It is a pre-requisite if the provisions are to have any impact that a "real life" disposition or transfer took place, so that the transferor can decide whether or not to make an election in order to trigger the deeming provisions.

As Mr R T Oerton put it in Capital Tax Planning July 1992, "In the real world of property law, where questions about ownership and the transfer of ownership are decided, the deceased does not make the changes : the beneficiaries do. And the deceased cannot be deemed in the true world to bring about effects which the beneficiaries cannot, or do not, bring about in the real world".

Let us take the situation in which, under the will of A, B has an interest in possession in settled property, and on its cesser the beneficial interest in possession passes to C. In other words A leaves a life interest in property to B, with remainder to C. Following B's death within two years of A, C makes a deed of variation – still within that two year period – which purports to vary the will of A by redirecting B's interest to C or to extinguish it totally. In the real world B's interest does not exist, there is nothing for the deed to bite upon, and so s.142 simply cannot apply. If the situation had been that it was possible for B's executors to disclaim his life interest as a matter of general law, then that should fall within the protection of s.142.

It has been found that some of these inoperative deeds have been accepted as effective variations. The inconsistency of treatment is regretted, and assurances that have been given in the past will be binding upon the Revenue.

Chapter 8

Failure

Introduction

8.1   Generally, it should be noted that the terms of any legacy must be sufficiently certain to be capable of being understood and construed by a court. If it is impossible to ascertain the subject matter because the testator has defined it inadequately, the legacy will generally fail. There are a large number of – largely nineteenth century – decisions that show the courts' willingness to establish what the amount of a legacy ought to be where the testator has not defined it but has given some yardstick to measure it by (see *Theobald on Wills* (16th edition Sweet & Maxwell) at 55-04; the yardstick is usually some purpose for the legacy). More recently, however, a gift to a wife of 'such minimal part of my estate . . .as she may be entitled to under English Law for maintenance purposes' has been held to be void for uncertainty (*Anthony v Donges [1998] 2 FLR 775*) as there is no entitlement for a spouse under English law. (The 'entitlement' of a spouse under English law does not equate to whatever a court may award to her under the Inheritance (Provision for Family and Dependants) Act 1975, as such awards are based on the individual factors of each claim and naturally vary in every case, particularly in amount).

Uncertainty of objects can also lead to failure of the bequest, but, short of failure of the legacy, problems with the identification of beneficiaries can more usually be resolved by the court. Identification of beneficiaries is dealt with at 5.11 above.

Disclaimer

8.2   No beneficiary can be forced to accept a benefit under a will (*Townson v Tickell (1819) 3 B & Ald 31*: 'The law is not so absurd as to force a man to take an estate against his will') or intestacy (*Re Scott [1975] 1 WLR 1260*). Disclaimer is usually by deed, but may be in writing under hand, or by conduct.

Disclaimer of benefit is effective from the date of death (i.e. the beneficiary is treated as never having had an interest) even though in reality the disclaimer is made subsequent to the testator's death. Disclaimer before the interest has arisen is not effective (*Re Smith, Smith v Smith [2001] 3 All ER 552*). In general terms, disclaimer must be made before the beneficiary receives any benefit from his interest under the will. However, it may be possible to renounce an interest in income only after having taken some benefit.

A disclaimer once given is final and cannot be withdrawn, save that where it was made without consideration, it may be withdrawn by the beneficiary if no one has altered their position in reliance on the disclaimer (including having accepted benefit) (*Re Young, Fraser v Young [1913] 1 Ch 272*).

Where there are two distinct gifts to the same person in the will, the beneficiary is able to accept one and refuse the other (*Guthrie v Walrond (1883) 22 Ch D 573*). The difficulty is in establishing whether or not the two gifts really are to be considered as two separate gifts.

Lapse

8.3   The most common application of this term to legacies is where the gift is to a beneficiary who has predeceased the testator. Unless a will makes alternative provisions, a legacy to someone who has predeceased the testator will lapse (*Elliott v Davenport (1705) 1 P Wms 83*). Where the legatee dies after the testator, the legacy will be saved for the benefit of his estate and be payable to his personal representatives, unless the legatee's death meant that he failed to meet a condition in the will (such as survival for a defined period). Whether or not the legatee predeceased the testator is generally a question of fact, arrived at from all available evidence (*Wright v Netherwood (1793) 2 Salk 593n*), but where there is uncertainty as to the order of deaths that cannot be resolved, the usual rules of *commorientes* will apply.

Where it is impossible to establish the order of death of two or more persons (*commorientes*) – for example, the testator and one of his legatees – the law will presume that they will have died in order of seniority (Law of Property Act 1925, s 184; *Hickman v Peacey [1945] AC 304*). The application of this principle will determine whether or not a legacy lapses, or is payable to the legatee's personal representatives. It may also determine which of alternative beneficiaries takes a legacy.

A gift to a class of beneficiaries will not lapse because one member of the class has predeceased the testator: the gift will be effective to the remaining members of the class. Similarly, a gift to one or more legatees as joint tenants will not lapse because of the death of one legatee, although by contrast, in the case of a gift to one or more as tenants in common, the individual shares can lapse because of the prior death of a legatee.

There is one important statutory provision affecting lapse when the gift is to a child or remoter descendant of the testator (Wills Act 1837, s 33(1)). Where such a gift is made, but the legatee predeceases the testator, the issue of the intended beneficiary will be substituted and take the legacy, in the absence of any contrary intention apparent from the terms of the will. The current terms of section 33 were inserted in the Wills Act 1837 by the Administration of Justice Act 1982 and took effect from 1 January 1983.

What exactly will amount to a contrary intention is to some degree ill-defined, although the question has been examined recently in *Ling v Ling [2002] WTLR 553*. There is no doubt that the preferred method of expressing a contrary intention is for section 33 to be specifically excluded. In *Ling v Ling* it was also accepted that if the original gift contained a contingency (such as attaining 21), the beneficiaries who are substituted are required to meet the contingency themselves, even if the original beneficiary had attained that age when he predeceased.

Ling v Ling did not, in fact, involve section 33(1) Wills Act 1837, but concerned section 33(2) which makes provision for similar substitution of issue in class gifts where the class consists of children or remoter issue of the testator.

Gift to an attesting beneficiary or their spouse

8.4   Any beneficial gift to an attesting witness, or their spouse, is void (Wills Act 1837, s 15) – unless there are sufficient other witnesses to give valid execution (within the terms of Wills Act 1837, s 9) – if the legatee's, or legatee's spouse's, attestation is ignored (Wills Act 1968, s 1(1)). A marriage between the witness and the legatee after the execution of the will will not void the bequest (*Thorpe v Bestwick (1881) 6 QBD 311*).

Where the gift is in a different testamentary document to the one that the legatee attests (i.e. the gift is in the will but the legatee attests only a codicil, or vice versa), the gift will be good (*Gurney v Gurney (1855) 3 Drew 208*). A legacy to an attesting witness can be good if the will in which the legacy is given is later republished by a codicil which the legatee did not witness (*Re Doland's Will Trusts [1970] Ch 267*). (Republication is outside of the scope of this book; for details see *Williams on Wills* (8th edition) Chapter 22.)

Gift to a former spouse

8.5   Where a will contains a legacy in favour of a spouse and the testator was, after the date of the will, divorced from that spouse (or the marriage was annulled), the gift will be construed as if the spouse/legatee predeceased the testator (Wills Act 1837, s 18A). This rule may not apply if the will is republished by later codicil after the divorce is completed. The legacy would also be saved if the will expressly provides that it should be payable notwithstanding any subsequent divorce.

Murder or manslaughter by a legatee of the testator

8.6   Where a beneficiary is convicted of the murder or manslaughter of the testator, the beneficiary is debarred by public policy from taking the legacy under the will and, as a consequence, the legacy fails (is forfeit). This rule applies to all types of manslaughter and includes aiding and abetting suicide (*Dunbar v Plant [1998] Ch 412*). Although the rule applies to manslaughter by reason of diminished responsibility (*Re Giles [1972] Ch 544*), it will not apply where the killer is found by the court to be insane (*Re Houghton [1915] 2 Ch 173*; there is also a New South Wales decision, *Permanent Trustee Co Ltd v Freedom from Hunger Campaign (1991) 25 NSWLR 140,* which holds that there is no forfeiture if the killing was not intended to bring financial benefit to the killer, but there is no support for this in the English authorities).

Where the legatee is convicted of the murder of the testator, the court has no power to relieve the beneficiary from the forfeiture. Where the conviction is for an offence which is less than murder, the court does have the power to modify the forfeiture rule, to the extent that they think appropriate, having regard to the conduct of the legatee, the deceased and any other material circumstances (Forfeiture Act 1982).

Where an interest which is forfeited is an interest in intestacy, the killer's issue will not inherit through him (as they would if he had predeceased; Administration of Estates Act 1925, s 47) as the killer's forfeiture is not the same as his having predeceased the intestate (*Re DWS, TWGS v JMG [2001] WTLR 445*; a rather harsh decision which literally involves the sins of the father being visited upon the child).

In practical terms this makes the distribution of an estate where the slayer is a beneficiary a delayed process. The executor will not know if the forfeiture rule applies until after the trial of the slayer and the verdict will then, if it is not murder, allow for the slayer to apply for relief from forfeiture under the Forfeiture Act 1982. There does not appear to be authority on what happens if the slayer is not tried (perhaps because of their own subsequent death), but it would seem that the act of the slayer is still capable of being proved sufficiently in other proceedings.

Bankruptcy

8.7   The bankruptcy of a legatee will operate so as to make a legacy payable to the trustee in bankruptcy.

An exception to this is where the legacy is on trusts which are expressly protective trusts within the meaning of section 33 Trustee Act 1925. Protective trusts operate to prevent the income beneficiary doing or attempting to do, anything that would alienate his interest. Such events could be sale, charging or assigning his interest as well as bankruptcy.

If one of these events occurs, the attempted alienation fails and the interest in income ceases, being replaced by a discretionary trust. This trust will last for the lifetime of the income beneficiary and after his death the distribution of the trust will be according to the terms of the original trust. During the period of the discretionary trust, income can be applied by the trustee for the benefit of the original beneficiary, their spouse and issue. In the absence of a spouse and issue those next entitled to the trust after the death of the original beneficiary are brought into the discretionary class.

Section 12 Insolvency Act 2002 inserted a new section 412A into the Insolvency Act 1986, in order to reverse the result achieved in *Re Palmer [1994] Ch 316*, where it was held that joint property owned as beneficial joint tenants was not available to the administrator of the insolvent estate of the first co-owner to die. This section makes provision, in certain circumstances, for joint property owned as a beneficial joint tenant, *which has already passed to the surviving co-owner*, to be made available to meet creditors' claims against the estate of the first co-owner to die. This can operate to deprive the beneficiary of that property under the will of the second co-owner to die.

The new section 421A applies where:

(a)   an insolvency order has been made in respect of the estate of a deceased person, and

(b)   the petition for the order was made after the commencement of this section (date not yet known) and within five years of the date of the insolvent's death, and

(c)   immediately before his death the insolvent was beneficially entitled to an interest in any property as joint tenant, and

(d)   the survivor who inherited by survivorship on the death of the insolvent is alive, or, if he is dead, died *after* the making of the insolvency administration order against the first co-owner.

If these conditions are met, the court *may*, on the application of the court appointed trustee for the insolvent estate, order the survivor or his personal representative to return a sum not exceeding the value which passed by survivorship. In making such an order the court is directed to have regard to all relevant circumstances, but unless there are exceptional circumstances, the section directs that 'the interest of the creditors outweigh all other considerations'.

There can be difficulties for the personal representative where he administers the estate of someone:

•   who inherited joint property by survivorship, and

•   where the first co-owner to die was insolvent, and

•   the first co-owner had an insolvency order made against his estate *before the second co-owner died*.

Under these circumstances, there is a real possibility that the second estate will receive a claim from the trustee of the first estate. Therefore it is important that the personal representative makes no distributions until the maximum value of the trustee in bankruptcy's claim has been calculated and reserved.

There does not appear to be any provision in section 412A for interest or appreciation on the inherited property after the death of the insolvent co-owner to be taken into account in the court's order. The value is therefore only that at the date of the first death.

The provisions of section 412A are not restricted to beneficial joint tenancies of land or interests in land. Section 412A(1)(c) refers to 'an interest in *any property* as joint tenant' (emphasis added).

The difficulty a personal representative will encounter is that he may not have knowledge of an insolvency order against the first co-owner to die. Obviously, if he is informed of such an order, he must make due enquiries to establish the true position. In other cases it is suggested that the deceased's papers should be examined for relevant information at the earliest possible time to establish if any property had accrued to the deceased by survivorship.

Where a personal representative is faced with a new estate, and his usual investigations into title and asset records reveal the likely earlier inheritance of joint property, it is recommended that he make enquiries as to whether or not there is an insolvency order against the estate of the first co-owner. The search becomes necessary to establish if such an order has been made, as registration of the order is deemed to be notice to all and lack of actual knowledge is no defence against it.

The safest way to address this issue is that, whenever the recent inheritance of joint property is identified, the personal representative obtains bankruptcy searches against the estate of the pre-deceased co-owner. It is difficult to be precise as to the meaning of recent in this context, but probably up to five to seven years previously ought to be safe. Where no insolvency is revealed by the searches the issue of section 412A does not arise.

Obviously there will be occasions where the personal representative can dispense with such searches because his own knowledge of his client is such that he is certain there is no such order.

Ademption

Ademption of specific legacies

8.8   The simplest form of ademption is the failure of the legacy caused by the disposal of the subject matter of the legacy by the testator in his lifetime. A legacy of 'my horse Arkle' is adeemed by its sale by the testator; there is no subject matter to give and the legatee has no right to the cash equivalent of the proceeds of sale (unless the will expressly provided for that to happen).

Destruction of the asset will have the same effect and again – in the absence of express provision for this in the will – the legatee will not be entitled to the proceeds of the insurance claim for the loss of the asset. Of more difficulty is where the testator and asset perish together. In these circumstances, if it cannot be established that the asset survived the testator, the asset is deemed to have perished before the testator (*Durrant v Friend (1852) 5 De G & Sm 343*). This problem is encountered in particular with fires. The practical importance in the order of destruction lies in the entitlement to the proceeds of the insurance claim, which will accrue to the legatee in the event that the asset 'survived' the testator and was therefore destroyed after his death (*Re Hunter (1975) 58 DLR (3d) 175*). If the asset was shown to have survived the testator before its destruction, but was uninsured or under-insured, the legatee is not entitled to any financial compensation out of the residue of the estate for the lost benefit.

> 'Every will shall be construed, with reference to the real estate and personal estate comprised in it, to speak and take effect as if it had been executed immediately before the death of the testator, unless a contrary intention shall appear by the will'. (Wills Act 1837, s 24).

This statutory provision requires careful consideration where the description of specific legacies and the possible ademption by disposal in the testator's lifetime are concerned. The authorities seem to be in agreement that the use of the possessive pronoun 'my' does not act as a contrary intention within the terms of the statute when it is applied to a generic gift such as 'my personal chattels' or 'my library', and that such specific legacies are of the chattels or library respectively as are owned at the testator's death.

The issue becomes more difficult when the specific legacy is of an object such as 'my car'. In the absence of any other contrary intention in the will, does 'my', indicating ownership at the time of the will, become a sufficient contrary intention to displace section 24? Some authorities have suggested that it does (*Emuss v Smith (1848) 2 De G & Sm 722*), but it is also suggested in one leading textbook that it does not (*Theobald on Wills* (16th edition) at 18-02). The point is probably best regarded now as uncertain and the modern practice of drafting such a legacy as 'such motor car as I may own at the date of my death' is good practice in order to remove the uncertainty. Alternatively, if the gift is to be of a specific car owned at the date of the will, then an accurate description is to be preferred, again to remove the uncertainty.

A particular issue arises where the nature of the specifically bequeathed property has changed between the date of the will and the testator's death. This is frequently encountered with stocks and shares. For example, would a specific legacy of National Westminster ordinary shares be adeemed by the take-over of that bank by Royal Bank of Scotland, when Royal Bank of Scotland shares were issued in replacement for the National Westminster holding?

The test for this issue was set out in *Re Slater, Slater v Slater [1907] 1 Ch 665*:

> 'You have to ask yourself, where is the thing which is given? If you cannot find it at the testator's death, it is no use trying to trace it unless you can trace it in this sense, that you find something which has been changed in name or form only, but which is substantially the same thing.'

This question has been examined in the context of other cases and the general proposition can be put forward (see Mellows: *The Law of Succession* (5th edition) at 30-41) that for the replacement holding to pass under the gift of the previous security there must be:

(a)   a unity of the company issuing the security in the sense that it has been either the old company or a new one formed just to take over the old one;

(b)   a similarity in the nature of the security itself; and

(c)   a similarity in the quantity of the holding before and after the change.

It would appear that if any part of this tripartite test fails then the legacy will adeem. (There is an absence of any significant modern authorities on this point and given the major changes in the securities market since *Re Slater*, there is some concern as to whether or not a court will find that case appropriate to legacies in the light of the modern securities industry.)

The change of security in this context may arise out of an Act of Parliament for the nationalisation or government-sponsored reorganisation of a specific industry. Under these circumstances, there could be statutory provision in the enabling legislation to prevent ademption, but there is no general statutory provision applicable to ademption by government action.

Ademption will occur where the testator has entered into a binding contract for sale of the subject matter of the legacy, even though in the case of land the sale may not have been completed (*Farrar v Earl of Winterton (1842) 5 Beav 1*).

The charging of an asset by a testator will not adeem a legacy of the asset, but the legatee will take the asset subject to the debt (*Brain v Brain (1821) 6 Madd 221*).

The disposal of the asset causing the ademption of the legacy must be an authorised act of the testator and an authorised act purportedly done on his behalf by a third party will not cause ademption (*Basan v Brandon (1836) 8 Sim 171; Re Jeffrey (1974) 53 DLR (3d) 650*). Similar unauthorised acts cannot increase the subject matter of the legacy (*Re Larking, Larking v Larking (1887) 37 Ch D 310*).

There is some statutory protection in the Mental Health Act 1983 to save legacies where the property of a mental patient is disposed of under the power given by that Act. The Act provides that, where property which would have been specifically bequeathed is disposed of, the legatee shall take the same interest in, if and so far as circumstances allow, any property which at death represents the subject matter of the original legacy disposed of (s 101(1)).

Demonstrative legacies

8.9   A demonstrative legacy cannot adeem as a specific legacy can. If the designated fund or property out of which the demonstrative legacy is to be paid does not exist, or is insufficient, the legacy will be treated as a general legacy and paid out of the estate generally. Thus it is possible for a demonstrative legacy to abate but not to adeem.

Election

8.10   Sometimes, intentionally or unintentionally, a testator may bequeath property which he does not own to a legatee (A) and at the same time leave a further legacy of his own property to the true owner of the first property (B). Would it, under those circumstances, be equitable to allow B to accept his legacy while retaining his own property so that A received nothing? The doctrine of election is the solution that equity has developed for this problem.

As a general rule, a person cannot take benefit from a will without conforming to its general provisions (*Codrington v Codrington (1875) LR 7 HL 854*), therefore in order to take his legacy B must either hand his own property to A or compensate that legatee as to the property's value. B is of course at liberty to take no action to compensate A and could, if he wished, disclaim his own legacy; A cannot compel B's choice of these options. B must make the choice and is referred to as having been 'put to his option'. The three options are known as follows:

- B may 'take under the will'; i.e. accept his legacy and transfer his own property to A.

- B may 'take against the will'; i.e. accept his legacy and keep his own property, but make a payment equal to its value to A (valuation to be determined as at the date of death of the testator: *Re Hancock, Hancock v Pawson [1905] 1 Ch 16*. The election relates back to the date of death. B must also account for the income between death and election: *Gretton v Haward (1819) 1 Swans 409*).

- B may 'disclaim' his legacy and therefore take no benefit under the will, in which case he makes no payment to A.

Where the person put to his election is a minor (*Streatfield v Streatfield (1735) Cas temp Talb 176*) or lacking mental capacity the court has the power to make the election on their behalf (Mental Health Act 1983, s 99).

For this doctrine to apply, the following conditions must be met:

1.   *The testator must dispose of his own property to the legatee put to his election.*

If for any reason the property given away to B by the testator is not disposable by that testator's will, there is no election for B to make as he will receive no benefit under the will (and consequently A will receive nothing as there is no election) (*Bristow v Warde (1794) 2 Ves 336*).

2.   *The legatee's property that is bequeathed by the testator must be freely alienable.*

If for any reason the property given away to A by the testator is not capable of being disposed of by B, there is no election for B to make, but he will keep his legacy from the testator. Similarly, if the legacy to B has adeemed (e.g. by prior gift to B) there is no election to be made (*Re Edwards [1958] Ch 168*). A will receive no compensation as there is no election to be made (*Re Lord Chesham, Cavendish v Dacre (1886) 31 Ch D 466*). If B does not own the whole of the asset given to A, but only a part of it, the election will extend to the part that he does own (*Re Dicey, Julian v Dicey [1957] Ch 145*). If B's property given away by the testator is a protective life interest, B cannot attempt to assign such an interest without causing forfeiture; this interest would be treated as non-assignable and B would not be put to his election (*Re Gordon's Will Trusts [1978] Ch 145*). (See 8.7 regarding protective trusts generally.)

3.   *Both gifts must be in the same instrument.*

For this purpose, a will and its codicils are considered to be one instrument (*Cooper v Cooper (1874) LR 7 HL 53*), as are two wills which deal with property in different jurisdictions (*Douglas-Menzies v Umphelby [1908] AC 224*). However, if the two gifts are not made in the same instrument, B would be capable of taking benefit under one and refusing the terms of the other.

This should be carefully distinguished from gifts upon condition. Election involves two separate gifts, as opposed to a will which bequeaths the testator's property to B upon condition that B conveys some part of his property to A. Such a gift does not give rise to an election: B has a simple choice either to comply with the condition or lose the gift (*Broughton v Broughton (1750) 2 Ves Sen 12; Central Trust and Safe Deposit Co v Snider [1916] 1 AC 266*).

4.   *Although the testator must intend to dispose of the property he does not own, it is not necessary that he should be aware that he does not in fact own it.*

This is illustrated by one of the most common instances of election in modern wills, the failure to understand, or even recollect, the manner in which property may be owned between spouses. The testator bequeaths his interest in his farm to his son and the residue of his estate to his wife. Where the farm is owned jointly as a beneficial joint tenancy between the farmer and his wife his estate will not own the farm (his interest having passed outside of his estate by survivorship to his wife). The widow would then be put to her election as she is bequeathed the residue, while the farm which she owns is bequeathed to the son (*Grosvenor v Durston (1858) 25 Beav 97*).

5.   *Must the testator intend to dispose of what he does not own?*

At law there is a presumption that a testator intends to dispose only of what he owns. Therefore, if he disposes of property in which he has only an interest, but uses words that are capable of meaning a wider interest, the courts will construe such words generally as meaning only the smaller interest that was actually owned (*Evans v Evans (1863) 2 New Rep 408; Lord Rancliffe v Lady*

Parkins (1818) 6 Dow 149). It will be the case that the doctrine of election will be difficult to apply where the testator actually owns part of the property which also belongs to B but the testator bequeaths to A. An example of where election can apply with part ownership is where the testator and B are co-owners as tenants-in-common of a property and the testator bequeaths the whole of that property to A and by a legacy to B (*Padbury v Clark (1850) 2 Mac & G 298*; *Re Dicey [1957] Ch 145*).

Timing of the election

8.11 If the will specifies any time within which an election should be made, and B does not elect within that time, he is deemed to have elected against the will (*Dillon v Parker (1818) 1 Sw 359*). Unless the will sets a time limit, the law does not prescribe one. It is possible that a court will deem there to have been an election because of the conduct of the person put to his election, but this will only occur where it can be shown that that person had full information as to his position (*Wake v Wake (1791) 3 Bro CC 254*). A court will be more ready to find election by conduct if it would be inequitable to others to find the contrary (*Tibbits v Tibbits (1816) 19 Ves 656*).

Anyone who is put to his election is entitled to be informed of all of the information relevant to the property and will in question. Any election made with this information not having been made available may well not bind the person making that election (*Pusey v Desbouvrie (1734) 3 P Wms 315*; *Kidney v Coussmaker (1806) 12 Ves 136*).

If a person put to his election makes that election, but dies before the election is completed by payments or transfers, the election is binding against his estate. However, if that person dies before making his election there are two possibilities for the election.

(a) If the property which is to be inherited and is the subject of the election passes to the same beneficiary as the property which the earlier will gave away and caused the election, then that beneficiary will be put to the election instead (*Cooper v Cooper (1874) LR 7 HL 53*).

(b) The property inherited and the property purportedly given away by the first testator may pass to different beneficiaries. In these circumstances, the beneficiary who is entitled to the property purportedly given away by the first testator takes the property free from the election and with no obligation towards the first estate. The beneficiary entitled to the property inherited from the first estate only takes that property with the obligation to compensate (elect against the will) (*Pickersgill v Rodger (1876) 5 Ch D 163*).

Satisfaction

8.12 The doctrine of satisfaction embraces four separate categories.

(a)   Satisfaction of debts by legacies.

(b)   Satisfaction of legacies by legacies.

(c)   Satisfaction of legacies by portion.

(d)   Satisfaction of portion debts by legacies.

Satisfaction of debts by legacies

8.13   The general principle is that where a testator owed money to another and by the terms of his will bequeathed that sum, or greater, prima facie the legacy given is in satisfaction of the debtor, so that the debtor would receive the legacy only and not the debt as well (*Talbott v Duke of Shrewesbury (1714) Prec Ch 394*; *Re Stibbe (1946) 175 LT 198*). At least one modern author regards this principle as having 'been so often disapproved of, and . . .held to be excluded by such slight indications of intention, that it is of small practical importance' (*Theobald on Wills* (16th edition)). It is probably also worth noting that many of the features of this doctrine derive from an age when personal credit was most often derived from borrowing from other individuals, which is very different from today's credit industry. Therefore, the conditions set out below are a brief summary only.

For this doctrine to apply, the following conditions must be met.

1.   *The legacy must equal or exceed the debt.*

If the legacy is less than the debt it will not be found to be in satisfaction of a part of the greater debt (*Eastwood v Vinke (1731) 2 P Wms 613*). When establishing whether or not the legacy is equal to or greater than the debt, outstanding interest is not included (*Fitzgerald v National Bank [1929] 1 KB 394*) and the interest will be discharged as a general obligation of the estate.

2.   *The legacy must be as beneficial to the creditor as the debt.*

There is no satisfaction of the debt if the legacy is not in every way as beneficial to the creditor as the debt (*Crichton v Crichton [1895] 2 Ch 853*).

3.   *The will must have been made after the debt was incurred.*

A legacy which predates (*Cranmer's Case (1702) 2 Salk 508*), or is contemporaneous with (*Horlock v Wiggins (1888) 39 Ch D 142*), the debt cannot be in satisfaction of the debt. It could be the case that a legacy of an amount equal to the debt is included in a will after the debt is incurred, but in these circumstances if the debt is repaid after death the legatee will not receive the legacy as it will, in the absence of contrary evidence, be deemed to be in satisfaction of the debt (which has since been repaid (*Re Fletcher, Gillings v Fletcher (1888) 38 Ch D 373*).

4.   *The doctrine is rebutted by contrary evidence.*

Direct contrary evidence in the will is easily apparent, but in addition a direction in the will to pay 'debts and legacies' can be sufficient to rebut the doctrine (*Chancey's Case (1725) 1 P Wms 408*), as can a mere direction to pay all debts (*Lee v Pain (1844) 4 Hare 201*).

Satisfaction of legacies by legacies

8.14   Sometimes known as the rule against double legacies, the presumption is concerned with the question: where two legacies are given to the same person, does the legatee take both or only one?

1. *Both legacies in the same will or codicil.*

Where there is no motive for the gifts expressed in the document, or the same motive is ascribed to both, a presumption arises that only one legacy was intended. If the legacies are of different amounts it is presumed that both were intended (*Curry v Pile (1787) 2 Bro CC 225*), but minor differences may not be sufficient for both to be payable (*Greenwood v Greenwood (1776) 1 Bro CC 31n*).

2. *The legacies are in different instruments.*

One gift may be in a will, and the second in a codicil and in these circumstances both will be payable, unless they are of the same amount with the same motive expressed for both (*Wray v Field (1826) 2 Russ 257*).

Satisfaction of legacies by portions and of portion debts by legacies

8.15   Both of these types of satisfaction can be considered together as similar factors apply. Both types derive from equity's presumption against double portions. This is therefore also known as the presumption against double portions.

1. *Example of satisfaction of a legacy by a portion.*

A parent by his will leaves legacies of £100,000 to each of his two children. Later he makes a gift of £100,000 to only one child. The parent then dies, having made no changes to his will. The gift would be deemed to have satisfied the legacy as there is 'a presumption prima facie that both gifts were made to fulfil the same natural or moral obligation of providing for the legatee' (Lord Selbourne LC in *Re Pollock, Pollock v Worrall (1885) 28 Ch D 552 at 555*). The legacy need not be pecuniary; it can be residuary (*Montefiore v Guedalla (1859) 1 De GF & J 93*).

2. *Example of satisfaction of a portion debt by a legacy.*

A parent, by a marriage settlement, covenants to provide each child of the marriage with a portion of £100,000. The covenant creates the portion debt. The parent dies before paying any portions, but leaving three children. Two children are each left legacies of £100,000 in his will, the third is left nothing. The two children who each receive the £100,000 legacies are deemed to have had their portion debt satisfied and cannot claim the debt against the estate. The third child's portion debt is still outstanding as no provision was made to satisfy it in the will and he can therefore claim the portion debt against the estate. The legacies do not have to equal or exceed the portion debt and if they are less the portion debt will only be partially satisfied.

3. *A portion.*

A portion is a substantial advance by gift in the lifetime, or by will or marriage settlement, by a person who is a parent or who stands in loco parentis to a child. (Although mainly about a father's provision for a child, anyone can stand in loco parentis to a child. Most of the older cases are about a father, but recently this rule has been applied in the case of a mother's will (*In Re Cameron deceased [1999] Ch 386*). This case also demonstrates that this doctrine is not quite as redundant as some would have suggested.) The aim is to make provision for the child or to establish them in life (portions are very much about future life rather than relief from the past; *Re Furness, Furness v Stalkart [1901] 2 Ch 346*). It is not necessary in the case of a gift by will that the legacy be described in the will as a portion (*Suisse v Lord Lowther (1843) 2 Hare 424*). The court will not aggregate a number of small gifts to make a portion (*Re Scott, Langton v Scott [1903] 1 Ch 1*).

4. *The rule cannot apply to benefit strangers.*

There are two aspects to this. Firstly the portion or portion debts cannot be created for a stranger, only someone to whom the donor stands in loco parentis. Secondly, as the doctrine is an attempt to give equality between children, a stranger cannot benefit from the rule being applied to children. Thus if the parent gives the residue of his estate equally to his two sons and his niece (to whom he does not stand in loco parentis) and one son and the niece received £100,000 gifts after the date of the will, the niece does not bring the gift into account and receives one third of the residue. The two sons would take two thirds of residue with an adjustment between only those two shares for the life-time gift to one of them (*Re Heather [1906] 2 Ch 230*).

Abatement

8.16   Where an estate is insufficient to pay all of the debts, taxes and legacies in full, the interests in the estate are said to abate. This is to say the legacies will be reduced in a certain order. This order will only apply in solvent estates; if the estate contains insufficient funds to settle the debts no gifts under the will will be payable and the estate will be dealt with as an insolvent estate.

Residue almost by definition must abate before any other gifts in the will (as residue is defined as what is left after the payment of the other gifts). All the interests in residue will abate rateably with each other.

General legacies are the next category to abate. Generally speaking this will be pecuniary legacies, any demonstrative legacies where the fund on which they were charged has ceased to exist and annuities. All gifts within this category will be reduced in proportion sufficiently to meet the funds available to pay them. Only after this category has been exhausted completely will the next category of gifts abate.

Specific and demonstrative legacies are the final category to abate, and again all of the gifts in this category will abate in proportion to each other (it should be noted that the old provision that regarded charging clauses for professionals and clauses authorising trust corporations' fees as being legacies (and thus liable to abate) was amended by section 28(4) Trustee Act 2000 so that such payments are no longer gifts and not liable to abate).

As it is common practice for testators to direct how the incidence of inheritance tax is to be varied between different interests in the estate, abatement calculations may have to take into account such directions. Where the burden of tax would fall on a specific legacy, but the testator directs that it should fall elsewhere (usually on residue), the amount of the burden of tax removed in this way amounts to an additional benefit to the legatee. For the purposes of abatement, this additional benefit is treated as a pecuniary legacy and if this abates before the specific gift the legatee will need to pay into the estate a sum equal to the amount that the free of tax legacy abates.

It is important to note that this order of abatement is subject any contrary intention in the will. Testators can, and often do, direct that a particular legacy is to be paid in preference to others.

Apportionments

8.17   There are two categories of apportionment, legal and equitable. The former, as applied today, derives mainly from the Apportionment Act 1870, whilst the second derives from decisions of equity, principally during the nineteenth century. For convenience, most modern wills expressly bar the application of both types of apportionments, but there are still occasions where both types of apportionment can affect legacies. The notes below illustrate their application to legacies, rather than their general application to estates. For more detailed information a suitable work on equity should be consulted.

Legal apportionments

8.18   This type of apportionment produces a division of income where the period from which the income arises contains a change of interest. Relevant examples are specific bequests of income-producing assets, such as stocks and shares or rented property, where dividends or rent for periods which include the date of death will be apportioned over the date of death. The effect of this will be to deprive the legatee of any part of the income from the asset bequeathed to him which is deemed to arise before death. Such 'before death' part of the income is credited to the residue of the estate.

Equitable apportionments

8.19   In the main these apportionments will affect the amount of income which is received by a life interest in a trust fund created by will. The underlying principle (if one can express it as strongly as being a principle) is to give a balance between capital and income interests, but the methods and the results are fairly artificial. Such apportionments are fairly routinely barred from operation by the terms of modern wills, but their application to life interest funds where the will does not bar them should be considered.

Joint gifts

8.20   Where an absolute legacy is left in favour of two or more beneficiaries it is important for those beneficiaries to establish the precise nature of the terms of the legacy; does it create a tenancy or a beneficial joint tenancy? In the case of a tenancy in common, death of the legatee before the testator will cause lapse (if there are no alternative provisions) while death after the testator will cause the interest to accrue to the legatee's personal representatives. A legacy which is in the form of a beneficial joint tenancy will, on the other hand, neither lapse (in part) nor accrue to the estate of the deceased legatee, it will accrue to the other joint beneficiaries.

When construing such gifts, the court will tend towards finding that the gift creates a tenancy in common, rather than a beneficial joint tenancy, where there is doubt (*Booth v Alington (1857) 27 LJ Ch 177*; *Oakley v Wood (1868) 37 LJ Ch 28*). However, where the words used direct a beneficial joint tenancy, or are capable of supporting such an interpretation, any or all of the joint legatees will need to consider severance of their interest. Whether or not a legatee wishes to continue to hold under a joint tenancy will depend upon his individual circumstances, but clearly preservation of his share of the legacy in the event of his death must be a factor, unless he is content that benefit could accrue to the surviving joint legatees in the event of his death.

The executors are of course also required to establish the nature of such a joint gift, as when they are able to distribute to the legatees they will need to know in what manner they are to vest the asset in the legatees. However, this may be some time after death.

Inheritance (Provision for Family and Dependants) Act 1975

8.21   A successful claim under the Inheritance (Provision for Family and Dependants) Act 1975 may result in the failure of the legacies specified in the will.

Whilst English law generally acknowledges that a testator may leave his estate in any way that he sees fit ('testamentary freedom'), this Act does give rights to certain defined classes of family and dependants to request the court to amend the provisions of a will if, in the opinion of the court, the will does not make adequate provision for them (claims may also be made against intestate estates). It must be stressed that this is not a right allowing a member of the specified classes to insist on provision being made for them, the right is only that the court should consider their claim.

The classes of person who may make such a claim are to be found in section 1 of the Act. They are:

(a)   a wife or husband;

(b)   a former wife or husband who has not remarried (and whose divorce was not on terms which expressly barred a claim under this Act);

(c)   a child (of whatever age);

(d)   any person who was not a child of the deceased, but was treated by him as a child of any marriage of the deceased;

(e)   anyone who was wholly or partly maintained by the deceased;

(f)   anyone (of the opposite sex) who cohabited with the deceased during the whole of the two years preceding his death.

This book is not the place to examine such claims in detail, but the practical implications for legatees can be noted. The right to make a claim under this Act should be exercised within six months of the date of a grant of representation (service of a claim before a grant has been issued is not valid). The court has the discretion to admit late claims where the circumstances warrant it. The legal personal representative is protected against the effects of late claims, but has no protection against claims where payments or appropriations are made in satisfaction of legacies before the six-month post-grant period has elapsed. Personal representatives will therefore act cautiously towards distributions during this period and, if there is the possibility of a claim, may defer any distributions until after six months has elapsed.

When considering an award in settlement of any claim under this Act, the court has discretion to reduce or remove bequests if it considers that a claimant's case is more deserving than those legatees named in the will. In any action, those who seek to protect their legacies have the right to have their interests represented if they wish. Legatees under wills where such claims are made against the estate should always consider taking legal advice as to whether to be represented in any action. The legatees should not assume that the terms of the will will be defended by the personal representative, as the position of the personal representative should be neutral.

Mutual wills

8.22   The subject of mutual wills is outside the scope of this book, apart from the issue of legacies that may be payable under such wills.

Mutual wills are wills made by – usually – two testators (but could be three or, most unusually, four), where they have agreed that the terms of their will will reflect a common intention and that the agreement they have reached is not to be revoked after the death of the first party to die. It is important to note that merely because the terms of two wills are a mirror image of each other does not necessarily mean that they are mutual; the agreement (contract) between the parties must also exist. Typically such wills are made by husband and wife or brother and sister, leaving their estates to each other and, on the death of the survivor, to a common beneficiary (whilst this is the typical framework, it is not essential that the surviving testator takes any benefit as the agreement could be to the entire benefit of a third party: *Re Dale [1994] Ch 31*).

If after the death of the first to die the survivor makes a new will on different terms, the court, whilst accepting the validity of the will, will impose a trust upon the personal representative of the terms of the original agreement (*Dufour v Pereira (1769) 1 Dick 419; Re Goodchild [1997] 1 WLR 1216, CA*). Thus legacies under the mutual agreement may become payable on the second death, although the will under which they should have arisen is revoked. However, in saying this, it must be noted that the reverse is true for the later will and that although that will may be admitted to probate the gifts under it will not be payable insofar as the court finds them incompatible with the original agreement and enforces the original agreement.

Negligence and wills

8.23   This is a recently developed area of law and it requires some comment in the context of legacies. Where beneficiaries fail to receive the benefit intended by the testator through the negligence of the will draftsman, the court can award damages to compensate the beneficiaries who suffered loss.

Thus in the leading case of *White v Jones [1995] 2 AC 207*, the testator died leaving a valid will which did not benefit his two daughters. The testator had intended to make a new will which would have benefited them. The House of Lords decided that it was the solicitors' failure of their duty towards the testator that caused loss to the daughters and found the solicitors liable to compensate the daughters for the amount of their lost benefit. Importantly, under these circumstances, the court does not have the power to vary the terms of the will with the effect that the legatees under the valid will still receive the benefit from their bequests. The sum paid to compensate the disappointed legatees comes from outside the estate i.e. from the solicitors (or more likely their professional indemnity insurers) and is not a legacy.

This principle is not confined only to a failure to prepare a will. It has also been applied to cases where there was defective execution which led to the will being invalid and thus giving no benefit to the intended beneficiaries (see *Esterhuizen v Allied Dunbar [1998] 2 FLR 668; Ross v Caunters [1980] Ch 297*); also where the solicitor failed to take reasonable steps to ensure that a bequest of property would take effect as the testatrix intended (*Carr-Glynn v Frearsons [1999] Ch 326*. It must, however, be stressed that the solicitor is not liable if there was no negligence on his part.

Debts charged on the subject matter of legacies

8.24   Where property that is bequeathed is subject to a charge created by the testator in favour of another, the general rule is that the legatee will take the asset subject also to that charge (Administration of Estates Act 1925, s 35). It is important to note that this is only the case where the asset in question is specifically charged with the debt.

In *Re Birmingham, Savage v Stannard [1959] Ch 523* the testatrix had bequeathed a house which she was in the process of buying. At her death she had contracted to purchase the property and paid a deposit. The legatee therefore took the bequest subject to the vendor's lien on the property for the balance of the purchase moneys. However, also outstanding in connection with the purchase were the testatrix's legal costs and expenses. Although liabilities are incurred by a purchaser they are simple contract debts that (in the absence of any express agreement) are not charged on the property being acquired. Therefore the legatee in *Re Birmingham* did not suffer these outstanding costs and they were payable from residue.

The general rule that the debt will pass with the asset that it is charged upon can be changed by the express direction of the testator. The contrary intention must be in writing but it may be in documents other than the will or codicil.

A contrary intention outside the will is frequently found where there is a mortgage protection or similar policy taken out to secure the repayment of a mortgage. Such policies usually contain an express provision that the purpose of the policy is for the repayment of the loan. Accordingly this will be a contrary intention so that the policy proceeds clear the loan and the legatee takes the property free of the now discharged debt.

As mentioned in the previous paragraph the wording of mortgage protection policies will usually amount to a contrary intention for these purposes. A life policy which does not contain such wording will not, in the absence of a written contrary intention, discharge the legatee's obligation, even though this may have been the sole purpose of taking out the policy or that the deceased had declared orally a contrary intention regarding the policy (*Perry v Hicknell (1982) 34 OR (2d) 246*).

If a charged property is bequeathed to more than one beneficiary, the beneficiaries bear the burden of the debt in the proportion that their benefits have to each other (*Re Major, Taylor v Major [1914] 1 Ch 278*).

Chapter 9

Charitable legacies

Introduction

9.1   Legacy income is a massively important source of funds for charities, often accounting for 80% – or even more – of their total voluntary income. An average 'Top Ten' charity will probably deal with around 2,000 cases every year and the UK's biggest charities each receive upwards of £50m per annum from this source. In the past, a legacy officer's role probably consisted of little more than saying 'thank you' for the cheques that were received. As with every other part of the economy though, the not-for-profit sector has been forced to work very hard in recent years to maximise its various income streams and the role of the legacy officer has, as a result, become of crucial importance. Although precise figures are difficult to establish, the entire sector is probably worth in the region of £1.5bn per annum. Given the scale of the operation therefore, it is perhaps not too surprising that many charities (certainly all of the major ones) now choose to employ qualified individuals to specifically administer their legacy income. No longer is the task limited to merely saying 'thank you' – although doing so, in an effective and sincere manner, remains a vital and integral part of the job.

A legacy officer's duty is, above all, to protect the position of the charity's trustees in the collection of bequeathed funds. It is perhaps a statement of the obvious, but worth mentioning nonetheless, that one of the fundamental differences between legacies and any other form of voluntary income is that a legacy is a legal entitlement; it is enforceable – if need be – through the courts. Charity trustees are legally obliged to ensure that their charity receives all that it is entitled to. Indeed, those trustees can be held personally liable for omitting to collect such sums. Given the specialist nature of probate work, sensible charity trustees will therefore generally delegate the task of administering legacies to a team of dedicated specialists.

A legacy department's role in the estate administration process is entirely unique. It operates at the precise interface between the commercial and charitable worlds. Legacy officers try to ensure – with very little actual support in terms of regulatory authority – that an independent third party (the estate administrator) complies with legislative requirements. In doing so they have to use commercial principles to protect charitable funds whilst, at the same time, being very conscious of the unique public relations aspect of their work.

The management of legacies is therefore a task that demands great tact, sensitivity, awareness and integrity – all combined with a fair measure of technical knowledge and legal awareness. Perhaps for these very reasons, many legacy officers are 'poachers turned gamekeepers'; they will very often have previously worked as professional estate administrators within the private sector. Whatever their background though, these individuals tend, by virtue of the sheer volume of cases they handle, to be very experienced beneficiaries and, with the larger charities in particular, well aware of their rights and entitlements. Their knowledge and expertise can often assist the estate administrator, particularly when dealing with some of the more awkward or unusual areas, such as contentious issues.

For many reasons, most charities will seek to communicate with the executor at a very early stage in the process. Perhaps because they are so dependent upon legacies as a source of funds, charities are especially grateful whenever they receive early intimation as to the value – and likely timescale for the eventual availability of – a bequest. The forecasting of likely legacy income levels is a crucial part of most charities' long-term strategic planning. Indeed, for those charities who maintain lower levels of reserves it is even a crucial part of short-term planning! By establishing contact with the executor, the charity can hope to make an early assessment of the issues likely to be involved in each individual case. In doing so, the hope is that a reasonably accurate estimate can be made for the likely receipt of the funds. In addition, there are certain specific areas where, because of their specialised knowledge, charities can perhaps provide guidance on how to deal with particular problems. Amongst these areas are:

(a)   claims against the estate;

(b)   saving charitable gifts from failure;

(c)   taxation issues;

(d)   dealing with realty (i.e. land);

(e)   probate fraud.

Claims against the estate

Moral claims – ex-gratia payments

9.2   This is a particularly thorny issue for many legacy officers – particularly because, in dealing with funds that have been bequeathed to their charity, they simply do not have the same discretions or privileges as a member of the public might have in the same situation. When a private individual who inherits under the terms of a will decides that nursing home staff, or even members of the deceased's own family, are morally entitled to some recognition of their efforts, he is entirely free to waive part of his entitlement in favour of the deserving party. Charities are more constrained in what they can sanction though – and their trustees do not have any power to unilaterally agree to make such ex-gratia payments. Indeed, up until 1969, the Charity Commissioners had always taken the view that not only did charity trustees have no power to make ex-gratia payments, but also that there was no way in which the Commissioners themselves could provide the authority for them to do so. However, this approach came to be questioned and, eventually, the Attorney General encouraged the plaintiffs in two separate cases to submit the facts to the court for determination. The resultant cases, *Re Snowden, Re Henderson [1970] Ch 700*, now govern the law in this area.

In deciding that the court (and, on behalf of charities, the Attorney General) *did* have the power to authorise ex-gratia payments, Cross J emphasised nonetheless that the power was not one to be exercised lightly, or on slender grounds. It was a power to be exercised only where it could fairly be said that, if the charity were an individual, it would be morally wrong for him to refuse to make the payment. In both of the test cases, it could clearly be shown that the testator had never intended the charity to receive as large a gift as it ultimately did receive. The distinction was firmly drawn between such a case and one where the testator's relations simply consider that he was not morally justified in leaving his assets to a charity rather than to them. In the latter case, no moral obligation will, as a rule, rest upon the charity and so authority to make the payment will therefore be withheld. The Charity Commission have published a booklet on this subject, CC7, which outlines their views and it is strongly recommended that any practitioner in this area should obtain a copy.

Before dealing with what *does* constitute a valid ex-gratia application, it is perhaps as well to consider for a moment those cases which do *not* qualify. In fact, very few of the cases initially represented as being suitable for ex-gratia treatment actually make it as far as the Charity Commission. This is because, in the vast majority of cases, it soon becomes apparent that the claim is in fact legal – rather than moral – in nature. This in itself is generally enough to prevent the operation of the ex-gratia procedure. Take, for instance, the situation of a surviving spouse. Here, claimants have a very obvious remedy available to them by way of the Inheritance (Provision for Family and Dependants) Act 1975. Any increase in financial provision for such a claimant would therefore be treated as a compromise of a legal claim and so would not require the sanction of the Commissioners (although independent legal advice will be required).

It is also often the case that disappointed family members, or close friends, will maintain that promises were made to them during the deceased's lifetime that they would receive some benefit from the estate. This might similarly preclude the matter being dealt with as an ex-gratia case because it raises the possibility of a legal claim under the heading of promissory, or proprietary, estoppel.

A growing area of difficulty is the situation where the claim might have legal status but the remedy does not actually lie against the estate. This can be slightly more awkward. Where, for instance, the testator gave instructions for a new will to be drawn up, but these instructions were not acted upon, it is possible that the disappointed beneficiaries might have a claim in negligence under the rule in *White v Jones [1995] 2 AC 207* against the testator's advisers. Morally, of course, one would have tremendous sympathy for the intended beneficiaries. However, the existence of the legal claim will, of itself, generally preclude the case from being dealt with under the ex-gratia procedure. Nonetheless, the intended beneficiaries have been disappointed and it is obviously preferable from the will-drafter's point of view if the claim can be settled out of the estate. As a result, legacy officers can often find themselves being put under some considerable pressure to support what is in fact an unjustified ex-gratia application.

Moving on to deal with situations which *are* suitable for ex-gratia treatment, the important point with any such payment is that it is the charity's trustees personally who must make the decision as to whether they feel themselves to be under a moral obligation. The trustees cannot delegate authority for making this particular decision to anyone – including the legacy officer. (The Charity Commission maintain that the ability to regard oneself as being under a moral obligation is a subjective question which cannot be delegated.) Once the trustees have decided that they do feel a moral obligation, they then have to seek the sanction of the Charity Commission – under section 27Charities Act 1993 – before the payment can be made. In order to obtain the sanction of the Commissioners, charity trustees therefore have to:

(a)   demonstrate that the intentions of the testator were perfectly clear;

(b)   explain why and how those intentions were thwarted;

(c)   show that the claimant has no other legal remedy; and

(d)   explain why they feel themselves to be under a moral obligation.

The first three of these headings are, basically, a question of fact and can therefore generally be dealt with by the legacy officer. The last, however, can only be addressed by the trustees themselves and the Charity Commission will expect to receive written confirmation that the trustees have dealt with it personally.

The correct procedure therefore is for the legacy officer to deal with the first three points and collate the documentary evidence to support the application. The case should then be referred to the charity's trustees (together, if it is felt to be helpful, with a formal recommendation from the legacy officer) for them to express their views.

In considering whether they should accede to the request, the charity will always regard the testator's wishes as paramount. It always has to be borne in mind that a testator has the right under English law to dispose of his property in the way that he wishes. The charity will in all likelihood therefore ask the executor (or the firm that drew up the will) for specific information about the intentions of the testator, and whether there were any factors that may or may not have prevented the testator from carrying out those intentions. Depending on the circumstances, it might also be appropriate for the charity to clarify the financial status of the applicant and also the value of any benefit that he already receives under the terms of the will or codicil.

Once the trustees have decided that they do feel themselves to be under a moral obligation, the Charity Commission can then be requested to make an order under the terms of section 27. The supporting documentary evidence will also have to be provided to the Commissioners. The Charity Commission's power in respect of ex-gratia payments is exercisable under the supervision of – and in accordance with directions given by – the Attorney General. It is of course open to the Commission to refrain from exercising the power or they may, on occasion, consult the Attorney General before doing so. If the Commissioners do refuse to make an order, this does not preclude the charity trustees from subsequently approaching the Attorney General direct if they do not agree with the Commissioners' view.

It is in the nature of a subjective decision that – even given identical sets of facts – different individuals, or groups of individuals, will come to different conclusions. Thus it is perfectly feasible that, where more than one charity is involved, the decision of one need not necessarily be reflected in the views of another. The case may well end up in a situation where the payment to the moral beneficiary is comprised of entirely unequal contributions from each of the donee charities.

In conclusion, it is important to realise that the number of occasions on which ex-gratia payments are sanctioned is, in fact, relatively limited. The requirements for a successful application are stringent and they are rigorously enforced by the Charity Commission. Early consultation with the legacy officer is essential in such situations because, if the executor does make an unauthorised payment, he could well find himself being held personally liable for the sum he has wrongfully distributed.

Legal claims

9.3   By contrast with the vagaries of the ex-gratia procedure, legal claims against an estate are usually fairly straightforward to deal with – provided they are identified and addressed as early as possible. In this respect, the recent Woolf reforms are both a help and a hazard for legacy officers. They certainly ensure there is less likelihood of litigation (or, worse, the mere threat of litigation) delaying the overall administration of the estate. However, they can also place severe demands on the legacy officer's ability to get the trustees' agreement to the terms of settlement of the claim. Because of the very tight time limits which now apply, it is important that, when confronted by a claim, the legacy officer should act swiftly and decisively.

Charity trustees do have the power to compromise a legal claim but this power is not unfettered. It is subject to a requirement that they must take qualified legal advice both as to the merits and strengths of the claim and as to the terms upon which it should be settled. Thus it is vital that the charity's legal advisors should be consulted and involved at as early a stage as possible.

Fortunately, because there is not the same 'subjective' element in dealing with legal claims as there is with ex-gratia applications, the trustees can delegate limited authority to agree the terms of settlement to the legacy officer. This can streamline matters somewhat and many legacy officers have extensive experience in facing such claims. Probably as a result, they will usually go to great lengths to avoid both the inevitable cost and the obvious uncertainties of litigation. This is not to say, however, that they will automatically back down when confronted by a claim. The qualified legal advice that they receive may well be such that they cannot justifiably settle at the level the claimant is expecting.

Once again though, it is important to emphasise the need for early consultation in order that an effective – and hopefully mutually agreeable – strategy can be developed.

Saving charitable gifts from failure

9.4   Occasionally, testators will leave legacies to charity which, on the face of it, seem incapable of fulfilment. This may be because the charity concerned no longer exists or it may simply be that the precise activity envisaged by the testator is no longer carried out. However, the courts do seem to tend towards construing testators' wills in such a way as to save charitable gifts from failure if at all possible. See, for example, *Re Broadbent's Will, Imperial Cancer Research Fund v Bradley [2001] EWCA 714; [2001] WTLR 967*, where the testatrix's gift (under her 1987 Will, with 1992 codicil) in favour of:

> 'The Vicar and Church Wardens of St. Matthew's Church Stalybridge for the general purposes of such Church but with the request that the money be used primarily for the upkeep of the fabric of the Church'

was upheld. This despite the fact that the Church was a mission church – and therefore had no vicar or churchwardens; the trustees of the Church had decided in 1990 to close and sell it; and that the building itself had been sold, demolished, and the site redeveloped, fully two years before the testatrix died in 1996. The court held that, because the gift was to a specified charity (rather than simply for a charitable purpose), for the gift to fail it would have to be shown that there was an exhaustion of assets and a cessation of activities. In this instance, although the church had been closed for worship in 1990 and the building itself had been demolished in 1994, the critical point was that there was still a charity in existence carrying out the general purposes of St Matthews' Church. This was sufficient to save the gift from failure.

Similarly in the case of *Re Chambers, Watson v National Childrens' Homes [2001] WTLR 1375*, the testator bequeathed half the residue of his estate to the National Children's Home, with the other half being left to the National Canine Defence League. However, this part of the gift was:

> 'on the condition that the said League will look after my domestic pets in their kennels during the remainder of their natural lives but in the event of the said League not agreeing to such condition I bequeath such one-half part or share of the residue of my estate to the National Children's Home.'

At the time the will was made, the testator owned a dog. However, that dog had, in the meantime, been stolen and Mr Chambers had not replaced it with any other pets by the time he died. Despite the patent impossibility of the League being able to fulfil the condition that was ostensibly attached to the gift, the court nonetheless held that the League should receive one-half of the estate.

Cy-près doctrine

9.5   The cy-près doctrine can sometimes provide a way to salvage a charitable gift that might otherwise fail. The doctrine has a long pedigree but the rationale behind it was originally a religious one:

> 'The donation was considered as proceeding from a general principle of piety in the testator. Charity was an expiation of sin, to be rewarded in another state; and therefore if political reasons negatived the particular charity given, [the] courts thought the merits of charity ought not to be lost to the testator, nor to the public, and that they were carrying on his general pious intention.' *A-G v Lady Downing (1769) Amb 571.*

Whilst 'general pious intention' may perhaps be a somewhat rarer commodity now than it was in 1769, the doctrine has nonetheless continued to ensure that many charitable gifts are preserved where they might otherwise have failed. The subsequent development and current scope of the doctrine is beyond the ambit of this chapter, as is a discussion of the law surrounding it. Such discussions have exercised far greater minds than the author's, for far longer than space here will allow! Suffice it to say that nowadays, for a cy-près application to be successful:

1.   there must be a designated charitable object, i.e. a charity;

2.   the situation must be one in which the law recognises that the doctrine can operate (as defined by section 13 Charities Act 1993); and

3.   in the event of an initial failure of the gift (although not in any other case) there must be a general charitable intent (Picarda prefers the term 'paramount charitable intent', on the basis that it confers a better understanding of what is required).

Provided these three requirements can be met, a scheme can be ordered which will allow the gift to pass to the charity and be applied as closely as possible to what the testator originally had in mind. It is possible, for instance, that a gift might be expressed to be for the benefit of a particular school for handicapped children. If that school has subsequently closed down but has transferred its pupils to a comparable establishment, it may be possible to apply the gift cy-près to the 'replacement' school, thereby continuing to assist those individuals (or ones very like them) that the testator originally had in mind.

This is an area where the legacy officer's ability to collate information relating to the charity's past and present activities, and combine this with an awareness of legal principles, may result in the salvaging of sometimes quite significant gifts. It is also vital, of course, to ensure that one has sufficient market intelligence to ensure that the charity is notified of any bequest that may conceivably relate to its past activities.

Royal Sign Manual procedure

9.6   The Royal Sign Manual procedure is another potential way of salvaging indefinite charitable bequests. Its use can be traced back to 1675 and the case of *A-G v Peacock (1676) Finch 245*, where Lord Nottingham upheld a bequest which was worded in favour of 'charitable uses for the good of the poor for ever' on the basis that 'the King by his prerogative could cure the uncertainty and apply the property cy-près to like charitable objects under the sign manual'.

Up until 1986 Directions were signed personally by the Queen but since then, she has delegated her powers to the Attorney General who now signs on her behalf. The Attorney General currently makes around 50 Sign Manual Directions a year and, in deciding how to dispose of the gift, the Attorney General adopts the same approach as would be adopted by the court. He will therefore take account of any evidence there may be within the will itself as to which charitable purpose the testator intended to benefit and also any clues there may be from the testator's lifetime behaviour (e.g. whether he had made lifetime gifts or pledged a legacy to a particular charity).

The Sign Manual Direction is intended purely to identify a charity whose identity was uncertain. It does not resolve any other dispute (indeed, if there is any form of dispute, the Attorney General will normally decline to make a Direction). Nor does it seek to construe the will. Perhaps more importantly, from the practitioner's point of view, it does not provide any protection for the executors if they decide to make a payment to charity in accordance with its terms and their decision is subsequently challenged. It is therefore for the executors to decide whether there is a risk of such challenge before going ahead with the payment.

Against these disadvantages, the procedure does have two considerable merits. Firstly, it is cheap – no fee is payable for the Direction. Secondly, it is a relatively quick answer to what might otherwise be a long drawn out affair. Directions are usually issued within a matter of weeks of the initial approach.

Taxation issues

Inheritance tax

9.7   Probably the single biggest area of concern where charitable legacies are involved is that of inheritance tax. Any gift to charity under a will is exempt from inheritance tax. Nonetheless, the Capital Taxes Office will not generally volunteer the exemption and it must therefore actually be claimed at the time the probate papers are submitted. It is certainly not unknown for estate administrators to forget to claim the exemption and thereby incur unnecessary inheritance tax.

Far more common though, is a failure to apportion the inheritance tax correctly amongst the beneficiaries. It seems eminently logical that, if one gift is given subject to tax and an equal amount is given free of tax, then the recipient of the taxable gift will actually receive less than the non-taxable recipient – the difference being the tax that is deducted. Parliament obviously felt this to be the case because section 41 Inheritance Tax Act 1984 states:

'Notwithstanding the terms of any disposition –

(a) none of the tax on the value transferred shall fall on any specific gift if or to the extent that the transfer is exempt with respect to the gift, and

(b) none of the tax attributable to the value of the property comprised in residue shall fall on any gift of a share of residue if or to the extent that the transfer is exempt with respect to the gift.'

The straightforward purpose of this rule is to ensure that the tax exemption for a gift to an exempt beneficiary will actually benefit that beneficiary and no other. In practical terms, what it means is that any inheritance tax that is payable on residue should only be deducted from the parts of residue that have actually given rise to the liability.

Example

If the residuary estate amounted to £500,000 and is bequeathed as to half to the deceased's spouse and the remaining half equally between his son and daughter, then inheritance tax of £6,400 will be payable. The calculation will run along the following lines:

Residuary estate	500,000
Deduct spouse exemption	250,000
Chargeable estate	250,000
Deduct Nil Rate Band	234,000
Tax calculated on	16,000
Tax due @ 40% thereof	6,400

The entire tax burden should fall only against the non-exempt share – because that is the share that has occasioned the charge to tax. Thus whilst the deceased's spouse in this instance will receive £250,000, the son and daughter will each receive (250,000 – 6,400)/2 = £121,800. Obviously, in the above calculations, one can substitute a charity for the spouse since both are exempt beneficiaries for the purposes of inheritance tax.

Unfortunately, ever since the case of *Re Benham's Will Trusts [1995] STC 210*, there has also been an alternative method of calculating both the amount and the apportionment of inheritance tax. Many learned tomes – and a great many opinions of learned counsel – have discussed the conceptual and practical difficulties that *Benham* created and it is not intended to rehearse them again here. Suffice it to say that, thankfully, *Re Ratcliffe (deceased), Holmes v McMullan [1999] STC 262* has subsequently rendered *Benham* all but irrelevant and, unless the wording of the will is especially specific, the 'normal section 41' approach is to be preferred. Nonetheless, for the sake of completeness, it is perhaps as well to mention the alternative method.

The end result of a *'Benham* calculation' is that all parties receive the same amount. However, this can only be accomplished by notionally grossing up the non-exempt share to such an extent that, after the payment of tax from that share, both parties receive equal amounts. In practice, what this produces is a circular argument because, in grossing up the non-exempt share, one changes the notional value of the estate. This in turn alters the amount of tax that is payable, thereby altering the amount by which the non-exempt share has to be grossed up. This alters the notional value of the estate . . .and so on. The calculation itself is probably best done by way of a computer spreadsheet. Using the same figures as in our previous example, the outcome will be as follows (and I make no attempt to explain the underlying calculations!):

Example

Residuary estate	500,000
Deduct spouse's proportion*	246,000
Chargeable estate	254,000
Deduct Nil Rate Band	234,000
Tax calculated on	20,000
Tax due @ 40% thereof	8,000

*the proportion passing to the spouse has to be amended downwards to accommodate the 'extra' which has to pass to the non-exempt share in order to cover the tax which is then deductible from that non-exempt share.

At the end of the calculation, the spouse will receive £246,000 (a decrease of £4,000) and the son and daughter will each receive £123,000 (an increase for them of £1,200 each); the amount of tax increases from £6,400 to £8,000.

Deeds of variation

9.8   Where an estate is liable to inheritance tax, it is always worth considering whether the use of a deed of variation might be able to diminish (or even eliminate entirely) the resultant tax liability. Again, legacy officers are always more than happy to discuss the possibilities.

Capital gains tax

9.9   Because charities are exempt from capital gains tax, it will normally be advantageous for the sale of any assets which are showing a gain over their probate value to be carried out by, or on behalf of, the charity itself. This is not as complicated as it might perhaps sound. There is no necessity for any actual physical transfer of the assets to take place. With Stock Exchange investments, there is no need to even complete stock transfer forms. What *is* essential is that the executor must have ascertained that the assets concerned are not required for administration purposes (i.e. for the payment of liabilities or administrative expenses). Where some of the investments need to be sold for administration costs or payment of legacies, the balance can still be appropriated to reduce the capital gains tax burden.

Once residue has been ascertained the executor should declare, ideally by way of a formal Memorandum of Appropriation, that he is henceforth holding the remaining assets as bare trustee for the residuary beneficiaries. (The ILM website http://ilmnet.org contains a model form for this purpose.) For capital gains tax purposes, the assets are deemed to have been acquired by the beneficiaries at their probate value. (Although, for the purposes of the estate accounts, values are usually taken to be the middle market price at the close of trading on the day of appropriation.)

The assets can then be sold or transferred in the normal way, directly from the executor's name. Most charities will greatly appreciate being consulted beforehand as to whether they wish to receive this part of their entitlement in cash or *in specie*. Where possible, it might be good practice to make such enquiries even before the issue of the grant. The rationale behind doing so is that many charities have a blanket policy of only taking the cash proceeds from the sale of investments. Making early enquiries would enable the executor to then carry out the necessary sales very shortly after the issue of the grant, thereby minimising the risk to the estate of short-term Stock Market fluctuations.

The procedure for dealing with real property is slightly more complicated. Here, it will be necessary for the executors to transfer the *legal* title (by way of a transfer form) out of their own names as executors, to themselves as trustees. In order to transfer the *equitable* interest in the property they then complete a declaration of trust confirming that they henceforth hold the property as bare trustee on behalf of the charities. (This latter step should, ideally, be supported by some evidence of acceptance of the appropriation by the beneficiaries). Each of these steps should be completed before contracts are exchanged. With effect from the date of the assent, both the executor and the charity will become subject to the provisions under sections 36 and 37 of the Charities Act. As a result, the sale price will have to be approved by the beneficiaries. It should also be noted that additional care is required where the property concerned is unregistered land. In that event, the assent of the legal title will trigger first registration which may well involve the estate in additional costs.

Obviously, there will be occasions when it is impossible for the executor to avoid incurring capital gains tax. Where substantial sums have to be raised from investment assets in order to discharge liabilities, administration costs, or pecuniary legacies, for instance, the executor will probably have little option but to realise some chargeable gains. However, even in these cases, sensible choice of which stocks to sell can often reduce the chargeable gain such that it falls within the executors' personal allowance.

Most charities, as a matter of course, now provide a simple checklist for administrators which details some of the more common areas of difficulty, including capital gains tax. If, as a result of an executor not taking the simple steps that are required, capital gains tax is needlessly incurred during the administration period then the executor will probably be in breach of his responsibilities to maximise the benefit to the estate. In such a situation, the charity will usually feel itself to be entirely justified in insisting (particularly in the case of a professional executor) that the executor, rather than the beneficiaries, should fund the resulting tax liability.

Income tax

9.10   Under section 700(5) Income and Corporation Taxes Act 1988, a duty is placed upon personal representatives to provide the beneficiaries of an estate with tax deduction vouchers. In the case of a charity these vouchers are of particular importance because they enable the reclamation of any income tax that may have been suffered on income arising during the administration. Whilst the individual amounts concerned are rarely by themselves significant, their cumulative effect can add substantially to charity income. In RNIB's case alone for example, more than £175,000 income tax was reclaimed during the year to March 2001.

The Inland Revenue publish a series of documents and booklets to assist executors in completing the Estate Tax Return. They also host a very informative website www.inlandrevenue.gov.uk/trusts/aps.htm whence all the relevant forms can be downloaded.

Dealing with realty

9.11   Even before the Charities Acts were implemented, many restrictions were already in place concerning dealings in charity property. It was generally accepted that, although there was no absolute legal prohibition against the sale of charity land, there was nonetheless a presumption that the person who donated land to charity intended that that land should be devoted to the particular charitable purpose in perpetuity. Nonetheless, charity trustees did have a general power to dispose of such property – provided it could be shown that the sale was beneficial to the charity.

These basic principles still remain and they now form the underlying basis of section 36 Charities Act 1993. As a general rule 'no land held by or in trust for a charity shall be sold, leased or otherwise disposed of without an order of the court or of the Commissioners'. The requirement to seek an order of the court or Commissioners does not however apply if (a) the disposition is made to a person who is not a 'connected person' (as defined by the Act), or to a trustee for, or nominee of, a connected person and (b) the statutory procedure and requirements have been complied with.

Whilst land remains in the name of the executors, section 36 will not apply – because it is not, at that stage, charity land. However, once the property has been appropriated, either into the charity's own name or into the names of the executors *as trustees for the charity* (see above re capital gains tax), then the requirements of section 36 must be complied with. Similarly, where land is being dealt with following the death of a life tenant, the requirements of section 36 must be adhered to.

Section 36 requires that, with the exception of the granting of a short lease (seven years or less), before any agreement is entered into for the sale, lease or disposal of the land, the charity's trustees must:

(a)   obtain an independent qualified surveyor's report;

(b)   advertise the property in accordance with that surveyor's recommendations; and

(c)   satisfy themselves that the proposed disposition is the best that can be achieved.

The surveyor who is instructed must be qualified in the sense that he should be either a Fellow or a professional associate of the Royal Institute of Chartered Surveyors, or of the Incorporated Society of Valuers and Auctioneers. However, these qualifications are not, in themselves, sufficient for the purposes of the Act. The charity trustees must reasonably believe that the individual concerned has ability in, and experience of, the valuation of land of the particular kind and in the particular area in question. The surveyor must also be seen to be acting for the charities alone – and not for any other party or vested interest.

Even in cases where the property is not, strictly speaking, charity land (e.g. where the executors are selling on their own account), the executor will often be asked to obtain at least two formal valuations from qualified local valuers. This ensures that any subsequent transaction can clearly be seen to have been made at arms length.

Probate fraud

9.12   Because most estates are dealt with by professional estate administrators, it is tempting to believe that the funds are in safe hands and that the proper amount will, in due course, be paid over in full to those who are entitled to receive it. Would that it were so. Unfortunately, it is impossible nowadays to write a chapter of this nature without making at least passing reference to the highly unpalatable subject of probate fraud, not least because it explains in part why charity legacy officers have to be quite so diligent in their approach. Whilst the vast majority of professional executors are entirely honourable and trustworthy, it has been an uncomfortable recent discovery that there are some individuals who do abuse the system for their own personal gain.

Although, numerically, these cases are relatively rare, the amounts concerned do make them disproportionately important. For instance, one charity alone has been involved with four cases in the last two years, where total sums in excess of £385,000 were stolen by various professional executors. By any stretch of the imagination, this is a substantial amount for any charity to lose. It is also, in part, why charities have to be so thorough in their checking of details as regards bequests that are left to them.

Nor is it necessarily a problem that is limited purely to charitable bequests. The cases of fraud that have so far been uncovered all involved very substantial sums and, for this reason alone, it is almost impossible to believe that they were the first attempt at fraud on the part of the individual concerned. By the time the crime is discovered, it seems probable that similar activity has been going on for years – if not decades. Although the nature of the relationship between a charity and its benefactors means that charities are more vulnerable to probate fraud than private individuals, this does not mean that family members are necessarily immune. The fraudster will almost certainly have 'practised' on some non-charitable estates. Indeed, charitable legacies as a whole account for only around 4% of the total value passing under wills every year, so any fraudster who limits him- or herself to only attacking charitable estates is passing up some very substantial opportunities.

Case study

A couple of years ago, a legacy manager took a telephone call from a lady who shared in the benefit from a particular estate. The conversation began along the lines of 'Mr X, I might be wasting your time with this and, if so, I apologise . . . but I just don't like this man'. She was talking about the solicitor-executor of her friend's estate. As the conversation developed, and the lady started referring to specific items within the estate accounts (which had just been delivered to the beneficiaries seeking their final approval), the legacy manager became more and more uneasy. It soon became apparent that the version of the accounts which had been provided to the charities was very different to the one that had been provided to the private individual. In fact, a comparison of the two revealed a discrepancy in excess of £60,000 – which was the amount by which the solicitor had enriched himself at the expense of the estate.

(The private beneficiary, of course, had known the deceased very well over a number of years and would thus have been able to spot any unusual 'liabilities'. Her version of the accounts was therefore, of necessity, relatively accurate. The charities, though, did not have such knowledge of their benefactor's financial circumstances and it was this area of ignorance that had been exploited.)

In fact, there can be few areas of the law quite so open to fraud as the probate sector. The difficulty for the legacy officer, of course, is to identify such cases – and enquire into them properly – without unintentionally offending the innocent. However, until such time as more effective institutional safeguards can be developed (perhaps along the same lines as those presently in use under Scottish law) the current, highly unsatisfactory, situation will continue. In the meantime, it can only be hoped that increased public awareness of the fact that charities *are* the victims of such professional fraud will result in a greater overall understanding of the need for a legacy officer to ask (what may at times seem to be intrusive) questions.

The Institute of Legacy Management (ILM)

9.13   ILM was formed three years ago with three fundamental aims:

1.   to raise awareness of and appreciation for the charity legacy officer's role;

2.   to provide job-specific training, tailored to the needs of individuals working in the sector; and

3.   to provide opportunities for liaison, both amongst members and with other professional bodies in the interests of establishing best practice.

ILM now has a membership of nearly 300 individuals, representing some 150 voluntary organisations, with total combined incomes in excess of £1bn. Although predominantly aimed at those people who are employed in administering legacies from within the not-for-profit sector, ILM also provides help and assistance to both professional and lay executors. A distance-learning Certificate of Competence course (produced in association with the College of Law) is available. They also have a website which provides advice and general assistance (including downloadable model forms) for legacy officers, fellow professionals and members of the public, at http://ilmnet.org

Further details about ILM, and membership application forms, can be obtained from The Administration Office, ILM, c/o Legacy Department, RNIB Peterborough, PO Box 173, Bakewell Road, Peterborough, Cambs. PE2 6WS.

Chapter 10

Legacies to unincorporated associations

10.1   Trust and estate practitioners (amongst whom are to be included judges) can take little, if no, credit for the state of our law relating to testamentary gifts to unincorporated associations. It is sad that in too many cases the complexity of the law contrives to defeat the simple objectives of the testator. Testators who wish to benefit organisations which may have given them pleasure in their lifetime – the classic gift to the tennis club or bowling club; or to assist groups who carry out worthy activities – for instance, benefiting the disadvantaged; or simply to do no more than make a farewell gift to an organisation with whom they have a nostalgic relationship – for example, Old Boys or Old Girls associations: all of these testators, acting from the highest of motives, find themselves looking down from on high at an unholy jumble of conflicting legal principles.

Testamentary gifts to unincorporated associations bring out the worst in the English legal system. There is a clash of legal concepts, leading to conflicts difficult to resolve in an obviously intelligent way and jurisprudential gymnastics are required to produce a result which Joe Public would have regarded as self-evident and obvious. To the trust and estate practitioner, and hence to the charity legacy officer, such gifts often raise difficult problems of principle and practice both as to the initial validity of the gift and as to the destination of funds of such associations on their dissolution. It is sufficient for us to confine ourselves to the former set of problems.

The classes of legal concepts involved in these problems include the perpetuity rules, issues of certainty of the bequest, the philosophical issue of when a trust is a purpose trust and when it is a people trust; and, if this were not enough with which to be coping, the law of unincorporated associations impinges at all times. These concepts run up against each other, collide and splinter into problems that medieval scholars would put into the same category as the number of angels capable of dancing on the point of a pin.

Finally, there is the problem of drafting. Most of the unnecessarily complex issues can be resolved by good drafting, but this area of the law is permanently bedevilled with bad drafting. If the drafting itself is not bad it is often inaccurate, possibly because those taking instructions did not appreciate the problems with which they were faced and possibly because the draftsman felt that he could easily assume (a fatal word in drafting as elsewhere) that what the client wanted was self evident on its face. Small errors lead to large problems. Too often we find ourselves trying to determine the intentions of someone now deceased based on inexact wording and a lack of written evidence as to what was the precise intention.

With these problems at the back of our minds let us turn to the so-called principles which govern this area of our law. Though 40 years old the issues involved were clearly summarised by Cross J in *Neville Estates Ltd v Madden [1962] Ch 832.* There are four possible ways in which a gift to an unincorporated association may be construed:

1. A gift to all the members of the association at the date of the gift (in testamentary terms the date of death) beneficially as joint tenants or, if words of severance are used, as tenants in common, and so that any joint tenant could sever his share and claim it whether or not he continued to be a member of the association.

2. A gift to members of the association at the date of the gift beneficially but as an accretion to the funds of the association. In this case the gift is not taken by the members as joint tenants but rather is held subject to their contractual rights and liabilities towards one another as members of the association. Here the member may not sever his share and take it for himself, but rather his share accrues to the other members of the association on his resignation or death even though the members of the association at that future time include persons who have become members of the association after the date of death of the original testator. If this is the effect of the gift in law then it will not be open to legal objection on the grounds of perpetuity or uncertainty unless there is something in its terms or circumstances or in the rules of the association which precludes the members at any given time from dividing the subject of the gift between themselves on the footing that they are solely entitled to it in equity. In other words the gift is to the association, and therefore to the members of it from time to time, but the rules of the association may permit the association to be wound-up and its funds distributed in specie or in cash to the members at the date of such winding-up. The testator may have had no such intention of benefiting the members in this way but this risk is implicit within any gift to any unincorporated association which, subject to its own rules, can be dissolved.

3. A gift to be held by the members of the association in trust or applied for the purposes of the association as a quasi-corporate entity. So if, unlike the gift described in the preceding paragraph, the terms of the gift or the rules of the association show that the property in question is not to be held at the disposal of the members for the time being but is to be held in trust for or applied for the purposes of the association as a quasi-corporate entity then the gift will fail under the rule against perpetuities or under the beneficiary principle or for uncertainty or any one or more of those three reasons unless the association is itself a charitable body. Thus gifts construed as trust gifts are the most likely to fail because the testator (and very often his advisor) will not have thought that what appears to be a simple gift (albeit in trust) to a benevolent body turns out to have perpetuity problems, beneficiary/purpose overtones or may simply not be worded with sufficient certainty.

4. In contrast to all of these problems a simple gift, without further instructions, to an unincorporated association which is a charitable body or a gift

on charitable purpose trusts to an unincorporated association will be valid as a charitable gift provided the trust is for the public benefit.

With these possibilities in mind let us look at some of the problems that have come before the courts. The following is no more than the author's subjective selection of relevant decided authorities and provides no more than a thumbnail sketch of the problems in each case.

Leahy v AG for New South Wales [1959] AC 457: A property was left 'upon trust for such order of nuns of the Catholic Church or the Christian Brothers as my executors shall select'. The property in question was a farm of 730 acres and a furnished homestead. The residue of the estate was bequeathed to the executors:

> 'upon trust to use the income as well as the capital . . . in the provision of amenities in such convents as my executors . . . shall select either by way of building a new convent . . . or the alteration of . . . existing building occupied as a convent or in the provision of furnishing . . . and I declare that my said executors . . . shall have the sole and absolute discretion of deciding where any such premises shall be built or altered . . . and the orders of nuns who shall benefit . . . the receipt of the Reverend Mother . . . shall be of sufficient discharge . . .'.

Inter alia, it was held that the bequest showed an intention to create a trust, not merely for the benefit of the existing members of the selected order but also for the benefit of the order as a continuing society and therefore, if the selected order were a non-charitable body, the bequest would fail as the trust infringed the rule against perpetuities.

Re Denley's Trust Deed [1969] 1 Ch 373: Land was conveyed to trustees upon trust that it was to be maintained and used for the purpose of a recreational sports ground primarily for the benefit of 'the employees of the company' and secondarily for the benefit of 'such other person or persons (if any) as the trustees may allow to use the same' . . .if at any time the number of employees subscribing should be 'less than 75% of the total number of employees at any given time' or if the land should at any time cease to be required or to be used by the employees as a sports ground it was to be conveyed to the general hospital at Cheltenham. The issue was whether the trust of the sports ground and the gift over were valid. It was held that the gifts were valid because where a trust, though expressed to be a trust for a purpose that was not in law a charitable purpose, was directly or indirectly for the benefit of individuals it was not invalid because of the absence of a beneficiary. *Re Astor's Settlement Trusts [1952] Ch 534* was distinguished. Goff J went on to hold that the employees of the company, being the beneficiaries, were sufficiently ascertainable so the trust was not invalid for uncertainty and, although there were words including in the class 'such other persons as the trustees might allow', these words created a power which was valid and it was not requisite to the validity of the power that all possible objects should be ascertainable. The trust was one that the court could control sufficiently by restraining any improper use of the land or by ordering the trustees to allow employees to use the land as a recreation ground.

Further, the concept of employees subscribing at a given rate was sufficiently certain to have the consequence that the gift over was not invalid.

Re Lipinski's Will Trusts [1976] Ch 235: This case related to a cricket and social club where the testator directed his residuary estate to be held on trust for the club in memory of his late wife, the funds to be used 'solely in the work of constructing the new buildings for the association and/or improvements to the said buildings'. At the date of his death the association occupied rented accommodation. Its membership numbered 41 at the date of the will and 26 at the date of death; there were patrons, numbering 20 and 12 at the relevant dates, who paid an annual subscription but were not members. The association never formally adopted a constitution but a document headed 'Proposed Constitution' was used. The document provided that the members could alter the constitution to provide for the division of the assets of the association amongst themselves. The objects according to the Proposed Constitution were to provide facilities for recreation subject to the Recreational Charities Act 1958 and to promote the education of and public advancement of religion amongst youth in the UK. The Judge held that despite the addition of some charitable objects the association was essentially a sports club for the benefit of its members. There was no evidence that, at the date of the death of the testator, the association had modified its constitution by restricting its objects to ones that were exclusively charitable. He went on to hold that a non-charitable purpose trust which was directly or indirectly for the benefit of ascertained individuals, particularly where they had the power to make the capital their own, was not unenforceable (the double negative means that the trust was enforceable). The gift to the association was for a purpose which was within the association's powers; the members of the association were both the trustees and the beneficiaries and thus able to vest the capital in themselves. Thus there was no question that the gift failed for perpetuity. Accordingly the proper construction of the gift was one of an absolute gift to the members of the association for the time being who were entitled to enforce the purpose or to vary it and so it was a valid gift.

The facts of *Neville Estates Ltd v Madden [1962] Ch 832* itself were as follows. The Trustees of the Catford Synagogue entered into a contract to purchase two pieces of vacant land adjoining the synagogue. The contract was subject to the consent of the Charity Commission 'so far as the same is required'. The Charity Commissioners refused consent but the trustees of the synagogue claimed such consent was not needed because the land was not held on charitable trusts and, if it were so held, it was exempt under the Charitable Trusts Act 1853, s 62. The Catford Synagogue was affiliated to the United Synagogues of the United Kingdom which had power to assist in founding places of worship for persons of Jewish religion who conformed to its rituals. The synagogue itself was an unincorporated association and its members were persons who were in occupation of seats at the synagogue and who paid a subscription. An appeal fund had been set up in 1941 to purchase a house which was thereafter used as a synagogue and the house was conveyed to trustees for sale on trust to hold the proceeds as 'the property of the members of the synagogue'. The building appeal fund moneys were kept in a separate bank account from the main account of the synagogue. In 1953, three adjoining plots of land had been acquired to be held on trusts under Settled Land Act 1925, s 29. The Court held that the moneys used for the purchase of the land in 1953, and the land bought with those moneys, were held on trust for the benefit of the members of the synagogue, from time to time and without limit of time, and the trust would accordingly fail unless the purposes for which the land was held were charitable purposes; the land purchased in 1953 was held for religious purposes notwithstanding the social activities carried on by members of the synagogue as part of its activities; the trust was for the benefit of the members of a private unincorporated association and the religious purposes had the requisite element of benefit to the public since members of the synagogue mixed with their fellow men and did not live secluded from the world – the trust was held to be charitable.

If it were thought that gifts to unincorporated associations which existed at the date of death of the testator were complicated how does English law deal with gifts to unincorporated associations which are either misdescribed in the will or did exist at the date of the will but ceased to exist at the date of death having been amalgamated with other like-minded associations in the intervening period? In this context does it matter that the testator knew the association in question had been dissolved and chose not to alter his will? Additionally what happens if the testator described the recipient of his bounty as a charity but it transpires that it was not a charitable body at all?

Let us begin with the case of *Re Recher's Will Trusts [1972] Ch 526*. There was a testamentary gift of residue to 'the Anti-Vivisection Society'. Before the date of the will there was in existence an unincorporated non-charitable association called 'The London & Provincial Anti-Vivisection Society'. This body had subsequently amalgamated with another unincorporated non-charitable organisation called 'The National Anti-Vivisection Society'. At a later date still the assets and activities of the amalgamated society were taken over by the 'Anti-Vivisection Company'. The court held that, if the London & Provincial Society had continued its separate existence, the legacy to it would have been a valid legacy to the members beneficially by way of accretion to the funds of the society subject to the contract that the members had been themselves as set out in the rules of the society. However, since before the date of the will The London & Provincial Society had been dissolved, and the contract binding the members together under its name and by its rules had been terminated, the gift to that society could not be construed as a gift to the members of the national society as an accretion to its funds subject to a different contract. So, the anti-vivisection company as assignee (of the assets of the amalgamated society) could not take the gift.

Re Finger's Will Trusts [1972] Ch 286: There was a gift to the National Radium Commission, an unincorporated charity, for the work of the Commission. This was clearly a purpose trust which did not fail as there was no indication in the will to make the existence of that body the essence of the gift. The National Radium Commission had been dissolved and its work carried on by the Secretary of State for Social Services. The gift was held valid in favour of the Secretary of State.

Now, by way of contrast, diversion and relief see what happens if a testamentary gift is made to an incorporated body. This is principle five. Take the case of *Re*

Vernon's Will Trusts [1971] 3 All ER 1061n. There, a share of residue was bequeathed to 'The Coventry Crippled Children's Guild'. The Guild was a corporate body with provisions similar to those contained in the Memorandum of Association of a Company Limited by Guarantee. The will in question was made before the National Health Service was brought into being on 5 July 1948 and at that date the Guild and its property vested in the Minister of Health. The activities of the Guild, via a hospital and the treatment of patients, continued under another name until the Guild was dissolved eight years before the testatrix died. A new unincorporated body was formed called 'Coventry and District Cripples' Guild'. The judge held that a bequest to a corporate body takes effect as a gift to that body beneficially unless there are circumstances to show that the recipient is to take the gift as trustee. There is no need in such a case to infer a trust for any particular purpose. The objects to which the corporate body can properly apply its funds may be restricted by its constitution but this does not necessitate inferring, as a matter of construction of the testator's will, a direction that the bequest is to be held in trust to be applied for those purposes. The natural construction is that that bequest is made to the corporate body as part of its general funds beneficially without the imposition of any trust. Had the incorporated Guild been other than a charitable body the bequest would have lapsed in this case on account of its dissolution before the death of the testatrix. The guild was however incorporated for exclusively charitable purposes and, thus, the court would not allow a charitable purpose to fail.

My colleague, Christopher J G Parker, wrote an excellent article on this whole topic in *Trust & Estates Law Journal*, March 1999 at p 202. With his kind permission I set out below the example that he gave of the problem and the issues involved in it. So suppose:

'By his will dated 3 September 1995, Y gave his entire residuary estate upon trust either to retain or sell it, and on trust to pay his debts, testamentary expenses and all taxes and duties, and to divide the net residue as to one-third to his favourite niece and as to two-thirds equally among eight named objects, which he described as charities, for their general purposes.

The testator died two years afterwards without changing his will, and the question which has arisen concerns one of the eight charitable beneficiaries, described in the will as "Charter House of Mons Gratia, near Stamfordham, North Coquetshire".

According to correspondence received by the personal representatives, it seems that Charter House is not a charity at all, but the name of a building at a particular location. However, it is claimed to be a building used by an institution known as Rural Care for the purposes of various "community services".

Rural Care is a company limited by guarantee and a registered charity whose objects are to provide a number of services beneficial to the local community. Apart from Charter House, there are a number of properties owned, leased or occupied by Rural Care in North Coquetshire, some providing sheltered, nursing and residential care homes, others providing community services such as retirement clubs, dance classes, music evenings, lunchtime gatherings and so on. There are also other services such as home care and visiting services.

The obvious difficulty is to ascertain what the testator intended when he used the words "Charter House" in his will, it being established that there was no material change in the status or use of the building between the date when the will was made and the date of death (for which relief much thanks). The normal approach is to establish whether the gift is to an institution or for a purpose. Here, it is unlikely to be construed as the former, as otherwise the testator would have, or perhaps should have, described it as "Rural Care" instead of "Charter House", and in that event the next question would be whether the gift should be taken beneficially by Rural Care, being a corporate body, or held by it in a fiduciary capacity.

However, given that it is highly unlikely that the gift should be construed as a gift to an institution, and in the absence of an identifiable beneficiary having legal personality, it is likely that the gift would be construed as a gift upon trust for the purposes, for which Charter House existed or was used, at the time the testator made his will. The obvious difficulty is knowing precisely what those purposes were, and whether they were capable of being performed at the date of the will, or are capable of being performed at the date the testator's death. For this purpose, any extraneous evidence which might shed light on exactly what the testator had in mind should be considered.

The first source of information will be the will file of the drafting solicitors, if it still exists (as it should, given the short lapse of time). Failing that, or in addition to such evidence, statements might be sought from relevant living persons who knew the testator well, and might be able to indicate what was so attractive to him about Charter House. Similar evidence might be forthcoming from members of staff at Charter House who might have remembered the testator and noted his interest.

Even if it can be established which purposes the testator had in mind when he named Charter House in his will, there then follows a subsidiary question: whether those purposes are or were wholly and exclusively charitable, or non-charitable, or possibly partly charitable and partly non-charitable. If the last alternative applies, then it will be necessary to consider whether the main purpose was charitable, with the non-charitable elements merely incidental to that main purpose, or whether the opposite was true. If it were the former, then the gift would most likely be treated as a valid charitable trust – if the latter, then as an invalid purpose trust. As is well known, non-charitable purpose trusts are generally either void or unenforceable, so, if that were the case here, then the likely result would be failure and lapse. In the context of this will, subject to the evidence, this is unlikely.

If the purposes which the testator had in mind, assuming that they can be ascertained, are wholly and exclusively charitable, then the next question will be whether those purposes are still capable of performance. If so, it must then be decided whether an application should be made to the Charity Commissioners, to establish a scheme facilitating the administration of the gift towards the achievement of those purposes, or whether payment should be made to Rural Care upon trust to apply for those purposes carried out at Charter House – purposes which were carried out at the time the testator made his will.

In the event that the purposes of Charter House are charitable but cannot be carried out or performed, the question would then arise as to whether the gift lapsed and passed on a partial intestacy, or whether there was a paramount charitable intention which permitted the gift to be applied cy-près. (For a thorough examination of the relevant cases, most of them dealing with "homes" and the various consequences, see Megarry V-C's judgment in *Re Spence's Will Trust [1979] Ch 483*).'

In spite of the problems as set out in this chapter and with which executors are faced they may well feel that they knew, at least in general terms, what it was that the testator wanted. Lay executors will often put down the problems to 'lawyers being difficult – again'. They will be happy to pay over the legacy to the body in question, sometimes irrespective of the niceties of the rules of perpetuity, the beneficiary principle and the concept of uncertainty. Happy that is until a lawyer reminds them that they will be personally responsible if they pay the wrong legatee. At that point the word 'indemnity' will spring to the collective mind of the executors. Now legacy officers of charities find themselves involved directly in the issues rather than reading about them with detached amusement or concern. The conversation is quite simple: Executors – We want to pay you, the unincorporated association, the legacy that we think the testator intended you to have – but our lawyers tell us that there is doubt about its validity – we have better things to do than spend the testator's money having the gift construed by the High Court – our lawyers have warned us that we are personally liable if we pay moneys to you incorrectly – but we will pay you subject to your giving us a full indemnity. Legacy officer – take centre stage in this discussion of the validity of gifts to unincorporated associations. Will you give an indemnity? How do you respond?

Chapter 11

Secret and half secret trusts

Introduction

11.1   The subject of secret and half secret trusts is relevant to a study of legacies because a legacy in a will is, in the majority of cases, the way in which the secret or half secret trust is completed, by the property that is to be the subject of the trust being transferred to the trustee. Secret and half secret trusts can be created other than by will, but they are most commonly to be found in wills.

Both these types of trust at first glance appear to be inconsistent with section 9 Wills Act 1837, because the devolution of the property after death is not by testamentary instrument. But a true analysis of these trusts is that the trust created is outside of the will and is not subject to that Act, apart from the requirement that if a will is to be used to complete the trust, then the will itself only must conform to the 1837 Act (*Blackwell v Blackwell [1929] AC 318*). If it does not, then the transfer of the intended trust property to the trustee that the will attempts to make fails. It has been found that if the will is witnessed by the beneficiary of the secret trust the gift in the will is good, as the witness is not a beneficiary under the will and section 15 Wills Act 1837 is not an issue (*Re Young [1951] Ch 344*, not following the earlier *Re Fleetwood (1880) 15 Ch D 594*, but interestingly there is no decision on the secret trust trustee/legatee witnessing a will.)

Secret and half secret trusts are traditionally used where the testator/settlor is eager to hide the identity of the trust beneficiaries and the terms of their entitlement from the public scrutiny that would follow the will being admitted to probate (e.g. *Blackwell v Blackwell [1929] AC 318* where the £12,000 legacy was to be used to maintain the testator's mistress and illegitimate son). It is therefore not surprising that many of the decided cases on these issues date from earlier times when such proprieties were considered to be more important than perhaps they are today. Secret and half secret trusts cannot be used as a vehicle to create an illegal trust, for in such circumstances the trustee/legatee would hold the gift on resulting trusts for the estate (*Moss v Cooper (1861) 1 John & H 352*).

If there are circumstances today when secret or half secret trusts are appropriate, it is recommended that, to remove the potential for unwanted and uncertain litigation, the terms of the trust are clearly evidenced, preferably in writing, at the time of the communication of the trust to the trustee – as should be his acceptance of them. Similarly, it is recommended that the uncertainties surrounding communication, especially of half secret trusts, are noted and avoided by clear communication prior to the will being executed.

Modern practice, particularly where the will is professionally drawn, is for the evidence of communication and acceptance and the terms of the trust to be put into a declaration of trust executed by the legatee/trustee shortly prior to the execution of the will and referring to the will about to be executed.

Secret trusts

11.2   For a secret trust to arise, the legacy must be an absolute gift to the legatee with no restriction or qualification being apparent on the face of the will. The terms of the trust are not contained in the will and the gift by the will is merely the method used to complete the constitution of the trust by conveying the trust property to the trustee. The terms of the trust will have been notified to the trustee either before or after the execution of the will (*Moss v Cooper (1861) 1 John & H 352 at 367*) but before the death of the testator. If the terms of the intended trust come to the notice of the legatee/trustee only after the testator's death, there has been no valid communication and acceptance of the trust and he is entitled to keep the legacy for himself (*Wallgrave v Tebbs (1855) 2 K & J 313*), there being nothing on the face of the will to indicate otherwise. It is possible that the legatee is aware that he is to hold as trustee, but that the terms of the trust were not communicated to him until after the testator's death. In these circumstances, the legatee will hold the legacy upon resulting trusts for the residuary estate, but if the subject of the trust was the residue of the estate then the legatee holds upon trust for those entitled upon intestacy (*Drakeford v Wilks (1747) 3 Atk 539*; *Re Pugh's Will Trusts [1967] 1 WLR 1262*; *Re Boyes (1884) 26 Ch D 531*).

If after performance of the secret trust there are funds unapplied, the trustee is entitled to retain them for his own benefit (*Irvine v Sullivan (1869) LR 8 Eq 673*).

The terms of the trust must be sufficiently definite to meet the usual requirements of certainty in a trust (*Knight v Knight (1840) 3 Beav 148*; for the application of those principles to a secret trust claim see *Kasperbauer v Griffith [2000] 1 WTLR 333*) and where there is a challenge, their existence is to be proved to the ordinary standard of proof in civil cases (*Re Snowden [1979] Ch 528*, which did not follow *Ottaway v Norman [1972] Ch 698* which suggested that the higher standard of proof attached to rectification should be applied) with the burden of proof being on those who seek to establish the trust (*Jones v Badley (1868) 3 Ch App 362*).

The death of the trustee/legatee prior to the death of the testator will defeat the trust as the failure of the legacy will leave the trust incompletely constituted (*Re Maddock [1902] 2 Ch 220*). The prior death of the object of the trust (the secret beneficiary) has been held not to defeat the trust, but this decision is widely regarded as eccentric and in all probability wrong in law (*Re Gardner (No 2) [1923] 2 Ch 230*). Although not free from doubt, the better view is that the death of the beneficiary will defeat the trust and the trustee/legatee will hold the property upon a resulting trust for the estate.

Half secret trusts

11.3   In appearance half secret trusts vary from secret trusts only in that there is some reference to the trust's existence on the face of the will, e.g. 'to A upon the trusts that I have already communicated to him'. As for a secret trust, the half secret trust by will does not reveal the identity of the beneficiaries or the terms of the trust, but it does reveal the trust's existence and, if the terms of the trust fail, this will prevent the legatee from taking absolutely.

Unlike a fully secret trust, it is doubtful whether there can be effective communication and acceptance of the trust after the date of the will, but the position is yet to be clearly resolved by the courts and should be approached with caution (see *Snell's Equity* (30th edition Sweet & Maxwell) at 7-22). The communication must, however, conform to the words of the will and thus 'which I have communicated to him' appearing in the will would prevent later communication being effective (*Johnson v Ball (1851) 5 De G & Sm 85*; *Re Bateman's Will Trusts [1970] 3 All ER 817*). This is on the basis that the court will not accept evidence that contradicts the terms of the will. Communication need not be any more explicit than handing an envelope to the trustee/legatee containing the terms of the trust (*Re Keen [1937] Ch 236*).

Two or more trustees/legatees

11.4   Concern by testators at the potential for fraud with secret and half secret trusts often leads them to conclude that such trusts are better created using more than one trustee. Regrettably the law on communication and acceptance by either or both trustees is neither clear nor logical.

Where there is a gift to trustees as tenants-in-common, only those trustees with whom there is the requisite communication and acceptance are bound by the trust and the others take their shares beneficially (*Tee v Ferris (1856) 2 K & J 357*; *Re Stead [1900] 1 Ch 237*).

Where the gift is to trustees as joint tenants, where there has been communication and acceptance with at least one of the trustees prior to the will then all are bound by it (*Russell v Jackson (1852) 10 Hare 204*; *Re Stead [1900] 1 Ch 237*); but where communication and acceptance are after the will, only those who have accepted the trust are bound by it (*Moss v Cooper (1861) 1 John & H 352*; *Re Stead [1900] 1 Ch 237*).

Half secret trusts should not be confused with the fairly common legacy where the testator bequeaths property to the legatee with a hope or wish expressed in the will that the legatee will apply or dispose of the property in a particular way (often in accordance with any letter that might be found after death). Such terms will not create a half secret trust and the legatee's compliance with the testator's wishes is optional. The legatee will take the gift absolutely and any gifts that he chooses to make to meet the testator's wishes are voluntary gifts of his own, not gifts of the testator under his will. However, if the gifts are of value the legatee may seek to give effect to them by deed of variation to the testator's will (made within two years of the testator's death), thus removing some of the potentially adverse taxation consequences for himself of making the gifts.

Chapter 12

Appropriation and payment

Appropriation of assets in satisfaction of legacies

Section 41 Administration of Estates Act 1925

12.1   Section 41 Administration of Estates Act 1925 provides the executors or administrators of both testate and intestate estates with the power to appropriate any assets of the estate in satisfaction of any beneficial interest in the estate. The appropriation under this power has the following features.

- It must not prejudice any specific devise or bequest of the property (although it will be possible for the devisee to give their consent).

- It should be made with the consent of the legatee who is to receive the property absolutely or, if the appropriation is in satisfaction of a settled interest, the consent of the trustee; but if the trustee is the personal representative then the consent of the person entitled to the interest in income from the settled legacy is needed.

- If the person whose consent is required is a minor or an adult incapable of managing his affairs, the personal representative should seek the consent of the parent, guardian, enduring attorney or receiver as is appropriate.

- Consent is not required if the beneficiary is not yet born or, being born, cannot be found.

- The personal representative shall determine the value of the appropriated property by using a qualified valuer when the nature of the property to be appropriated requires it.

- The personal representative, when using this power, must have regard to the rights of any other person, born or unborn, whose consent is not required.

- This power is in addition to any express powers to be found in the will.

Section 41 does not specify the form in which the consent to appropriation should be given, but good practice is to obtain consents in writing whether the consent is required under section 41 or under an express power of appropriation.

Once carried out, the appropriation is conclusive to discharge the liability of the personal representative. Subsequent appreciation or depreciation in the value of the asset appropriated is for the advantage/loss of the beneficiary alone.

Express powers of appropriation

12.2   These are commonly used in modern wills. They often remove the need for consents to appropriation and also extend the power so that it may also apply to trusts after the administration period of the estate has been completed. The statutory power is not available to a trustee.

Valuation

12.3   Unless the asset is one specifically bequeathed, the personal representative should revalue the asset being appropriated as at the date of its appropriation (*Re Charteris [1917] 2 Ch 379; Re Collins, Robinson v Collins [1975] 1 All ER 321*). Probate value is not the correct value to use, but it might conveniently be used to avoid the expense of a revaluation where the valuation has no consequence for the different interests affected, for example where:

(a)   assets are being appropriated to a sole residuary legatee; or

(b)   assets are being appropriated in equal shares to all the residuary legatees.

There is no judicial authority for not revaluing in such examples, but it is common practice and of no financial consequence. However, care should be taken with intestacies where it is thought that the estate is sufficiently small to pass entirely as part of the spouse's statutory legacy. Accurate values become important in case post-death appreciation increases the value above the statutory legacy limit and the administrator is then faced with considering the interests of those others entitled to part of residue under the intestacy. A similar point will arise when dealing with appropriations in estates where there is abatement.

Some modern precedents for wills contain express powers of appropriation that permit the appropriation, often to nil rate band trusts, to be made at values that may be less than market value at the time of appropriation. Other powers permit the executor to choose the value at which the appropriation is made. This approach is fairly recent and, in the author's opinion, is flawed. The views of the Revenue on these precedents are not known, but it is believed that the value at the date of appropriation is one of fact and if a value of less than market value is used, the true value of the property appropriated will always be the value for tax purposes. Thus if a nil rate band legacy is apparently satisfied by appropriating shares at probate value (which for example is half the value at the date of appropriation) the nil rate band legacy fund will have a true value of twice the nil rate band with the consequence that it will become taxable.

Section 41 requires the use of a qualified valuer where the nature of the asset makes it appropriate. Although most express powers do not contain similar requirements, appropriation – without being able to show an acceptable basis for valuation – would in all probability breach the personal representatives' common law duty of care to the beneficiaries and be in breach of trust if a loss to the estate or other beneficiaries occurred. If the beneficiary who took such an appropriation was aware that the absence of an accurate valuation worked to his advantage, he would also become liable to make good the breach (*Re Lepine, Dowsett v Culver [1892] 1 Ch 210*).

Where assets are being appropriated by a personal representative in satisfaction of his own interest as a beneficiary in the estate, self-dealing questions arise (*Kane v Radley-Kane [1999] Ch 274*). If the personal representative wishes to take the asset himself, agreement to the act of appropriation and to the valuation used, with all the interests affected by the appropriation, will be necessary. This is because the transaction places the personal representative in a position of conflict between his personal interests and his duty towards the other beneficiaries of the estate. Without the agreement of those also interested, the personal representative must satisfy his beneficial interest by the appropriation of cash or assets which have an open and independently verifiable value such as quoted stocks and shares.

Evidence of valuation

12.4   The appropriation of assets does not generally require any particular formalities. However, best practice will be to record the decision (and the date of appropriation) in a suitable resolution of the personal representatives. A written resolution is not essential if there is enough evidence with the estate file to substantiate the appropriation, its value and the date.

The appropriation should always be recorded in the estate's books of account showing the value at appropriation and the date. Apart from the need for the estate accounts to recognise the reality of the estate transactions, the evidence of the transaction within the estate accounts is important if the Inland Revenue require evidence of the appropriation in order to accept that subsequent dealings in the appropriated asset are on behalf of the beneficiary and not the estate.

In addition to the act of appropriation the personal representative also has to transfer the title in the appropriate asset to the beneficiary. This is an act subsequent to the appropriation. The method of transfer will be what is required for any particular asset. However, where the interest is one in real property, the personal representative will need to consider the necessity of vesting the legal title in the beneficiary as soon as possible, as Revenue practice is not to accept an interest in land as being appropriated without the change of title insofar as the appropriation affects taxation issues. Therefore, in order to maintain that a sale of the land subsequent to the appropriation is on behalf of the beneficiary and not the estate, the legal title must have been transferred out of the name of the personal representative. This can be particularly important where a transaction is intended in respect of which the gains expected to arise must be on behalf of the individual beneficiaries and not the estate. If it is not suitable at the time to vest the legal title to land in the beneficiaries to which it has been appropriated, the personal representative may, for example, transfer the legal tile to a nominee (perhaps himself) to be held under a declaration of trust for the beneficiaries.

Effect of appropriation

12.5   Once property has been appropriated the personal representative ceases to hold the asset in the capacity of a personal representative. If the asset is not immediately transferred to the beneficiary (or trustee, if the legacy is settled) the personal representative holds the appropriated asset as trustee for the beneficiary and not as an asset of the estate. This means that personal representatives need to be aware of the consequences of the act of appropriation and should not undertake it without satisfying themselves that the reserves held for estate liabilities are sufficient. The assets appropriated are not then available to meet the general liabilities and expenses of the estate. (The recovery of sums distributed in error by a personal representative is possible (see *Ministry of Health v Simpson [1951] AC 251* and *Kleinwort Benson v Lincoln City Council [1999] 2 AC 349*), but this process is outside the scope of this book and is by no means an easy or ready remedy for the personal representative who appropriated too much or too hastily.)

Minors' legacies

12.6   Before section 41, a personal representative could not appropriate assets to satisfy an immediate vested legacy to a minor, but section 41 now permits him to do so with the requisite consents (s 41(1)(ii)). Usefully, section 42 Administration of Estates Act 1925 also gives power to a personal representative to appoint trustees (two or more individuals or a trust corporation) of such legacies, but this section only permits this in respect of vested legacies.

Care is needed for minors' legacies which do not carry intermediate income. Not only can the power under section 42 not be used to appoint trustees, but also it is in practice difficult to segregate these from the residue of the estate by appropriation (*Re Hall [1903] 2 Ch 226*), given that the intermediate income belongs to others and that the remainder of the estate is still charged with the payment of the sum on the contingency being met. The minor is not able to agree to a suitable sum being appropriated to secure the legacy, but if he were, then the residue could be exonerated from further liability.

Fairness

12.7   Section 41 requires a personal representative to consider the interests of all present and future beneficiaries when making an appropriation. This can be characterised as a duty to act fairly between all the interests, although acting fairly does not require the personal representative to hold a balance between all of the competing interests when acting fairly (*Re Charteris [1917] 2 Ch 379; Re Hayes [1971] 1 WLR 758*). In *Lloyd's Bank v Duker [1987] 1 WLR 1324* it was necessary to sell a majority shareholding in a hotel company rather than appropriate it. The personal representatives had a 99.9% shareholding in the company which when appropriated would give a 57.44% interest to one beneficiary and leave 42.46% to be divided equally between five other beneficiaries absolutely entitled. After appropriation, the 57.45% holding would have been worth significantly more per share than the other holdings (such being the disparity in values between majority and minority holdings) and for this reason the court ordered an open-market sale (at which any of the beneficiaries could bid) with the proceeds then to be distributed proportionally among the interests.

Intestates' Estates Act 1952

12.8   On intestacy a surviving spouse has a statutory right (Intestates' Estates Act 1952, Sch 2) (should they elect to exercise it within twelve months of the grant of letters of administration), to have the deceased's interest in the matrimonial home appropriated 'in or towards satisfaction of any absolute interest' (Sch 2 para 1(1)) the spouse has in the estate. Although this right is usually considered in the context of the spouse's other rights in the estate, the cash part of the statutory legacy is often an important part of the value of their interest. This schedule gives the spouse a right to require appropriation and this appropriation, unlike other appropriations considered in this section, is not at the discretion of the personal representative.

If the surviving spouse makes this election, the value of the interest in the property is, as usual, to be determined at the date of appropriation, not the date of death (*Re Collins, Robinson v Collins [1975] 1 WLR 309*). If that value exceeds the total value of the spouse's absolute interests in the intestate estate, the spouse can introduce the balance of funds needed from their own resources (*Re Phelps [1980] Ch 275*).

In this Act the matrimonial home is defined as 'a dwelling-house in which the surviving husband or wife was resident at the time of the intestate's death'. It is to be noted that this definition may not necessarily accord with how a matrimonial home is usually defined and indeed may allow an interest in a property which was not the usually accepted matrimonial home to be appropriated. Where the dwelling forms part of a larger building which is owned by the intestate, the spouse's right to elect for appropriation must be approved by application to the court (Sch 2 para 2), as it must where part of the dwelling was used by the intestate for purposes other than domestic.

Time of appropriation

12.9   An executor may appropriate assets at any time after he has proved title to them (i.e. obtained a grant of representation). Appropriation before then is not possible, given that he cannot transfer title to the legatee in the absence of the grant.

In addition, a personal representative is unwise to appropriate assets before such time as his statutory notices (see Trustee Act 1925, s 27) to creditors have expired without claims having been made under them.

These notices should be made as soon as possible after death by an executor or, in the case of an administrator, as soon as possible after the date of the grant. A notice should in all cases be placed in the London Gazette and, where the deceased had an interest in land, in a paper circulating in the district where the land is situated. Each notice must give a clear two months, from the date of publication of the paper in which they appear, in which claims against the estate should be made to the personal representative (or his agent).

In the event of a claim being made distributions will not be made until the claim has been resolved, unless it is for a small amount which does not materially affect the distribution. If no claims are made and the personal representative distributes the assets he is protected against claims made later. Later claimants may follow the assets into the hands of the trustees.

Income considerations

12.10 When an appropriation is made in favour of a beneficiary, that beneficiary will normally become entitled to the interest or income on the assets appropriated with effect from that next paid on the appropriated assets.

Where quoted investments are involved, if they are quoted 'XD' as at the date of appropriation, that first dividend payment will usually be due to the estate, not the beneficiary.

If tenanted property is the subject of the appropriation, and there are arrears of rent outstanding, the right to those arrears is an asset separate to the premises and the personal representative will need to consider if such right should also be appropriated. If the arrears are not appropriated, though, issues may arise as to how the personal representative might recover them once he no longer holds the property title.

Where the appropriation is in satisfaction of a specific gift in the will, the act of appropriation will trigger the doctrine of relation back (*IRC v Hawley [1928] 1 KB 578*). In other words, the effect of the appropriation will be to pass to the beneficiary the income or interest payable on the specifically gifted asset(s) since the date of death. If the asset has been sold by the personal representative without appropriation, the beneficiary will be entitled to the income and/or interest received on the proceeds, in addition to that generated by the asset itself, when those proceeds are appropriated to him.

Taxation comments

Inheritance tax

12.11 Appropriation has no inheritance tax consequences, provided that it is made at current value (*Re Charteris [1917] 2 Ch 379*). As previously identified (see 12.3 above), where appropriation is made at a value to be determined by the executor, and the executor selects a value other than the then current market value, this may result in an element of bounty between the differing interests.

The beneficiary(s) who receives less may be deemed to make a transfer of value for the purposes of inheritance tax, depending upon the particular circumstances that apply.

Where the basis of valuation for appropriation effectively inflates the amount that enters a 'nil rate band' discretionary trust, the Inland Revenue might look to apply the standard principles of valuation and assess tax accordingly, both at the date of death and upon any subsequent occasion of charge (e.g. periodic or exit charge). Should the beneficiary who receives a lesser interest as a result of the basis of valuation selected by the executor also be a beneficiary of such discretionary trust, it might also be arguable that he is a settlor for taxation purposes.

Capital gains tax

12.12   Until such time as an appropriation is made in favour of a beneficiary, the beneficiary has only a chose in action for the due administration of the estate (*Marshall (Inspector of Taxes) v Kerr [1995] 1 AC 148*). That chose in action is equal to the value of the beneficiary's (remaining) interest in the estate at any particular point in time. When the personal representative appropriates any asset(s) to the beneficiary, whether cash or any other form of asset, the value of the chose in action is reduced by the value of the asset appropriated. The chose in action remains as a single, indivisible asset until such time as the beneficiary has received his full entitlement from the estate, at which time it is extinguished.

The appropriation of assets to a beneficiary in satisfaction of his interest in the estate will usually result in his taking those assets at the date of death value, as 'legatee' for capital gains tax purposes under section 62(4) Taxation of Chargeable Gains Act 1992 (TCGA 1992).

Where any asset is disposed of by the personal representative, without it first being appropriated to a beneficiary, the sale will be made by the personal representative in that capacity. If the asset sold is the subject of a specific gift, the doctrine of 'relation back' does not apply for capital gains tax. Accordingly, the disposal will be made by the personal representative, and any gain or loss will accrue to him, and not to the specific legatee or devisee.

There will be occasions where the residuary beneficiary will introduce cash into the estate so as to avoid the need to sell particular assets, with a view to those assets being transferred to him in specie at the end of the administration of the estate. This most frequently occurs where he wants to keep the house, which would otherwise need to be sold to discharge the liabilities of the estate, whether they be outstanding debts, administration expenses, inheritance tax or prior legacies.

Where a beneficiary introduces cash to enable the liabilities of the estate to be discharged and, as a consequence thereof, for land (such as the deceased's house) to be appropriated to him, whilst the transaction is characterised as a sale

(*Passant v Jackson (1986) 59 TC 230*, per Slade LJ at 240G), it would appear to be settled law that the beneficiary will acquire the property as 'legatee' under section 62(4) TCGA 1992 (*Passant v Jackson*). The amount paid into the estate cannot be used to reduce any gain upon the eventual sale of the property, although it is treated as 'consideration' for stamp duty purposes (*Passant v Jackson*), so that ad valorem duty is payable upon the transfer of the property to him, calculated by reference to the amount paid into the estate.

Where the beneficiary introduces cash to enable investments to be transferred to him in specie, this is a sale to the beneficiary by the personal representative, to the extent of the moneys paid in. As a sale, the personal representative will be assessable for any gain arising on the disposal, so that they may need to carefully consider which investments will be 'purchased' by the beneficiary. If it is possible to 'cherry pick' the investments to be 'purchased', there might be merit in selecting those which give rise to the least gain within any capital gains tax allowance available to the personal representative (taking account also of any other disposals the personal representative may have made, or might make, during the same tax year). The moneys introduced will be treated as consideration for stamp duty, so that ad valorem duty will be payable on the transfers to the beneficiary, or his nominee.

Income tax

12.13   Where the appropriation is in respect of a specific gift, this will trigger the doctrine of relation back, so that the income or interest payable on the specified asset(s) since the date of death, or interest generated by the proceeds of sale thereof, will belong to the specific beneficiary (*IRC v Hawley [1928] 1 KB 578*). As a result of the 'relation back' the beneficiary will be deemed to have received the income and/or interest as it arose and be subjected to income tax accordingly.

The appropriation of assets to residuary beneficiaries and general legatees does not trigger the doctrine of relation back, so that such beneficiaries are subject to tax on such assets only in respect of the income or interest payable upon those assets after the date of appropriation (except the first interest payment or dividend on any investments quoted 'XD' as at the date of appropriation).

Stamp duty

12.14   Other than where assets are appropriated to a beneficiary who has introduced cash to satisfy any liabilities of the estate (including the satisfaction of prior legacies), transfers to beneficiaries are exempt from stamp duty under the Stamp Duty (Exempt Instruments) Regulations 1987 (SI 1987/516).

The document effecting the transfer should contain a certificate under the appropriate category, as follows:

Category

B	The conveyance or transfer of property the subject of a specific devise or legacy to the beneficiary named in the will (or his nominee)
C	The conveyance or transfer of property which forms part of an intestate's estate to the person entitled on intestacy (or his nominee)
D	The appropriation of property within section 84(4) Finance Act 1985 (death: appropriation in satisfaction of a general legacy of money) or section 84(5) or (7) Finance Act 1985 (death: appropriation in satisfaction of any interest of surviving spouse and in Scotland also of any interest of issue) NB Strictly, where an appropriation is made under the statutory power in section 41 Administration of Estates Act 1925 and is subject to the consents of the beneficiaries, the appropriation is a sale and ad valorem duty is payable.
E	The conveyance or transfer of property which forms part of the residuary estate of a testator to a beneficiary (or his nominee) entitled solely by virtue of his entitlement under the will. NB This form of wording specifically excludes a transfer to a beneficiary entitled under a partial intestacy (category 'C'); or to a person entitled by virtue of a deed of variation (transfer is subject to £5 duty as 'a conveyance of any other kind').

Where a transfer is made to a beneficiary (or his nominee) and the stamp duty exemption certificate is omitted, the transfer document should be submitted for adjudication and will be stamped at £5.

Payment of legacies

12.15   A personal representative should not pay legacies until he is satisfied that there is a sufficiency of assets to meet the debts, taxes and administration costs of the estate. It is not necessary that these need all have been paid, as the competent personal representative should be able, under normal circumstances, to identify the liabilities and retain and manage reserves to meet them, leaving the excess available for distribution. Unusual circumstances, particularly litigation and disputed debts or tax liabilities, or even assets that are difficult to realise, will of course mean a degree of prudence with reserves that might prevent any distribution until the issue is resolved. Because of this one cannot say that legacies should be paid within a specified period of time after death.

Once the personal representative is satisfied that he has a sufficient reserve for outgoings, he can distribute the remainder in whole or part satisfaction of the legacies including residue – and also provided that, for his own protection, he has placed section 27 Trustee Act 1925 notices which have expired without claim. (NB Some trust companies do not place these notices in all estates, relying instead on commercial insurance against claims. The individual premium payable by the estate is normally less than the cost of statutory notices. The additional advantage of such insurance is that there is no two-month period to wait, as there is with statutory notices, before distributions can be made.)

Normally a personal representative will distribute in favour of all the other legatees before making distributions of residue, but this need not be the case in practice, provided that the personal representative is fully satisfied that he holds sufficient reserves to meet the legacies. This may happen, for example, when there are business assets which the personal representative wishes to transfer very quickly to a residuary legatee to enable a business to continue more smoothly. It is not something that a personal representative should take on lightly or carelessly, for if his reserve to meet the other legacies is insufficient and he has made a residuary distribution, he will be exposed to personal risk for the shortfall.

An older, and more formal approach to distributions has been to wait until all liabilities have been settled before making a simultaneous, or near simultaneous, distribution to all legatees, including residuary legatees. Whilst this may be simpler for the personal representative, it does have several drawbacks in practice.

- The extra time that the legatee may have to wait for payment, which prevents him using or applying his inheritance as he may want, when he wants.

- The risk – to the residuary legatee in particular – of adverse stock exchange movements, unless all such investments have been sold.

- The risk to the personal representative of a claim if he fails to manage the cash balances properly during the wait before distribution.

Receipts

12.16   The personal representative is entitled to a receipt from a legatee for payment or for assets transferred, but only in exceptional circumstances to a discharge by deed (*Re Roberts (1869) 38 LJ Ch 708*). A receipt for an interest in residue may take the form of a signed approval to the estate accounts, or it may be expressly incorporated in such approval. There is no authority for the personal representative to require any form of indemnity or discharge from liability for his actions from the legatee, either separately or as part of the receipt.

A receipt cannot validly be taken from a minor unless the will expressly authorises it. Similarly, unless the will expressly authorises it the personal representative cannot take a receipt from the minor legatee's parent or guardian.

Bankruptcy searches

12.17

'nothing in this section –

(b)   frees the trustees or personal representatives from any obligation to make searches or obtain official certificates of search *similar to those which an intending purchaser would be advised to make or obtain.'* (emphasis added) (Trustee Act 1925, s 27(2)(b)).

Although the correct placing of section 27 advertisements would normally deal with potential creditors' claims, the advertisements would not give protection against a claim from a trustee in bankruptcy where the personal representative has made a distribution to a bankrupt. Searching the Charges Register for notice of the bankruptcy of a beneficiary is the only way to safely ascertain bankruptcy, as the statute, by its wording, does not operate to make section 27 notices *by themselves* effective against claims from trustees in bankruptcy. The implications of this restriction on the operation of section 27 are considerable. Many personal representatives carry out searches when distributing land or interests in land, but this restriction applies to all distributions, including those of personalty.

It may well not be practical for the personal representative to search for all distributions but in formulating a policy it would perhaps be reasonable to omit:

- searches for charities;

- searches for small distributions;

- searches where the personal representative is closely and reliably informed as to the financial circumstances of the beneficiaries.

Persons of unsound mind

12.18   Distributions should not be made to legatees lacking the ability to handle their own affairs as they are neither able to give a valid receipt nor approve the estate accounts. Payment should instead be made to their receiver or attorney (under a registered enduring power of attorney). If there is neither a receiver nor a registered enduring attorney, payment should be withheld pending the appointment of a receiver. In the event that no such appointment is made, the personal representative has the option of paying the sum due into court (Trustee Act 1925, s 63).

Costs of distribution

Vesting specific gifts

12.19   Much of the law in this area is of some antiquity and arises pre-1925 (see *Sharp v Lush (1879) 10 Ch D 468*; *Re De Sommery, Coelenbier v De Sommery [1912] 2 Ch 622*; *Re Grosvenor, Grosvenor v Grosvenor [1916] 2 Ch 375*) and in view of that it is to some extent unreliable, given that post-1925 the practice regarding assents of assets has changed. The following is a general statement of the current law.

'The general principle is that the estate must bear the expenses incident to the proper performance of the duties of the personal representative as personal representative but not the expenses involved in the execution of

trusts which arise after the estate has been administered or an assent given.'
(*Halsbury's Laws of England* (4th edition) volume 17 para 1185).

The difficulty lies in the practical application of this principle. It is difficult to
see that personal representatives can be criticised with any degree of validity for
their decisions regarding the usual fairly minor costs of transfer, but where the
costs are significant the legatee and the personal representative need to be aware
of the position. The two tables below are an attempt to summarise the author's
view on typical expenses, but the information should be treated with some
caution given the uncertainties of this area.

Table A

*Incidence of expenses when vesting assets (unless the trust instrument directs
otherwise)*

Type of gift	Type of expense	Incidence
Specific legacy	Packing and delivery	Specific legatee
Specific legacy	Preservation and upkeep, e.g. storage charges and insurance	Specific legatee
Specific legacy where legatees have a right of selection	Preservation and upkeep before selection	Residue
	Income before selection	Residue – costs arising after selection fall on the specific legatee as above
Specific legacy of shares	Registration by the company	Specific legatee
Appropriation of an asset not specifically bequeathed to a beneficiary	Expenses before appropriation	Residue
	Expenses after appropriation	Beneficiary
Generally	Costs of getting in any part of the real or personal estate in the UK or in a foreign country	Residue

Table B(i)

Summary of costs on property transactions – sales

Interest	Cost of sale	Cost of registration
Specific legacy	Specific devise/legacy	Purchaser
Trust legacy	Trust devise/legacy	Purchaser
Residuary asset	Residue	Purchaser

Table B(ii)

Summary of costs on property transactions – transfers

Interest	Cost of assent	Cost of registration
Specific legacy	Residue	Devisee
Trust legacy	Residue	Trust fund
Residue (in trust)	Residue	Residue
Residue (distributable)	Residue	Residue

Table B(iii)

Summary of costs on property transactions – part sale/part appropriation (i.e. a beneficiary introduces some cash)

Interest	Costs of sale and assent	Cost of registration
Part sale/part appropriation	Residue	Beneficiary (beneficiary is also liable for any stamp duty arising)

Costs of cash payments

12.20   Under normal circumstances there are no costs associated with making payments of pecuniary residuary legacies. Very often these are paid by cheque – although for security reasons direct payment to a beneficiary's bank account is preferred by many institutions – but neither method contains any inherent cost. Were there to be minor banking costs these would be borne by residue. However, should the beneficiary request payment in a manner that imposes cost on the personal representative then the cost should fall on the legatee and be deducted from the payment.

More common costs are those involved with foreign transactions in making payment to a foreign account or in foreign currency. The banking costs involved are considered to fall on residue as a testamentary expense, whilst any loss/gain on the currency conversion is that of the legatee (unless the will directs payment in a particular currency, the currency for payment should be that of the domicile of the testator).

The costs of assenting title to assets, both specifically devised or part of residue, will, in the absence of express directions, generally be payable from residue, rather than individually by the beneficiary. However, where the asset in question is land, the costs of the first registration will be the beneficiary's.

Where, after appropriation, the beneficiary requests that the asset is dealt with in a particular way (sold, for example) the costs of dealing with the asset post-appropriation will be those of the beneficiary.

Distribution of settled legacies

12.21   There are some differences in the distribution of settled legacies which provide a contrast to the distribution by executors of legacies to which the beneficiary is absolutely entitled.

The statutory powers of appropriation that an executor has under section 41 Administration of Estates Act 1925 (see 12.1 above) are not available to a trustee under the terms of the statute. It is therefore quite common to find those powers expressly extended by the terms of the deed to apply to trustees. Even without express powers, trustees have some powers, although their exercise is generally bound by the same conditions of consents, fairness and equality as an executor's (see in particular *Kane v Radley-Kane [1999] Ch 274* on self dealing, *Re Brookes [1914] 1 Ch 558* on fairness and *Re Beverley [1901] 1 Ch 681* on consents).

The effect of appropriation of part of a settled legacy to those absolutely entitled to the assets is the same as an appropriation of any other type of legacy, especially in the beneficiaries' rights over the property and their right to require that the title is vested in them once appropriation has been made by the trustee.

Until appropriation of the assets the trustee has a lien over them for the discharge of the proper liabilities of the trust fund. These would usually be tax liabilities, pecuniary legacies which become payable out of the settled legacy fund on its distribution and the costs of distributing the settled legacy fund. They may include potential liabilities of less certain amount. A trustee's right to retain and manage funds for potential liabilities for contaminated land under Part IIA Environmental Protection Act 1990 was recently established in *X v A [2000] 1 All ER 490*. Where a trustee retains funds to meet potential liabilities in this way, his interest in how the funds are to be invested, as a safeguard for the funds being available for payment, may outweigh the wishes of the beneficiaries, although he is bound to consider them.

Valuations

12.22   These are governed by the same general principles as valuations for appropriation by executors (see 12.3 above).

Notices to creditors claiming against the trustee

12.23   The protection considered earlier under section 27 Trustee Act 1925 for personal representatives is also available to trustees in order that they can protect themselves against unknown liabilities (see 12.17 above).

Taxation comments

12.24   Settled legacies become distributable upon the happening of a specific event. This may be pre-ordained (e.g. the death of the income beneficiary) or elective (e.g. absolute appointment of the whole of a discretionary trust or the partitioning of the trust fund at the instigation of the beneficiaries).

The more frequent events that give rise to the distribution of a settled legacy are:

- death of an income beneficiary;

- termination of an income entitlement by agreement (i.e. a 'trust bust');

- termination of a discretionary trust legacy.

Let us consider how the four major taxes, inheritance tax, capital gains tax, income tax and stamp duty are applied in each of the above events.

Death of an income beneficiary

12.25   The same general principles apply whatever the nature of the income beneficiary's interest, provided that it is a vested interest in possession. This section will therefore apply equally upon the death of:

- a life tenant;

- a tenant for life under the Settled Land Act 1925;

- the holder of a lease for life; and

- an annuitant.

The deceased income beneficiary's interest may not extend to the whole of the trust fund maintained for them; for example, they may be entitled only to a share of the income or to an annuity (which is less than the income generated by the trust fund). In those cases a disposal will be of only the appropriate proportion of the trust fund (inheritance tax); or of each individual asset in the trust fund (capital gains tax).

NB The right to the income of a defined share of the trust fund means that the capital can be divided into the relevant number of shares; however, if the income beneficiary is entitled to a share of the income, the capital remains a single undivided fund: *Re Freeston's Charity [1978] 1 All ER 481, Ch D*.

Inheritance tax

12.26   On the death of the income beneficiary, the value of the trust fund, to the extent that he is interested in it, is aggregated with the value of the other assets and interests which form his estate (as defined by section 5 Inheritance Tax Act 1984 (IHTA 1984)). If the deceased beneficiary is entitled to, say, the income of a third share, then the relevant share will be valued and aggregated; if his entitlement is to, say, a half of the income, a half share of the value of the trust fund will be aggregated; where he is an annuitant, then the share of the trust fund to be aggregated will be the proportion that correlates to the ratio that his entitlement bears to the income of the fund over the preceding 12 months.

(NB Whilst the value of any lifetime gifts made by the income beneficiary may affect the amount of inheritance tax payable, by reducing or extinguishing the available nil rate band on death, they are not aggregable with the estate and may be ignored for this purpose.)

The inheritance tax charge is then allocated between those various parts of the estate in the proportion that the taxable value of each bears to the total taxable value passing on the income beneficiary's death. To the extent that any exemptions may be claimed, they will be applied to that part of the estate by reference to which they arise, although the effect of such exemption(s) might also be to reduce the overall inheritance tax charge on other parts of the estate.

The main exemptions are:

- funds passing to charities (IHTA 1984, s 23), political parties (IHTA 1984, s 24), housing associations (IHTA 1984, s 24A), or gifts for national purposes, etc (IHTA 1984, s 25);

- funds passing to the spouse of the life tenant (such a transfer is wholly exempt if both spouses are domiciled within the UK; if the surviving spouse is domiciled outside of the UK, and the deceased income beneficiary is domiciled within it, then the exemption is limited to £55,000: IHTA 1984, s 18(2));

- where the income beneficiary's interest in the trust vested in possession on the death of their spouse before 13 November 1974 (in such cases, estate duty would have been chargeable upon the death of the first spouse and the death of the surviving spouse would have been exempt from estate duty; transitional provisions have preserved the exemption on the second death so as to avoid the potential double charge to tax: IHTA 1984, Sch 6, para 2);

- where the deceased income beneficiary is domiciled outside of the UK and tax exempt government stocks are held (IHTA 1984, s 6(2)). (Strictly, this is not an exemption; the assets will be 'excluded property' for the purposes of inheritance tax, though the effect is much the same as far as the tax charge on the income beneficiary's death is concerned. The holdings in question are frequently referred to as FOTRA securities: 'Free Of Tax to Residents Abroad'.)

- in relation to any transfer of value or other events occurring on or after 22 October 2002, a holding of any authorised unit trust or open-ended investment company will be 'excluded property' if the person beneficially entitled to it (e.g. the life tenant) is an individual domiciled outside of the UK (new s 6 (1A) Inheritance Act 1984 to be inserted by clause 183 Finance Bill 2003).

Within the trust fund itself, any exemptions will be applied to the individual interest from which they arise. If, upon the death of the beneficiary with the income entitlement, the trust fund passes equally to, say, his son and a charity, the son's share will be subject to inheritance tax, but the charity will receive its share without any inheritance tax charge (subject of course to there being no specific direction otherwise).

If any particular asset attracts relief from inheritance tax, the relief will be restricted by the extent that the asset is deemed to pass on the death to an exempt beneficiary (i.e. if one half of the interest in remainder is exempt from inheritance tax, then the relief will extend only to one half of the value of the asset). If the remaindermen subsequently decide that no part of the asset will pass to the exempt beneficiary, this will not affect the amount of the relief.

Where gifts of specific assets, or of sums of money, are to be satisfied out of the trust fund upon the death of the income beneficiary, they will each bear their proportionate share of inheritance tax (subject of course to an allowance for any exemption or relief attaching to the beneficiary and/or asset in question), unless specifically directed to be paid free of tax. Section 211 IHTA 1984 applies only to inheritance tax payable by a personal representative, and not to that paid by trustees.

Where any gift is directed to be paid out of a mixed fund comprising assets subject to tax in another jurisdiction, the donee will be liable to pay the proportionate share of the foreign tax (or duty) also.

The liability to interest chargeable upon the inheritance tax or any other tax/duty will follow the liability to the tax/duty.

If a loss arises on a sale by the trustees, relief against inheritance tax may be claimed of an amount equal to the difference between the date of death value and the gross sale proceeds under:

- section 179 IHTA 1984: sale of investments (as defined in IHTA 1984, s 178) within 12 months of death; or

- section 191 IHTA 1984: sale of land within three years of death (in certain circumstances, this may be extended to four years: IHTA 1984, s 197A).

Only the person who is assessable to the inheritance tax on that asset may claim either relief, provided that the sale is made by them in the same capacity in which such tax is assessable upon them. For example, if the trustee has appropriated the asset to any beneficiary (even to himself) he will no longer be able to make the sale as trustee of the trust fund, as he will then be bare trustee (or maybe even the absolute owner) at the time of the sale. Accordingly, relief will be denied.

Capital gains tax

12.27 Upon the death of an income beneficiary, the trustees are treated as having disposed of the assets of the trust fund, and immediately reacquired them, as at that date (TCGA 1992, s 71(1)). In most cases, though, no charge to tax will arise as the gains are specifically exempt (TCGA 1992, ss 72–74). Upon the death of an income beneficiary whose entitlement extends only to part of the trust fund, it is only that part which may qualify for a capital gains tax free uplift.

If the trust fund is absolutely distributable as a result of the death, the trustees will be deemed to hold the assets upon 'bare trust' for capital gains tax purposes (the trustees will continue to hold as trustees under general law, irrespective of the deeming provisions of the taxation legislation).

Capital gains tax on gains arising as a result of the deemed disposal will be assessable upon the trustees in the following situations:

* where the right to income had been purchased at any time;

* where any gains were held over on assets entering the trust (although this would apply to inter vivos transfers, perhaps under an instrument of variation);

* where the trust fund is distributable upon the death of a person who does not have an interest in the income of the trust, or of that part or proportion of the trust (this will include not just interests pur autre vie, but also, for example, that part of an annuity fund correlating to the surplus income).

In the second and third of these situations, provided that an inheritance tax charge arises, it may be possible for any gain arising to be held over (TCGA 1992, s 260). The trustees and the beneficiary(s) entitled will need to join in the relevant election and, until the end of the sixth full tax year following the year of assessment in which the gain arose, the trustees can be assessed in respect of such of the gain as has not been crystallised by a sale of the assets (i.e. if the income beneficiary died on 1 June 2002, under certain circumstances, the trustees would remain potentially liable until the end of the 2008–09 tax year).

Subject to the following exceptions, any gains or losses arising upon any subsequent disposals will be gains or losses of the beneficiaries, in proportion to their interests in the trust fund:

* the sales are made by the trustees to settle the trustees' obligations to discharge prior interests (e.g. legacies payable upon the death of the income beneficiary), or administration expenses (which does not include any inheritance tax charge);

* the trustees have claimed loss on sale relief under either section 179 or section 191 IHTA 1984 (in this case the beneficiaries will be deemed to acquire the assets for capital gains tax at the value accepted for inheritance tax after the relief has been applied).

If the beneficiary is entitled to an annuity, then the capital gains tax free uplift will apply only to that proportion of each asset that the annuity bears to the total income of the fund in the 12 months before death. If upon the death the entire fund is distributable, the remainder of the fund will be subject to a capital gains tax charge on the basis that the beneficiaries are absolutely entitled against the trustees (TCGA 1992, s 71(1)). If not absolutely distributable, there will be no deemed disposal of the remainder of the trust fund.

Where the deceased income beneficiary was entitled only to a share of the income (as opposed to the income of a share (*Re Freeston's Charity [1978] 1 All ER 481, Ch D*)), again the capital gains tax free uplift can apply only to the relevant proportion of the individual assets. If absolutely distributable following the death, the remainder of the assets will be subject to a capital gains tax charge on the basis that the beneficiaries are absolutely entitled against the trustees (TCGA 1992, s 71(1)). If not absolutely distributable, there will be no deemed disposal of the remainder of the trust fund.

In cases where the trust is not wholly distributable and one of the assets is indivisible, such as real property, then, applying the 'rule' in *Crowe v Appleby [1975] 3 All ER 529*, no disposal of any part of the asset can occur, so that the capital gain tax charge will arise only upon the eventual sale, or when the trust fund becomes fully distributable.

The beneficiaries entitled upon the death of the income beneficiary will take the assets at the value at which the trustees are deemed to have reacquired them (TCGA 1992, s 274). If the assets of the trust are distributed between the beneficiaries other than on an aliquot basis, there will be deemed to be a sale between the beneficiaries of the excess over their individual proportion of the individual assets. That 'excess' will be acquired at market value by the beneficiaries, applied as at the date of appropriation. Those beneficiaries receiving less than their aliquot entitlement will have made a chargeable disposal as at that same date.

Income tax

12.28   Income tax follows capital gains tax to the extent that following the death of an income beneficiary, if the trust fund, or a defined part of it, becomes absolutely distributable, the trustees are deemed to hold it upon 'bare trusts' for income tax purposes, but remain as trustees under general law. Accordingly, whilst they are required to submit trust tax returns up to the date of death, it is for the individual beneficiaries to submit details of the post-death income to their own Inspector of Taxes.

To the extent that the trustees are required to apportion the income over the date of death of the income beneficiary, they must provide the personal representatives of the deceased income beneficiary with the appropriate income tax certificate. If those personal representatives agree to accept a capital sum in lieu of the apportioned income, this will not be subject to income tax in their hands. It will also enable the trustees to distribute the underlying assets to the beneficiaries entitled in a more timely manner than might otherwise be the case.

Stamp duty

12.29   Provided that the interest of a beneficiary has not been acquired for money, or money's worth, any asset transferred to him, or his nominee, in satisfaction of his interest will be exempt from stamp duty if it carries the appropriate certificate under the Stamp Duty (Exempt Instruments) Regulations 1987 (SI 1987/516). If the appropriate certificate is omitted, the transfer or conveyance should be submitted to the Stamp Office for adjudication and will be subject to duty at the fixed rate of £5.

The applicable exemption categories are:

Category	Origin of Interest
B	Will: gift of specific asset
C	Intestacy: any statutory entitlement
D	Will: satisfaction of general legacies
	Intestacy: satisfaction of the statutory legacy to the surviving spouse
E	Will: interests in remainder
F	Inter vivos settlement: all interests

NB Where a trust fund has been created by an instrument of variation, whether or not effective under section 142 IHTA 1984, the distribution of assets will be subject to a category F certificate. Whilst, for inheritance tax purposes, the terms of the instrument might be 'read back' into the will (or intestacy) so that they are deemed to be treated as though they were made by the deceased, the gift is in reality made by the person making the instrument and is, therefore, an inter vivos settlement.

The above apply where the trustee transfers the assets to the beneficiaries in proportion to their interests. Where a beneficiary takes more than his aliquot proportion, the excess is treated as though a sale and is subject to ad valorem stamp duty on its value as at the date of appropriation.

If the beneficiary has acquired his interest for money, or money's worth, the transfer of assets to him will be subject to ad valorem stamp duty.

Termination of income entitlement by agreement

12.30   The income beneficiary may terminate his entitlement by agreeing with the remaindermen to divide the trust fund between them. The division may be in accordance with actuarial advice; all to the income beneficiary; all to the remaindermen; or in such other proportion as they might agree. The basis of division may affect the taxation aspects, as discussed below.

If the beneficiaries are, together, absolutely entitled to the whole of the trust fund, they may terminate the trusts by agreement (*Saunders v Vautier (1841) 4 Beav 115*), provided that none of them is under a legal incapacity (e.g. any of them is a minor, or a 'patient' within the meaning of the Mental Health Act 1983).

Where a beneficiary is a 'patient', the Court of Protection may give any necessary consents on his behalf. If consent is given, then the court will direct someone to execute any documents on behalf of the 'patient', so as to give effect to the arrangement.

If any beneficiary is under any other form of legal disability (or there are, as yet, unborn beneficiaries), a termination of the trust might only be effected upon an application to the High Court under the Variation of Trusts Act 1958.

Any attempt to terminate a trust fund where the beneficiaries are not absolutely entitled to the fund between them, or some are under a legal disability (and the necessary steps are not taken), will invariably result in the beneficiaries' expectations not being fulfilled. The assignment or surrender by some of the beneficiaries may be ineffective. If the class of remaindermen has not closed, the distribution will in any event be deferred at least until it does close, and maybe for even longer if the beneficiaries are also required to fulfil certain other conditions (e.g. attain the age of 18 years).

If the income beneficiary has a power of appointment exercisable over the trust fund, so that he might select the parties between whom the trust fund will pass upon his death, it may be necessary for such power to be released before any termination can be effective. Care should be taken not to exercise the power as a prelude to the termination, as this might constitute a 'fraud upon the power', resulting in the appointment being ineffective.

Whilst, below, reference is made to the income beneficiary assigning his interest to the remaindermen, if the whole of the income entitlement is to be gifted, this may often be achieved by a release of the entitlement. The effect is generally the same.

Inheritance tax

12.31 The income beneficiary is deemed to have an interest in possession in the trust fund, or the relevant proportion of it that produces the income to which he is entitled. Any assignment by way of gift of that interest during his lifetime, to the extent that it is neither exempt (see 12.26 above, for commentary on exempt transfers) nor gifted into a non-interest in possession trust, will be a potentially exempt transfer (PET) (IHTA 1984, s 3A) and will affect his inheritance tax position if he dies with seven years of the date of the gift.

If the remaindermen assign their rights in remainder to the income beneficiary, so that the trust fund vests solely in him, there will be no inheritance tax implications. The remaindermen's interest is excluded property (IHTA 1984, s 48), unless it had been acquired for consideration in money, or money's worth.

Where the trust fund is partitioned between the income beneficiary and the remaindermen, the income beneficiary will have made a PET to the extent that the value of his estate has been reduced. The PET will be reduced to the extent that such transfer of value is to exempt beneficiaries.

If the income beneficiary dies within seven years after the date of the PET, any inheritance tax payable will be assessable upon the trustees. They would therefore be well advised to consider the extent to which a reserve should be retained, or insurance purchased out of the trust fund, to cover the possibility of any inheritance tax liability falling against them.

If any of the assets attract relief (e.g. agricultural relief or business relief) as at the date of the PET, such relief might be lost if, at the date of the income beneficiary's death, the nature of the asset is such that it no longer qualifies for the relief.

Relief under section 179 IHTA 1984, or section 191 IHTA 1984 is not available to reduce any potential inheritance tax charge if relevant assets are sold by the trustee at a loss. The reliefs only apply where the tax charge arises in respect of a transfer on death, not an inter vivos transfer.

Where the income beneficiary has made a PET, he may assign to the trustees of the trust some or all of the annual allowance available to him as at the date of the PET (IHTA 1984, s 57). Notice of such assignment must be given to the trustees within six months of the date of the PET, and be in the prescribed form.

Capital gains tax

12.32   A capital gains tax charge arises under section 71(1) TCGA 1992.

Provided that no consideration passes, and the beneficiary entitled upon the termination is a charity, or the gift is for 'national purposes, etc' (as defined in IHTA 1984, Sch 3), the deemed disposal will be treated as a no gain/loss transaction to the extent that it relates to the charity's share, or the gift for national purposes (TCGA 1992, s 257). Accordingly, no capital gains tax charge will arise on the disposal in favour of such beneficiaries.

Where assets which qualify for relief under section 165 TCGA 1992 are held, a claim for holdover relief may be made.

In the absence of any specific direction in the documentation setting out the division of the trust fund between the beneficiaries, the capital gains tax liability will be borne by the beneficiaries in proportion to their respective interests, post termination, subject to the benefit of any relief under section 257 TCGA 1992 accruing to the relevant beneficiary.

Upon the termination, the trustee will hold the trust assets as 'bare trustee' for capital gains tax purposes. The beneficiaries' acquisition cost will be the market value as at the date of the termination.

If the assets of the trust are distributed between the beneficiaries other than on an aliquot basis, there will be deemed to be a sale between the beneficiaries of the excess over their individual proportion of the individual assets. The beneficiaries will acquire the 'excess' at market value applied as at the date of appropriation. Those beneficiaries receiving less than their aliquot entitlement will have made a chargeable disposal as at that same date.

Income tax

12.33   Income tax follows capital gains tax to the extent that following the termination of a trust, if the trust fund, or a defined part of it, becomes absolutely distributable, the trustees are deemed to hold it upon 'bare trusts' for income tax purposes, but remain as trustees under general law. Accordingly, whilst they are required to submit trust tax returns up to the date of termination, it is for the individual beneficiaries to submit details of the post-termination income to their own Inspector of Taxes.

Stamp duty

12.34   The assignment of the beneficiary(s)' interest which gives effect to the termination of the trust fund will normally contain a category L certificate under the Stamp Duty (Exempt Instruments) Regulations 1987 (SI 1987/516). If no such certificate is included, the assignment should be submitted for adjudication and subject to £5 fixed duty.

If the termination is effected by the income beneficiary executing a release of their interest, such instrument should contain a category L certificate.

To the extent that assets are transferred to the remaindermen in proportion to their interests in the trust fund, the transfers or conveyances to them, or their nominee(s), will be subject to stamp duty as if they had acquired the assets upon the death of the income beneficiary (see 12.29 above). Any excess over their aliquot share will be subject to ad valorem duty.

The transfer or conveyance of assets to the former income beneficiary, or the assignee (other than for consideration) of any remainderman, will be subject to the fixed stamp duty of £5 as a 'conveyance of any other kind'. The nature of the interest does not fall within any of the criteria in the Schedule to the 1987 regulations (Stamp Duty (Exempt Instruments) Regulations 1987, SI 1987/516).

If any person has purchased his interest, any transfer or conveyance of assets to him will be subject to ad valorem duty.

Termination of a discretionary trust

12.35   The power to terminate a discretionary trust is usually vested in the trustees, who may use it to give limited or absolute interests to such of the beneficiaries as they might decide.

In this section we will consider an absolute appointment of the entire trust fund.

Inheritance tax

12.36   Upon the exercise of the trustees' power of appointment, an immediate charge to inheritance tax will arise (IHTA 1984, s 65). The rate of charge will be calculated by reference to:

- the effective rate as at the date of the last periodic charge, and

- the length of time that has elapsed since the last periodic charge (IHTA 1984, ss 68, 69).

If the termination occurs within three months of the valuation date upon which the last periodic charge was calculated, no additional charge to tax will arise.

Where an appointment is made in favour of an exempt beneficiary, no inheritance tax is payable in respect of the benefit received by that beneficiary (see ss 76(3)–(8) IHTA 1984).

To the extent that a capital gains tax charge arises on the appointment, this is an allowable deduction when calculating the inheritance tax liability. However, if the gains arising are held over (for more detail, see 12.37 below), no allowance is made for the possibility of the capital gains tax liability crystallising.

Capital gains tax

12.37   The exercise of the discretion by the trustees of a discretionary trust will result in a deemed disposal of the assets in question under section 71(1) TCGA 1992. Any gain or loss will be assessable upon the trustee and the beneficiary(s) will acquire such assets at the trustees' disposal value.

Subject to compliance with the provisions of either section 165 TCGA 1992 (relief for gifts of business assets), or section 260 TCGA 1992 (relief for gifts on which inheritance tax is payable, etc), any gains arising upon the assets of the trust fund may be held over. Such gains will crystallise upon the disposal of such assets by the beneficiary, or upon the beneficiary ceasing to reside in the UK for the purposes of capital gains tax. The trustees and the beneficiary(s) entitled will need to join in the relevant election and, until the end of the sixth full tax year following the year of assessment in which the gain arose, if the beneficiary ceases to reside within the UK, the trustees can be assessed in respect of such of the gain as has not been crystallised by a sale of the assets (i.e. if the appointment had been made on 1 June 2002, under certain circumstances, the trustees would remain potentially liable until the end of the 2008–09 tax year).

Once the trustees have exercised their discretion to terminate the discretionary trust and distribute the trust fund absolutely, they will hold the trust assets as 'bare trustee' for capital gains tax purposes. The beneficiaries' acquisition cost will be the market value as at the date of the termination.

If individual assets are distributed amongst the beneficiaries other than:

- in the proportions set out in the trustees' memorandum or minute of appointment of the trust fund, or

- in accordance with the default provisions of the trust,

there will be deemed to be a sale between the beneficiaries of the excess over their individual entitlement of the individual assets. The beneficiaries will acquire the 'excess' at market value, applied as at the date of appropriation. Those beneficiaries receiving less than their entitlement of each asset will have made a chargeable disposal as at that same date.

Income tax

12.38   Income tax follows capital gains tax to the extent that following the termination of a trust, if the trust fund, or a defined part of it, becomes absolutely distributable, the trustees are deemed to hold it upon 'bare trusts' for income tax purposes, but remain as trustees under general law. Accordingly, whilst they are required to submit trust tax returns up to the date of termination, it is for the individual beneficiaries to submit details of the post-termination income to their own Inspector of Taxes.

The tax charge at the rate applicable to trustees will also cease on the date of termination.

Any 'tax pool' accumulated during the currency of the discretionary trust will be lost once the discretionary trusts have been terminated. Accordingly, the trustees might be advised to make a distribution of income so as to reduce the extent to which any tax paid under section 686 Income and Corporation Taxes Act 1988 may become forfeit.

Stamp duty

12.39   The transfer or conveyance of an asset to any beneficiary under the appointment, or his nominee, in satisfaction of his interest, will be exempt from stamp duty if it carries the appropriate certificate under the Stamp Duty (Exempt Instruments) Regulations 1987 (SI 1987/516). If the appropriate certificate is omitted, the transfer or conveyance should be submitted to the Stamp Office for adjudication and will be subject to duty at the fixed rate of £5.

The applicable exemption categories are:

Category	Origin of Interest
B	Will: gift of specific asset
D	Will: satisfaction of general legacies
E	Will: interests in remainder
F	Inter vivos settlement: all interests

NB Where a trust fund has been created by an instrument of variation, whether or not effective under section 142 IHTA 1984, the distribution of assets will be subject to a category F certificate. Whilst, for inheritance tax purposes, the terms of the instrument might be 'read back' into the will (or intestacy) so that they are deemed to be treated as though they were made by the deceased, the gift is in reality made by the person making the instrument and is, therefore, an inter vivos settlement.

The above apply where the trustee transfers the assets to the beneficiaries in proportion to their interests under the power of appointment, or the default provisions of the trust. Where a beneficiary takes more than his due proportion, the excess is treated as though a sale and is subject to ad valorem stamp on its value as at the date of appropriation.

Income and interest on legacies payable after the death of an income beneficiary

12.40   Unless the trust instrument provides otherwise, the beneficiary entitled to a specific or general legacy upon the death of an income beneficiary is entitled to income or interest from the date the legacy become payable, i.e. the date of the income beneficiary's death (*Re Scadding (1902) 4 OLR 632*).

A specific legacy will carry with it the right to the income (if any) generated by the specified assets. However, in the absence of an effective non-apportionment clause, the income beneficiary's estate is entitled to the income earned on the assets up to the date of his death, even though it may be due and payable some time after that date.

Where a legacy is contingent, it will not generally carry the right to income or interest until the happening of the specified event, unless it is directed to be set aside following the death of the income beneficiary (other than for purely administrative reasons).

If the gift is a general legacy, such as a cash sum, simple interest will be payable at 6% (Rules of the Supreme Court (Amendment No 2) Order 1983, SI 1983/1181), even if the fund out of which it is to be paid has achieved a higher rate (*Re Campbell, Campbell v Campbell (1893) 3 Ch 468*). The statutory rate is, in effect, a default rate, which applies unless the trust instrument specifies a different rate (which very few do).

Interest is due upon the balance of the legacy which remains unpaid and is calculated by reference to the date upon which it first became payable. Where a legacy is paid in more than one instalment, which may often be the case following the death of an income beneficiary, the payments are first applied to discharge the outstanding interest. Only once that has been satisfied is the payment applied to reduce the balance of the unpaid legacy (*Re Morley's Estate, Hollenden v Morley [1937] 3 All ER 204*).

If the legacy is payable upon the death of the income beneficiary, and the trust is terminated during his lifetime, the right to income or interest will only arise when the legatee becomes entitled to the capital of his legacy. The question of whether or not such termination accelerates payment of the legacy will depend upon the terms of the trust instrument and is outside the scope of this text.

Income tax

12.41   Interest on general legacies is payable to the legatee without the deduction of tax (Income and Corporation Taxes Act 1988, ss 348, 349), even though the trustee may be paying it out of taxed income.

There is an exception, though, where the interest is due to a person 'whose place of abode is outside of the United Kingdom' (Income and Corporation Taxes Act 1988, 349(2)). In such instances, interest is paid after deduction of tax at the 'rate applicable to savings' (20% in the tax year 2003–04). The trustees must account to the Inland Revenue for the tax deducted (Income and Corporation Taxes Act 1988, s 350) and provide the legatee with a tax deduction certificate.

In the hands of the legatee, the interest is treated as income of the year of receipt, irrespective of the period during which it might have accrued.

Any interest paid on legacies may be claimed as an allowable deduction against the trust income in the hands of those beneficiaries entitled to the remainder. Whilst there is no statutory authority for this practice, the Inland Revenue has confirmed that interest due to a legatee should be treated as a trust expense, reducing the taxable income of the person out of whose interest it is paid in the same way that would be allowed in an estate under (Income and Corporation Taxes Act 1988, s 697(1)).

Index